LET'S HANG ON

Let's Hang On

Mudhuts, Bets and Beers on the Road to Division One with Wigan Athletic

Martin Tarbuck

MAINSTREAM PUBLISHING
EDINBURGH AND LONDON

First published in Great Britain in 2003 by
MAINSTREAM PUBLISHING (EDINBURGH) LTD
7 Albany Street
Edinburgh EH1 3UG

ISBN 1 84018 784 0

A catalogue record for this book is available from the British Library

Typeset in Badhouse and Berkeley

Printed in Great Britain by
Mackays of Chatham plc

ACKNOWLEDGEMENTS

MASSIVE THANKS TO JOHN HEELEY FOR THE COVER DESIGN, PROOFREADING, photographs and contributions. To Paul Simpson for the photographs. To Vaughanie for the initial proofreading and submission and also for being the drive behind *Cockney Latic*. Thanks to Les Bagg for the contributions and also to my contact at Blackpool. Thanks to everyone at Mainstream Publishing for agreeing to publish this nonsense, especially Bill, Tina, Ken, Ailsa and Graeme. Respect to the *Cockney Latic* team including Neil M., Chocker, Joe Hawkins, Brasso, Pompey Lil, K21, Golly, Blugirl, Mr and Mrs Wiggin Omen, Doris the Bookmaker, Griff, Dave, Brad and the V100s, Baker, Penk and many others for keeping the whole thing ticking over. Dell, Gal, The Banker, Oldham Geoff and all the original Cockney Latics. Thanks to numerous people at the club and especially Stu H – top Latics mon. Matt @ WISH for the publicity and for backing Latics. Thanks to Trevor at Smith's for the guidance and support. Respect to Arky for the away travel and the many loony occupants including Caddy, Jonesy, CB, Beany, Rammy, Shannon, Irv, Stey, Bric, Col, Carl H, Shawy, Sedge, Manny, Dean, Martin and Sheila, the Chorley Latics, the Tyldesley Latics, Howard, Malc, Griff, Greeny and the Springfield Latics, Duffy, Peety, Gareth, Statto, Clandon, Morgy, Dean, Purdham,

Rob, Louise, Les, Pilps, Tufty and Foz, Giz, Wiggy, Parky, Freddie, Frankie, Cainy, Mitty, Sharpy, Colonel Jay T and Tim, Shed and Parky, Pez, Shannon and 'yoof' and many other nutters too numerous to mention. Respect to all my matchday chums and The Pagefield Crew: Naylor, Moore, Ian T, Neil Goon, Canny, Liam, Chris and Ant Mushy, Martin, Ang, Donna, Michelle, Gom, Chris, the Joynt brothers, Sparky, Hughes the Booze, Meehan, John, Craig, Stu, Faz, Lindsey, Liam Faz, Andy, Webby, Carl, Liam, Dave Dickie, Phil and Mick @ Micron, Spen, Beckham, Bentley, Myers, Karen, Gorey for the music, along with Bri Cannon and Dylan at the Lux club, Dave for the bottles of Pils, Ian @ Fever for the hospitality. Thanks to my wife and kids for not existing and therefore not preventing me from getting away with it all. Thanks to my family for putting up with my rampant mood swings. Thanks to the bloke who picked me up out of the gutter on Boxing Day. Thanks to all the lads and lasses on the *Cockney Latic* message board for the inspiration (and abuse). Thanks to Oldham Athletic for six points. Thanks to all the tight gits for picking up this copy, scragging the ends and putting it back down again. Thanks to coppers everywhere for not nicking me when me mouth's got the better of me. Thanks to pub landlords and landladies everywhere for treating us with respect. Huge, huge respect to Dave Whelan for making it all happen, Paul Jewell and the players for having the belief and ability to do the business. Respect to *Cockney Latic* readers and true Latics fans everywhere for keeping the faith and getting behind them. Humble apologies to those whom I have foolishly omitted, and even humbler apologies to those I've mentioned and shouldn't have. See you all in Division One.

CONTENTS

FOREWORD

AS ALL TRUE FOOTBALL FANS IN ENGLAND KNOW, THE SEASON STARTS IN EARNEST IN the third week in June. This is when the coming season's fixture lists are released and for those next few weeks (on paper at least) all teams are equal. 'It's going to be our year' is heard throughout the pubs and clubs up and down the country. Lists are studied with a vengeance, journeys planned, weddings postponed and holiday request forms and potential 'sickies' are marked down at work. After a week the true football fan will be able to tell you without hesitation that: 'Huddersfield away is 19 April 2003.' Ask him or her the date of their wedding anniversary and they'll struggle.

Some people even utter that enduring phrase, 'I'm going to every match this season.' I do it every summer. I once made it to the end of September when the lure of a cheap fortnight in the Balearics got the better of me. The fact that we were playing shit also helped. I even toyed with the idea of doing a diary on a couple of occasions, but realised what a stupid idea that was when it was pointed out to me that I'm usually that drunk on a Saturday that I can't remember to take my baseball cap home with me after a match, never mind note down what happened during the day and, more specifically, the 90 minutes of football.

Therefore when Martin (Jimmy to everybody but his mum) said he was going to diarise the coming season I took not a blind bit of notice. I mean, this is the man that has single-handedly kept the Park Road Chemist in business for the last 30 years. If there's an illness or bug about your man has got it. He would also have played for England at football if it hadn't been for his groin/hamstring/cruciate ligament/bunion injury. I could have also included that other common football injury 'lack of talent' but that would be cruel. It was only when he was trying to rally the troops to go to Colchester at the end of August that I realised he meant it. Amazingly, he did it, and this is his story.

But it's more than his story. It's our story as Wigan Athletic fans and it's a story for all like-minded fans across the country. It's a story for fans of all clubs that don't buy into the merchandising culture of modern football and it's for everybody that's been stuck on a train or in a traffic jam checking their watch as kick-off time approaches. It's for people who have sacrificed perfectly sane existences to travel 500 miles in a day and been rewarded with a 1–0 defeat. It is for all those fans who study league tables in the firm belief that their team is going to blow a 14-point lead and it is for all those people who have had a can of Stella at eight in the morning!

The photographs on the cover of this book give you a good idea how the season ended. How the team, and us supporters, got to that magical moment is featured herein. Experience the highs and lows (and yes there were some lows) in Jimmy's superb tale of the greatest season in the history of Wigan Athletic Football Club.

Vaughanie
Founder of Wigan Athletic fans' quality, premier, best-selling (OK then, only) fanzine *Cockney Latic*

PREFACE

I HATE ALDERSHOT WITH A PASSION

WHY WOULD A NONDESCRIPT RYMAN LEAGUE OUTFIT INSTIL SO MUCH HATRED IN A young man? Well, it's simple. Back in 1987, they prevented me from completing the Holy Grail which all true football fans aspire to achieve: to attend every game, home and away, of your favourite team's football season. I was still at school and Aldershot was deemed to be too far to travel on a Tuesday night. It was the only game I was to miss that season. The season afterwards I only missed one game as well. It was, again, on a Tuesday night, our opponents were Aldershot. Yes, them again.

In the subsequent years I never got close. Different events got in the way from 1989 onwards, such as discovering dance music, discovering alcohol, playing football, going away to university. Of course, for the largest part of the next ten years, the team was quite simply terrible and not worth dedicating every Saturday for nine months towards. As you get older, responsibilities start to burden you; although I have actively avoided responsibility all my life, I still occasionally found myself with 'other things to do' on a Saturday. I simply picked and chose my games, as did many others. This was borne out by Wigan Athletic's home crowds, which began to plummet below the 1,500 mark (and they weren't exactly massive beforehand!). Five years ago, in our Championship season, I only missed a handful, and then two years ago I got close as well, only missing eight games.

Last season, 2001–02, Wigan Athletic fans were put through the mangle. Sorry defeats to the likes of Wrexham (three), Blackpool (three) and Canvey Island (isn't once enough?) tested all our faith, only for the team to come around at the end of the season with an impressive run of form. This gave Latics fans everywhere renewed optimism for the forthcoming 2002–03 season. We believed this could be our year after so many recent disappointments.

'I'm going to every game next season, me, you just watch' is the oft heard cry of (usually) drunken fans. I wish I had a pound for every time I had heard, or indeed, said it myself. Well, this year, I'm going for it: armed with a reasonable disposable income and no bloody Aldershot to screw it up for me, this year I'm going to do it.

There will, inevitably, be obstacles along the way: drunkenness, travel problems, and although I have sworn that this book will not see the light of day should I miss just one game, I am pretty sure that, knowing what a cowardly liar I am, I will simply give you the sob story in the hope that you take pity on me. Or I could make it up, which wouldn't be the first time. My excellent review of our game at Blackpool last year won wide accolades yet was actually produced from the comfort of my bed following eager listening to the radio commentary due to my not receiving one of the woefully inadequate ticket allocation of 1,000.

Not this time. No lies, no confessions; load up the camper van, it's gonna be a bumpy ride . . .

AUGUST

TEAR GASSED IN TEWKESBURY

10 August 2002, Cheltenham (a). Won 2–0.

OH, TO BE IN MALIA IN SUMMER! MY GOOD MATE DORIS THE BOOKMAKER'S PROBABLY still there, working on the beach, stacking sun loungers and chatting up birds from Worksop. The World Cup was out of the question, out of my price range, so Crete was the next best thing. Football or sunshine? It's a tough one. From Crete to Cheltenham in a matter of days and you'll have to bear with me if I'm not exactly ecstatic about the impending football season. Still, at least there's no Cockney losers in Hackett on our coach shouting 'oi-oi' and offering free slammers, or silly Home Counties birds with their 'Good Girls go to Heaven, Bad Girls go to Malia' T-shirts. Piss off – come September you'll be loading up the 4x4 Daddy's bought you and hotfooting it to the Halls of Oxbridge to do a BA (Hons) in Modern Pavement Design or summat. The worst we've got to put up with is Beany charging down the coach demanding a 'dump stop' when we've barely hit the M6.

10.55 a.m. and 50 faces peer through the window of Ye Olde Black Bear, 'Gloucestershire's oldest pub' being its proud boast. There are shadows moving about inside so we knock on the door and the attractive young lady inside looks very pleased to see us, although probably not as pleased as we are to see her. She's gorgeous, and zooms straight to the top of the Away Day barmaids' chart. An easy achievement on the first day of the season, but she'll take some shifting regardless. It's a marathon not a sprint, remember. After a couple of minutes during which we speculate as to whether she is actually bolting or unbolting the door, we are let in as she gives us her best 'Hello Boys' impression. She knows it, and on later inspection it turns out she is all over one of the impressionable spiky-haired youths who are also behind the bar. Boo to them.

There is the inevitable dual rush for the bar and the bogs (well, it has been a long journey), a swift couple here, a couple in The Anchor down the road and then we return to the first pub where we were dropped off by the river. I've been commenting all morning how great it is just to be able to have a few beers in a foreign town without getting any hassle off the locals or the police. It's half past one and the beer is flowing when someone announces: 'The Old Bill's here.' Sure enough, several vans have come all the way from Cheltenham to escort us to the ground, there's also a group of TAGs filming us across the road from behind a Ford Focus. What have we done? You tell me.

The bobbies come into the pub and tell us to drink up. I can't help thinking a coach full of boozed up rugby union fans on their way to Gloucester wouldn't get this treatment, but it's the price you pay for being a football fan and it leaves a sour taste in the mouth. The fact that we were invited back after the game shows exactly how much bother we were causing. There are big queues at the turnstiles, only two of them, but a heavy police presence again, and a good away following of 1,000 or so from Wigan. Being the bunch of tarts that we are, we sorted out our tickets on the Friday for the seats because it looked like it was going to piss down, and we didn't want to get wet due to our 'Disco Dave'-ing it back in Wigan later that night. Fortunately, Cheltenham's one of those grounds where you can either stand or sit if you have a seat ticket, so I spend half the game stood up behind the goal yapping anyway.

Whaddon Road is a tight, homely, ramshackle ground. I wouldn't exactly call it plush, but then two years ago Cheltenham were a non-league team. It's also probably better than our old ground, the beloved Springfield Park. We have seats in the bottom end of the best stand, not a bad view and considerably better than the terrace behind the goal, where the size of the following makes it difficult to see on the shallow terrace. Wigan start brightly, and take the lead after a

Nathan Ellington cross is converted six minutes in by 'Sir' Andrew Liddell while there are plenty still queuing up outside to get in. There is some debate as to whether the ball has crossed the line, but the linesman flags to give it the OK, and we're 1–0 up and pogoing on the terraces. It's all Wigan from there on in, and Cheltenham, in their first game ever in Division Two, must be pining for the Third.

In the seats we're right next to the Cheltenham lot and, much to our amusement, two kids (probably aged about 15) have been giving us verbals and insinuating that they are going to cut our throats. Now, we're no hard men and not really interested in this sort of thing at all, but the threats this little mob are issuing are a source of immense comedy rather than terror. The more we laugh, the more they try to intimidate. We've been to Millwall, we've been to Stoke, we've been to Cardiff, we've been to the old Bolton ground at Burnden Park – now they are scary places. Personally, I had to walk away over to the terraces to go to the toilets as I was in danger of pissing myself at the thought of these teeny terrors waiting for me outside. Yeah, it's a fair cop, I was shit scared.

After 25 minutes our young friends get even more agitated as the Wigan pressure tells again as Matt Jackson crosses the ball in from a cleared corner, which Lee McCulloch bullets into the net. 2–0 and we're coasting! I try to queue for some food at this point, as I have had nothing to eat all day as per usual. I am under the illusion that with Cheltenham being on the way to the West Country, there will be a tasty selection of pasties akin to the excellent ones available at Bristol Rovers. Alas, all I can see is two young lads flipping burgers, tossing them about like they're working in a cocktail bar! Tom Cruise with BSE!

For reasons best known to myself, I twice wait in the queue for five minutes and walk away to get a bit more of the game. Each time the queue gets bigger. I don't seem to be getting the hang of this at all, so give it away. Who needs food? The first half sees no more goals, although Latics have quite a few chances to pull further in front, and a very, very clear penalty appeal is turned down as Nathan 'The Duke' Ellington is tripped in the box. Cheltenham must be pleased to hear the whistle for half-time.

The second half sees Latics content to catch the Robins on the break, but as Cheltenham's firepower consists of Julian Alsop, who is the size of an airport hangar, the Wigan defence holds firm, save for a late scare as Devaney clips the post with a beautiful drive. The better team wins, and this is borne out after the game as Cheltenham fans surreally wave and clap us on our way with no hostility at all. Apart from the Cheltenham Youth in the ground they have been very genial hosts and we look forward to welcoming them to the JJB Stadium in February. That's what football is about: no animosity, just appreciation of good football. And bowls! There's a bowling green at the back of the away end so we amuse ourselves for ten minutes or so. One of the geriatrics who plays a bad 'wood' is treated to a chorus of 'You're shit, and you know you are!' as his octogenarian opponent celebrates with a little jig for us. We have a good laugh at the scores, with Millwall losing 6–0 at home to Rotherham and Oldham losing, full stop. As for us, well it's one down, forty-five to go.

The coach eventually pulls off to leave, closely escorted by several vans full of the boys in blue. They escort us out of Cheltenham, out of Gloucestershire and halfway to Birmingham, finally leaving us to our own devices a good 40 miles away and spoiling our plan to return to Tewkesbury for a couple more beers. No pub stop then, so we detour to ASDA in West Brom, in return for a healthy tip for the driver. Being a health-conscious individual, I purchase a tea of a Double Cheese Dairylea Lunchables pack and a large bag of 'posh' Walkers crisps, plus a little something to wash them down with for the remaining hour and a half back to Wigan. Others are sat around me eating McDonalds, sausage rolls and half a chicken with the obligatory tinnies for accompaniment. The occupants of this coach are not in danger of being mistaken for a bunch of travelling triathletes.

On arrival back in Wigan, we all stay out and go on a mini pub crawl around the back end of the town, ending up in Rik's Bar, the only place which really welcomes football fans who have been out since eight that morning. Not surprisingly, the rest of the evening is a blur, and I can't remember how I got home. When I do finally awake, at 8 p.m. Sunday night (a personal best, thanks very much), the paint and cuts on my hands indicate to Detective Tarbuck that he has fallen over drunk at some point. I really should give up this drinking lark. In about nine months.

On inspecting the pockets of my Paul Smith jeans, which are strewn on the bedroom floor, I can see that I have spent £80 the previous day. The significance of this I will now explain, but before continuing I would like to suggest that if you go to football matches and are reading this out aloud and have a wife, husband, partner or significant other in close proximity, either be quiet or cover their ears. Failure to do so will mean that you will ultimately have attended your last ever football match.

I often find myself setting budgets for things. Typically, my football-related budget is £100 for an away game and £30 for a home game. Home matches would typically include three pints before and after, £12 entrance fee and a few quid left over for either food or a bet. Don't ask me to even begin to explain where the money on an Away Day goes. Take a whole season, chuck in an optimistic eight cup games, and this comes to around £3,500. Taken over the 20 years I've watched Wigan and you are looking at £70,000. No further comment needed, except you can uncover those ears now. It's going to be a long and expensive season!

THE DUKE IS ON FIRE!

13 August 2002, Mansfield Town (h). Won 3–2.

Oh blimey, the debt collectors are back. A particularly odious company have been blacklisting me for a debt incurred by a dead relative; the bastards won't go away and clearing my name is akin to trying to chuck an elephant over the Great Wall of China. I didn't even live here then, I was away at college in Nottingham, sharing a flat with three Geordies of questionable personal hygiene and a green-fingered penchant for growing the sort of plants which rarely feature on *Gardeners' World*. I have explained this to the pig-ignorant bastards, but still they hound me. I had my car nicked last year, couldn't get a loan and had to spend several months travelling to work on the bus in some of the shittiest weather the West Pennines have to offer but I eventually, and I mean eventually, cleared my name and laughed it off. And last night I opened a letter telling me I was right back to square one. After spending most of Tuesday afternoon on the phone to people with harder faces than The Man in the Iron Mask, I'm in the pub pre-match and getting pissed. Bollocks to the £30 budget.

7.25 p.m. I'm selling fanzines on the Bridge over the River Kwai, which actually goes over the Douglas, but that hasn't quite got the same ring to it. My perch is at the end of the bridge, slightly elevated so that I command respect from my customers (?), and is a good spot as a lot of the home support comes past this way. There is a minor problem tonight as two teenage girls are sat nearby, asking everyone who walks past 'Who do you support?' Those replying with an alternative answer to Wigan Athletic are treated to a mouthful of abuse. 'Go on, clear off,' I say authoritatively, but my voice knows there's no escape.

'We'll help you sell them!'

To avoid incessant mithering, I give way immediately. They are bloody good too, running over to blokes twice their size, tugging on their shirt ends and saying, 'Buy one of these! Call yourself a Latics fan!' while I stand there swaying slightly due to inebriation. Back they come for more, miles better than me! This is all great amusement to all the passing Latics fans, the ones that know me and the ones that don't. The more genteel ones are content to accuse me of exploiting child labour laws, while the more obnoxious are insinuating something more sinister. Mr Glitter I ain't! Still, they are good for business, as the bulk of the hundred or so I have carried are gone in minutes. As kick-off approaches I make my way into the ground and think about offering them a couple of quid apiece for their assistance, but they just pop the money into my top pocket and are off into the night, muttering something about 'going around to Anthony's'. Later that night, the takings seem at least a tenner short. Tsk, young enterprise, I hope the cider was good. I convince myself otherwise – that a note must have fallen out of my pocket. It wouldn't be the first time.

The atmosphere at the JJB isn't the best at times and is even worse for evenings as people roll up from work at the last minute. Although it would be great if the crowd were to fire the players up, I am afraid at the JJB it often takes the players to fire the crowd up. Twenty-five minutes in, Scott Sellars of Mansfield obliges, when he sees red for a foul, backed up with lip to the referee. The usual jostling between players, the Mansfield fans give the ref a load of abuse, the home fans cheer and goad the Mansfield lot, who are now roaring their team on due to the perceived injustice. Next minute, their manager's off as well.

Ho ho ho. Our manager sympathises. 'It makes a change from it happening to me,' are Paul Jewell's words. Regardless, it's now game on.

Latics win a free kick on the edge of the box. While the Stags are still picking up their collective dummies, Jason De Vos nips in with a diving header which the keeper can only parry to the feet of 'The Duke' who tucks it away. 1–0! Five minutes later and it's that man Ellington again with a looping header to make it two, and Mansfield might as well go home. But they don't, and on the stroke of half-time some sloppy defending leaves Mansfield's Colin Larkin open at the far post, from where he nods home. Here we go again. Wonder if his nickname's Pop? The inevitable happens in the second half as Latics concede another soft goal to the same man to let ten-man Mansfield equalise. I look at the jubilant Mansfield lot, there's a few hundred of them, and I can tell every one of them thinks it's their night now. Jason De Vos, Wigan Athletic's new captain and an absolute giant of a man, then powers home a header with aplomb. 3–2 and the Mansfield fans are not so smug.

The Duke misses numerous chances to get his hat-trick, some are easy, others are athletic, audacious attempts. It would be unfair not to acknowledge the contribution of the Mansfield goalie, Kevin Pilkington, who makes several top-class saves. Right at the end, Mansfield break and Larkin, also on a hat-trick, narrowly shoots wide from the edge of the box. The threat is over, but Mansfield have shown tonight that they have plenty of fight, and are obviously still buzzing from their promotion. Still don't know what happened with Sellars, but we can expect a hot one at Field Mill later in the year, I should wager. We've got the three points tonight, however, so bollocks to 'em!

Good performances all around for the boys in blue tonight, although the plaudits will undoubtedly go to Nathan Ellington, who has had an outstanding game. For several years we have waited for a centre-forward of The Duke's calibre. He gets everywhere, he is hungry and he is a constant threat to the opposition's back four. Compared with the player he effectively replaced, Simon Haworth, he is a breath of fresh air. Haworth was loathed by the majority of the Wigan crowd. Like all the best lazy footballers, he was capable of moments of pure brilliance, but in between those there were a lot of mediocre performances which frustrated the Wigan public. Ellington never stops running and always looks desperate to score, he's got great skill, he is a natural athlete and must be a nightmare to play against. He's also black, which I know shouldn't come into it, but historically Wigan Athletic hasn't had many black players, and certainly not many good ones. Don Page, signed from Runcorn, was an idol of sorts, but generally they have been few and far between.

Wigan, as a town, has always had a very small percentage from ethnic groups in the population. It's hardly a hotbed of racism, it is the home of Wigan Casino and Northern Soul remember, but the club has been known to attract a small but vocal racist element over the years. I'm not about to get into a discussion here, because I personally believe that all political figures, be they far left, far right or slap bang in the middle, are as useless as each other, as is the playground that is the House of Commons. Grown men doing all that hollering and bickering, and they are in charge of our country. What I am saying is that if The Duke can stay free from injury and carry on in the vein that he has been, then he's going to be a legend. The monkey chants heard at many football grounds for many a year were still heard at Latics up until recently, but now you're more likely to hear the uncannily similar-sounding thrust of 'Duke! Duke! Duke! Duke!' ringing around the stands. Signing him has dragged the club into the twenty-first century and, in return for a healthy weekly wage, we'll be looking to this young man to shoot us to promotion.

NINE OUT OF NINE

17 August 2002, Bristol City (h). Won 2–0.

An upbeat mood prevails. It's easy to get cocky after a couple of wins, and boldly predict that this is our year. Somehow, it never is. Don't forget this is the team that has played in nine play-off matches and only won one.

The first half is terrible.

The second half is marginally better. The Bristol City team are intent on kicking lumps out of The Duke despite him having an off day. They only succeed in getting one of their number sent off, and once again we find ourselves playing against ten men. For about 15 minutes, City parry everything we throw at them. Finally, a well-worked passing move cuts them to ribbons and Scott Green is the first of a mêlée of Wigan Athletic players gleefully charging the ball into the net. Belting!

Ten minutes later, and Lee McCulloch is holding the ball twenty yards out while a man creates an overlap on the wing. Thankfully, he ignores my yelled advice to 'Give it, man!' and thumps a screamer into the corner. Great finish! Now he's on the left wing, the pressure to score seems to be off him, and conversely, he's now started to chip in with a few more goals. The team does have the feel of a 4-3-3 formation at times, and yet we still have four in midfield. Many Wiganers were questioning Jewell's tactics last year when we were struggling, nevertheless, he appears to have pulled a masterstroke here with a player who looked all at sea for most of last season.

2–0 will do us against one of the other clubs I fancy to do the business this season. They are another club, like ourselves, who are tipped every year, but cost the punters a fortune. A shame really, because I generally like Bristol City; they are a proper football club who play proper football. It's not for me to say why they are crap, but their support deserves better. A noticeably poor turnout at the JJB today compared with previous efforts, they are normally good for a thousand or so foaming-at-the-mouth cider-swigging loons, but it's still a better turnout than we usually take to their place so I can't be too critical. We do, however, amuse ourselves with the sight of the 30 or so 'teeny terrors' sat nearest to us, all with cute matching Stone Island jumpers and Aquascutum caps, posing and gesturing like Chris Eubank.

Bit disappointed with the home crowd. During the week people were talking to me saying that there might be 10,000 for this game, when in fact there were actually 6,548. It's poor, we know it's poor and we don't need fans of other clubs telling us that, thank you. The geographical location of Wigan doesn't help. Being halfway between Manchester and Liverpool we suffer far more than most as regards the number of glory-hunting armchair wankers in the town. Hanging's too good for them, but the sad truth is that we need them yet they only want to watch Premier League football, and lower division clubs everywhere feel the squeeze.

When the JJB Stadium was opened in 1999, we were lucky enough to play Manchester United in a friendly with Beckham, Solskjaer and Scholes on display. David Beckham played the whole game, and was booed for the duration. This did my box in: a full year had passed since France '98, but being a (bad) footballer myself and a football fan, watching him play was special. How often do we see world-class talent at the JJB, but all people can do is boo him? He might dress like a tit, but he does so safe in the knowledge that millions the world over will follow suit. Or sarong, as it were.

That night we got beat 2–0, one goal undoubtedly handled on the way in by Solskjaer, but I wasn't the slightest bit bothered because I had watched a quality football match and seen quality football players in our fantastic new stadium. It's doubtful whether we will ever play in the Champions League or have players such as Beckham wearing the blue and white, but we are entitled to dream nevertheless. As a kid, Kenny Dalglish was my first footballing idol and I used to badger family friends to take me to Anfield at a time when Liverpool conquered all. So there you go, I was a glory hunter, but at least I saw the light, which many in the town haven't. However, in the '90s I drifted away a bit, playing football on Saturdays, and it was Cantona I had to admire: stood in the middle of the park with his foot on the ball, team-mates and opponents in awe of him. To pull him to pieces, he wasn't a brilliant technical player. He didn't have the pace of Michael Owen, the instincts of Robbie Fowler, the aerial ability of Bobby Campbell, but he had so much presence that you knew he could win a game with his mind alone.

It would have been the same with George Best had I been older. I like United in a perverse way and have massive respect for the 67,000 that fill Old Trafford every week. Yet I'm also an ABU (Anyone But United) of the highest order when it comes to dealing with the twats sat in Wigan pubs with their United shirts on watching the big game, while ignoring their local team. I'll not even get started on the complete bakes in Wigan who follow Manchester City, but at least they can't be termed glory hunters. If one of them hits me as a result of saying this I will be amazed, because it will be the first time any of them has actually got off their backside. The rest will presumably subscribe to watch it on pay-per-view. It's people like this who have directly resulted in clubs like Maidstone and Newport County disappearing, and have put Wimbledon in their current plight.

This does bring me back around to Bristol City, though. They are a very well-supported club in Second Division terms, and you can't help but think that a city the size of Bristol should have a Premier League club. It is ludicrous that they have two average clubs in City and Rovers, when they could merge the two and make one big club able to sustain life in the top flight. Of course, any passing Bristolians will be appalled with that concept, but it makes perfect sense in a footballing economy. Having said that, Hull's a bloody big place but that has not got them anywhere. Football doesn't operate on logic, it's about tradition and passion. Just because Wigan don't get 67,000 every week doesn't make any one of those that do go any less worthy of the term 'fan'.

Today is also the day I reaffirm my tragic affliction of football betting. Let's kick it off with a simple straightforward bet – put three homes down and add an away to bump up the anticipated return. It should be easy enough to find three dead cert home wins and just one away. A £10 stake will return a sum of around £200. Piece of cake, eh? Coupon hard-luck stories are always the topic of conversation come six o'clock. Fulham to beat Bolton. Notoriously difficult to break down, and Bolton Scumderers are always likely to concede on their travels. They have also outstayed their welcome in the Premier League and deserve to get tonked every week this season for moving their ground closer to Wigan than it is to Bolton. 4–1 Fulham. Even forgot that Fulham are currently playing at Loftus Road thus throwing their home form out of the window.

Crewe look good at home. They got turned over 3–0 by Notts County last week, but that isn't going to happen again, certainly not against a team who don't travel too well as a rule. A 2–0 win is secured by the trainspotters. Now the tricky away – a bit impulsive this one. Portsmouth away at Crystal Palace. I figure that Pompey have bought a lot of players recently, including some big names, and would therefore be too strong for Palace, who have signed someone from Brentford and Dele Adebola, who is crap. He's not going to score past the fantastic ex-Wigan centre-half Arry De Zeeuw, and indeed he doesn't. Portsmouth go from 2–0 down to 3–2 up, up Pompey indeed. Now that's what I call good betting, just a home banker left!

Cardiff, Second Division title favourites, at home to one of the weakest teams, Northampton. Dead cert, offering a measly 2/5. The Taffs, however, let me down for £200 as Marco Gabbiadini scores twice for Northampton to bag me out of a healthy beer fund. Still, Cardiff's defeat puts us two points clear at the top. Bastards.

GRASS ROOTS

19 August 2002, Aspull 2 Appley Bridge 1 (Wigan Cup).

The football obsession continues: I've got a new second team, up in Aspull. Quite a few play for our crack Wednesday night indoor league outfit, Cockney Latic FC, reigning Division One champions, I'll have you know. The only prerequisite for us is that you must be a Latics fan to play, although we may have bent that rule once or twice. Oh, and an ability to play like Ronaldo, or take fearful abuse. As an obsessive who reads all the local league results and digests the tables, I thought I'd pop along to watch them play on a Monday night.

Aspull Juniors have a good set-up and run kids' teams from Under-7s to Under-16s. I think the senior committee members got a bit fed up with their players hopping over the border to play for Blackrod Town when they hit 16. The villages are next door, but one's in Wigan and one's in Bolton. Enough said. Over the summer, they have set up their own open-age club, originating in the somewhat humble surroundings of the Wigan Amateur League Division Two, but with designs on getting up to at least West Lancashire League level (an amateur/semi-professional gateway league). From there the North West Counties League, Unibond and Conference undoubtedly await, simple isn't it? They've got some shit-hot players together, including a few of the heads from Blackrod and elsewhere and a few up-and-coming youngsters. They train properly, have got a well-respected manager in Terry Gaskell, and have wiped the floor with everyone in the league so far. They turned over Wigan Rovers 8–1 on Saturday, a team who, 40 years ago, were in the same division as Wigan Athletic! Rovers still have their own pitch and clubhouse, and I always used to like going to places like this. They may pale into insignificance compared to Old Trafford, Highbury et al., but what they have is theirs and has been proudly built and supported by the local community. This is the ethos behind Aspull.

In my playing days I've been fortunate enough to play at the homes of footballing giants such as Formby Town, Garswood United, and even, when much younger, Deepdale and Leeds Road (Huddersfield's old ground) while briefly on Chorley's books. I say briefly, because I was stitched up, someone grassed that I had skipped training to watch Latics in a Rumbelows Cup game at Anfield, like I was going to miss that! I had a good spell of playing on Saturdays at Uni and also for local sides who would scout at college games on Wednesday for Saturdays. Great fun going to rough mining towns in Nottinghamshire as they always had a little shitty clubhouse serving pies and ale, although a bit more serious than my Sunday League team, the legendary and now sadly defunct Swinley FC back in Wigan. I lasted about a month, turned up pissed once or twice and got slated in a game where we lost 7–0. I played alongside a lad called Turner in midfield who made it clear he didn't like 'student wankers' being recruited for the team after having 'played for this club for 12 years'. 'I heard you were even fucking good once,' I said. Two minutes later, the centre-half was dragging him off me. I didn't return and they got relegated. A few weeks later I was walking along Mansfield Road on my way into college, when the binmen were driving slowly by and who should I see picking up the shit-filled green bin bags but my former midfield chum. Well, it gave me a laugh anyway. I wondered why he always bloody stank. 'All right Turner? Thought you played sweeper.'

I could write a book on local football tales alone but I'd sound like one bitter bunny. I'll not witter on about how I could have made it professionally because, to be quite honest, I was and still am complete shite and at the time I was forever disappearing on Saturdays to go and watch a team in blue and white, even driving back from Nottingham and returning on Tuesday when sober.

And so to tonight's prestige fixture, with much better players than me on show, who should and indeed have, in many cases, played semi-professionally recently. Appley Bridge were last year's defeated finalists and are one of the top outfits in the Preston League, and are probably expecting an easy ride tonight. In the first half they should be 5–0 up, but just cannot put the thing in the net, much to the amusement of the watching crowd. There's a rope around the pitch and Aspull are sporting a brand new Brazil-style kit. On the next pitch there are around 60 or so youngsters training, dozens of junior players and potentially future stars, all in 'rugby mad' Wigan. My mate, Joynty, by his own admission, is having a bit of a 'mare in the first half. In fact, Aspull are all at sea generally – there is plenty of neat passing from both sides, but with Aspull it's three good passes then one goes astray. I don't think it's the technical ability that is lacking, but the fact that they have only played together for a month or so, whereas the Appley Bridge lot have been together for years. The half-time score is 1–0 to Appley Bridge: a well-executed free kick is popped into the far corner while the keeper is still trying to organise his wall.

I've watched the first half stood behind Terry, and the ref's bearing the brunt of his wrath. Terry has 'done the non-league circles', as they say, for many years, both as a player and latterly manager of outfits such as Daisy Hill, Mossley and Manchester City's youth team. He is also one of the hardest trainers I have ever played under, a right evil bugger, in the best possible way. For all my talk on a Wednesday about 'going training with Aspull to get fit' I know that if I did I'd end up requiring breathing apparatus after five minutes. He nearly killed me when I was a 16-year-old whippersnapper at Chorley, so he definitely would now. Joynty told me he nearly passed out the first time he trained with them over the summer.

The second half starts and Aspull look more up for it this half, the tackles are flying in. It doesn't boil over at any point but it's more of a contest now. Merse, another Cockney Latic FC star and a cracking player, sends one man sprawling and gets up to walk away. The ref's had enough. 'Yellows, let's have your captain please.' 'He IS the captain,' is the predictable reply from the touch-line! Soon after, an Appley forward breaks free, he squares it to an oncoming player and the ball is in the net. The dozy bugger had, however, played the ball to a man in an offside position, and the goal is disallowed. 'Tell him to read up!' howls Terry. A turning point? I think so, as the home crowd perks up a bit. Joynty tricks his way into the box, jinking past a couple of men until a stray leg catches him, Merse slots away the resulting penalty and at 1–1 it's getting interesting. Ten minutes later, the young forward, Ruddy, who has been causing all manner of problems fires Aspull ahead. A good contest to watch for nowt!

The score remains 2–1, and despite rarely being one to miss a post-match pint, I fire off straight after the whistle. I'm not a part of this club. It looks a great set-up, but of course they are a Saturday outfit, and Latics come first for me. Looking at the squad they've got and with my fitness level, I've no chance anyway. I'm still hoping that Terry will come over and ask what I'm up to these days, even though I've not played competitively for three years and my legs are knackered, but he's too hyped up by the match. He's acknowledged me earlier – one of the few people apart from my family who calls me Martin rather than Jimmy, but he soon turns back to the pitch to bark some more orders at his team. Roll on the Wigan Cup, and maybe I'll offer to become Aspull's commercial director when the all-seater stadium goes up at Dukes Row in a few years.

FROM THE SUBLIME TO THE RIDICULOUS

24 August 2002, Notts County (a). Won 2–0.

There's something about Notts County I can't help but like. They've not beaten us in 14 years and it's also a great city, where I lived for three years, so the memories come flooding back at the mere sight of the place. Half past nine and in good time for the coach at ten, so I'm in McD's stuffing my face. It's a 15-minute walk to the pick-up point, so no problems on that score, except that the heavens open and deposit half of Lake Windermere over Wigan town centre within minutes. Welcome to August in Wigan! I ring up my travelling companion, who's getting a lift in, and his dad picks me up while I wait huddled in McDonald's doorway watching the pavement get pounded into submission.

The coach is half empty, the others are on their way but they've been in a certain, unnamed pub since 8 a.m. for 'breakfast'. Not a long trip by any means, just time to read the paper and the filthy text messages Ian is sending, and indeed receiving, from some bird. Next stop is the Cavendish Arms in Doveridge after briefly pausing to utter choice expletives on passing the Britannia Stadium. In contrast to the earlier downpour, we're now in the beer garden amidst tropical sunshine and there's another tidy barmaid, which several others, not I, are leching over. She's not in the Tewkesbury class, she just looks mucky. Six beers later and it's two o'clock, farewell to another fine hostelry.

After spending 20-odd minutes sat in agony because I'm desperate for a slash, someone kindly informs me there is in fact a toilet on board, tucked away near the back. Relief turns to horror, as I hear laughter before persons unknown carry out the predictable task of barricading me in. A valiant attempt boys, but it's only a matter of seconds until the next person needs it. These toilets on coaches are just about the darkest, scummiest there are but a coach without a bog would result in a lot of en route morris dancing. Reminds me of the tale of the lads who go everywhere on the Scooby Doo bus. They were getting escorted out of Millwall with all the coaches a couple of years back when the locals came bouncing out of a pub while the minibus was stuck in the post-match traffic. On some of the longer trips it had become necessary to provide their own toilet facilities, otherwise they'd be stopping every ten minutes. Therefore, on their minibus there was, what can only be charmingly described as a 'piss bucket'. Oh, you can work the rest out! We never did get on with Millwall!

Back to Notts County, and amazingly, time for a pint in the ground. As lager goes, it is on a par with the stuff which drenched the Millwall fans, but it's still something of a novelty actually being able to have a drink in a football ground, so we take up the offer and join the mêlée to get served. There's a good 1,500 or so present to savour the first half. Notts County are battering us, they've got two good forwards in Danny Allsopp and Mark Stallard although it seems that their entire team are camped in our half. Thankfully, their best opportunities do not fall to their forwards but to the ridiculously named Marcel Cas. He blazes one over and the Latics keeper, John Filan, pulls off a great save to deny him soon after. Just before the half-time break, as we're about to make our way back to the bar for more bad beer, Nathan Ellington hits the bar with a header, our first real chance of note. It's 0–0 at half time, and I will settle for that – we'll hold them for an hour and then break away and score one, because that's the Wigan way.

Lidds is up front, he's never been a 20-goal-a-season man, but he's real quality on his day. Today is going to be one such occasion, when he produces something out of the ordinary. I have always been an advocate of playing him behind a front two in a free role. When you've got a gifted player like Andy Liddell, you should build a team around him, but the team has played 4-4-2 in recent years with wide players, so it doesn't really work; we've also a shortage of decent centre-forwards. He loves the club, having been here a few years now, and loves scoring goals for the club. I haven't asked him to verify this statement, it's written all over his face when he scores. A well-spoken, intelligent chap, but when he scores, he's mad for it, man.

His first is a brilliant finish. He has the ball 25 yards out and is running across the pitch with the ball at his feet, parallel with the edge of the box. He looks up to check the keeper's positioning, but carries on running further out wide. Then, he half turns and launches the deftest of chips over the stranded goalie's head and the ball is nestled in the net. Celebration time – the players come charging over and the fans charge down to the front, much to the consternation of the stewards. The newspapers term it an 'exquisite' chip and I'm not going to argue with that, it was worth the entrance fee alone.

The breakthrough has come and Notts County are torn apart. Their fans are now muted, whereas ours sound like a Welsh choir. Ten minutes later and the Welsh choirboy himself, Mike Flynn, drives through from midfield. He tricks his away to the edge of the box, helped in no small way by Nathan Ellington dragging the Notts County defence left, right and centre off the ball, and he is fouled. Play on, and the ball runs right into the stride of Liddell, who curls a beautiful right-footed shot into the far corner. Cruising. Flynny goes off to a cracking ovation, he looks pleased with his contribution, a young lad who was playing non-league last year. He's probably still clapping 20 minutes later when he comes out of the shower. Other clubs are always slating us for spending money, yet Mike Flynn cost £15,000 from Barry Town.

Unsavoury scenes in the away end at full-time, all because the stewards decide to confiscate a drum off a young lad, followed by a bit of 'all pile in' from the usual suspects. Only the flash of a few police batons prevents a free-for-all. It could all have been avoided by the stewards using a bit of common sense. We've had run-ins with this lot before, though, and know that they don't have any. I remember us going there on Boxing Day a couple of years ago, all in fancy dress, where we saw the surreal sight of a 'Copper' and a '1970s Bovver Boy' being thrown out by another 'Copper' while 'God', 'Superman' and a (male) cheerleader were all hurling abuse at them.

Sainsbury's Castle Boulevard for us. Stella, Monster Munch and a sneaky squirt of Lynx off the shelf. Ian is berating a shelf stacker because the only aftershave we can pilfer a squirt of is Brut. 'Haven't you got any Cool Water or owt?' A certain tour organiser has bought six bottles of Beck's on special offer. 'You lot don't know a bargain when you see one,' he crows, until someone points out the blue 'alcohol-free' label on them. The 'Karaoke Challenge' gets underway, led by Pem's answer to Elvis (Caddy) leading with 'Suspicious Minds' and 'In the Ghetto'. Others chip in with 'Saturday Night at The Movies' by The Drifters, a couple of Jam classics and a bit of Erasure (!) for good measure. Back in Wigan for half seven and not in the best of states. Now I'm getting older I am finding it much harder to combine having a good day out with having a good night out, and an eyewitness confirms that I am seen 'stumbling around the Walkabout without a leg under me'. I reckon I last till about midnight, and I'm amazed I last that long. Another day, another dollar, more importantly, another three points. The league's wrapped up already!!

FUNNY OLD GAME – IS IT BOLLOCKS!

26 August 2002, Port Vale (h). Lost 0–1.

Not at the races at all. Port Vale (played four and lost four) versus Wigan Athletic (played four and won four). Only one result there then! As Neil M called it: 'A classic Latics occasion: top of the league, gorgeous weather, a few extra on the gate, and a complete and utter let down.' Drunkenly predicting a 1–0 Vale win on the website the night before comes back to haunt me. A couple of my non-Latics-watching mates, one a Blackburn fan, the other with no interest in football, lump on Vale at 6/1. The Faroe Isles are only 5/1 to beat Scotland! (And they nearly did!)

Port Vale battle hard, and fully deserve to win. We just look lacklustre and completely out of sorts, nothing is coming off apart from the froth on the Foster's as disgusted patrons storm off to the bar with 30 minutes gone. After four wins on the spin, it may well be deemed acceptable for us to have an off day, but this is just clueless and woeful. I thought that we had put the inept, underachieving days of Wigan Athletic behind us. Second to everything, hoofing it forward, players hiding, a complete contrast to the previous four and just when we think that it cannot get any worse, Vale take the lead on the stroke of half-time. Bloody rubbish Wigan, not coming again!

We'll come out all guns blazing second half, I expect. Sadly it's more pea-shooter-like. Vale have got their lead and defend it using some of the most blatant time-wasting tactics I have ever seen, plus quite a few I haven't. They take it in turns to lie on the floor and feign injury under the most innocuous of challenges. We're not going to get past their keeper anyway, the way he's playing, so why blot the copy-book by taking hours to take goal kicks. I'd rather see a team come here and win with dignity, but we cannot break them down. We only really go for it in the last five minutes of normal time, plus the five minutes the ref has added on due to gamesmanship. We hit the post and force a succession of corners, but their keeper is equal to everything. The crowd, who have been moaning all afternoon at wayward passing, make one big effort to get behind them. We agree that we don't deserve even a point out of the game, but on a personal note we just want Latics to equalise to piss the smugsters off in the pub who have backed against them.

We take heart from the view that it's better to lose to Port Vale than a team who are likely to be up there challenging us, or, heaven forbid, Blackpool or Oldham, from whom we'd never hear the last of it. And at least we don't have the millstone around our necks of a long unbeaten run. Losing every now and then will do us good and make us stronger in the long run. Sorry, it's not working: that was rubbish!

JOURNEY TO HELL AND BACK

31 August 2002, Colchester (a). Lost 0–1.

Trying to fill a coach for Colchester is like trying to get Dracula to give blood. Trying to fill a minibus is marginally easier, say like trying to find a Bolton fan with a GCSE, so still very, very difficult. OK, so Colchester United isn't exactly Galatasaray but it's a horrible place, although it's probably perceived that way in our eyes due more to its location than anything else. As Vaughanie always says, Colchester are there to remind us that, despite all the millions we have spent, we have failed miserably. We'll be there again next year if this performance is anything to go by.

It was looking like filling a minibus would be easy after the Notts County result, when everyone was high as kites (literally, in the case of most of the back-seat boys). Everything is shelved after Port Vale. A few of the lads at the Soccerdome on Wednesday night went last year and confirmed it's a 'nightmare of a trip' so you can understand the apathy. The train's a six-hour, six-connection and (probably) six-hundred-bleeding-quid job. The Supporters' Club do a very good job, but it just isn't my cup of tea, I'm afraid. Sod it, looks like the car it is then.

I only travelled from Nottingham last time, so maybe I'm being naive in deciding to drive down, but nevertheless I find myself working out the best route to take. A search for Colchester brings up the 'Colchester Youth Offenders' website, with pictures of their 'mob' rampaging around such ghettos as Cambridge and Wycombe. I'm more wary of what they'll do to my car with its inconspicuous 'We Come From Wigan And We Live In Mudhuts' sticker plastered on the back. Apparently, the Colchester mob like trashing northern monkeys' cars while the game is going on. Still, the faint heart never drilled the pig and I manage to entice Canny, Penk and Pez along for company. Felt bad about leaving Brasso out (who helped me arrange the minibus) as someone told me 'he doesn't want to go really'. He did, but 24 hours later, I think I could safely say that I did him a big favour.

An eight o'clock start and, despite getting briefly lost in the poxy Potteries, we hit Cambridge at eleven and have a brief stop at a Little

Chef/Burger King. I have meticulously planned the route out (M6–A50–M1–A14–M11–A120) complete with mileage and time travelled estimations. 'Ten minutes maximum stop,' says Mother Goose here. At half past we hit Stansted Airport, and are cruising, but the A-road out to Colchester is a slow, sprawling one, as painful as watching rugby league, and I can now understand why people consider it such a horrific journey. We do about 20 miles in an hour and finally stop at a pub just outside Braintree.The Dolphin is a Royston Vasey pub by all descriptions, full of farmers who all seem to know each other, but they're friendly enough. I think the only woman in the place is locked in the kitchen serving up nosh. It's not the first or last bad decision of the day. Another car load of Wiganers turns up, as directed by us, and moan about the ale while soaking up the sunshine.

A few beers later, at quarter past two, we set off for Colchester with my car following the others. Sharpy, along with Les Bagg, Mitty and Heeley rarely miss a game and have been to Colchester many times before. So I have no need to question why they have driven past the Colchester South turn off, despite having studiously examined the map and various websites and recognising that this would be the best way in. It is, yet still I follow them along this bypass until Colchester Centre and Colchester North have been ignored. Eventually, they turn off and see a road heading back to Colchester town centre. I stay on the road with the intention of turning around, retracing my steps, avoiding the town centre traffic, and using the bypass for its intended purpose. But there is no opportunity to turn around – it's one long road to Clacton, 13 miles away, with absolutely no junctions, a central reservation and it's quarter to three. Looks like a day at the seaside then. The bastards in the other car ring up to take the piss.

After delivering some ridiculous speeds in an already weary motor, I eventually manage to get back around in the direction of Colchester, not before nearly killing the lot of us by going through an unseen red light. On arrival in the town, the ground is very well signposted, and it's in quite a pleasant leafy area. This turns into a red herring as the signposts take us all over the place, no doubt designed to prevent travelling hoolies passing any local public houses. I knew beforehand that there are no car parks near the ground, so I have already made a mental note to park on the side of the ground away from the town centre.

Unfortunately, due to it now being quarter past three, I am forced to park bastard miles away and we face at least a half a mile walk to the ground, getting in at 3.30 p.m. They could have delayed the kick-off. How can we be half an hour late for a game we set off for seven hours ago? Pez tries to get in for a half but the Colchester steward, Martina Navratilova, isn't wearing it. I decline to attempt this trick, although I did once get in through the kids' turnstile at Hartlepool aged 26. In the home end as well. Must have been seriously pissed that day.

We've missed nothing, though. I arrive just in time to see former Ipswich player Micky Stockwell go down screaming in the box under a heavy challenge from Matt Jackson. 'Yer maud squealed like that last night, lad,' chirps I, which raises a few giggles but no penalty. There's only a few hundred here from Wigan, some of the regulars and the southern-based fans who have moved away from Wigan. Mick Geordie (from Sunderland obviously!) is present and as I'm back to goal talking to him, I turn around just in time to see the ball rocketing into our top corner. That is less than fucking ideal. A great goal, begrudgingly, struck by some pimply teenager who has never scored before, ever, not even in that hotbed of Essex, Hollywood's in Romford, I should wager.

Although in the first half Wigan are just a bit mediocre, in the second half they are absolutely terrible and cannot string two passes together. Maybe it's the very unfamiliar red kit we are wearing? Colchester's a tight, partisan ground with much of the noise coming from the 'Barside'. They are giving the ref a hard time, strange really because from where I am standing he seems to be giving them everything. They are a loud, rowdy bunch for whom the word 'lairy' was invented, whereas our fans are struck dumb by our team's ineptness. 'In Your Northern Slums' is sung, how original, along with anti-IRA songs, which I suppose I can understand from such a big army town. We have enough chances to win the game in the second half: Nathan Ellington hits a free kick just outside the post; he also disappointingly lobs wide when clean through; and, right at the death, Andy Liddell hits the post. But Colchester grow in confidence as the second half unfolds, and totally dominate in the face of our meagre attempts to get back in the game.

The biggest cheer of the day from the away end comes when the crowd is announced – a paltry 2,721. A bit hypocritical really, as a few years ago we would have been pleased to get a crowd like that, but it's the first time all day we've been able to give them stick back so a rousing chant of 'shit ground, no fans' is belted out for good measure. I badly want us to equalise just to shut the mouthy Essex boys up.

The frustration begins to boil over as Wigan Athletic midfielder, Tony Dinning, aims a reckless lunge at a Colchester player, earning himself a straight red card. That's not going to help at all Tony, although we do rally a bit after it. I doubt he's cost us the game, because we've never really had it, but I'm unsure about him. Does he do it just because he's a head case, or is it genuine frustration because he wants to win so much? If it's the latter, he's certainly not going to help us by getting sent off. Dinning looks like the one who could be a leader in the midfield, he's certainly got the ability, but he hardly sets a good example. Third straight red in less than a year at the club: grow up or get out!

The journey home takes five hours and is proper suicide tackle. I feel guilty for talking the other three in my car into travelling away with me, like it's my fault that the football team I support are shit. We pass on a beer stop and I just get my head down and drive while reflecting on the day's events. We don't have a divine right to win every game, but the least we expect is for the team to have a damn good go and show commitment, and that looked discernibly lacking today. The few hundred who have travelled the length and breadth of the country to see the game deserve much better than what was served up.

Physically exhausted on arrival back in Wigan, my mood is worsened following a visit to Jumpin' Jaks, paying £2.40 a pint. A load of St Helens rugby players are in, and are putting unravelled condoms (hopefully unused ones) on people's shoulders, proving themselves to be as equally thick a bunch of oafs as their Wigan counterparts, who we frequently see uptown. One question keeps recurring, 'Why bother?' The season is over in August on today's performance. I spend large periods of Saturday night wondering why I've completely wasted a day of my life. I look and feel like shit but still find myself fending off a female's attention. Not exactly Caprice, before you start. I get home drunk (and alone) about 4 a.m., a complete waste of a Saturday. I'd rip my season ticket up if I had one.

SEPTEMBER

LAWRIE'S NOT CRAZY, HE'S A MORBID GIT

7 September 2002, Wycombe Wanderers (h). Won 3–0.

PRE-MATCH BOOZING JUST AIN'T WHAT IT USED TO BE. I'M DRINKING ON ME TOD again, there used to be a whole host of us banging on the pub door at eleven bells in days gone by. It's only half past twelve, but kick-off is at two due to England playing. At quarter to two, one, and only one, of my mates turns up, another one has gone straight to the ground (it's not the hardest place to find your friends when you turn up on your own). Mind you, quite a few work on Saturday mornings, whereas I fell out of my pit at 11 a.m., so maybe it's me who's the lazy bastard. There's still a dedicated group who can be found in The Moon at opening time, but I get in a bad enough state at away games to bother with this for homes.

Wycombe are playing three up front and are going for it, great stuff. They take it to Wigan in the early stages and have plenty of early pressure. Unfortunately for them, the first chance Wigan have is bundled into the net by Lee McCulloch following good work by Andy Liddell. Three minutes, 1–0, and a dream start. This doesn't ruffle the Choirboys' feathers and they continue to attack, the home crowd all know that 1–0 is not going to be enough to win this game, but the Latics players soak up the pressure very well and don't concede.

Just before half-time, the usual time when we concede a goal, we get another. It's that man Liddell again, smacking home a fierce shot after De Vos bravely wins a header. A hammer blow for Wycombe, which in truth, they probably don't deserve. Although the sneery, sheepskin-wearing, gamesmanship master that is Lawrie Sanchez is almost universally disliked amongst the Wigan support, you've got to give him credit for bringing his team here to attack. Maybe next time Lawrie, you should play five at the back, come for a draw, and you'll probably sneak all three points *à la* Port Vale. In the last two games we've resorted to the big hoof upfield as soon as we've been unable to find a way through the middle, and it's both distressing to watch and completely ineffective, due in no small part to the general titchiness of our forward line. Today is different, we are playing football, using the wide open spaces afforded at the JJB.

Half-time and we stay upstairs in our seats rather than venture downstairs for the usual fodder. Just what does half-time entertainment consist of these days? The 'Jumpin' Jaks' Crew, that's what! A bunch of '70s-attired bar staff from the aforementioned bar in Wigan (somewhat cruelly dubbed 'Jumpin' Spaks' by a certain *Cockney Latic* contributor) are dancing about to Steps and S Club 7 in front of the family stand (somewhat cruelly dubbed the 'Gary Glitter Stand' by the aforementioned warped individual). We also have the personality DJ, 'CJ the DJ', parading around the pitch with his bright turquoise suit and spiky hair. Camper than a row of chiffon tents but, hey, if it's what the kids like who am I to argue?

The second half follows a similar pattern in terms of possession. Wycombe have a go but are overwhelmed several times by a stronger Wigan attack who force many corners but fail to add to their tally until the very last minute. After two defeats, it's great to see them bounce back, and at least part of it can be put down to Paul Jewell completely re-jigging his midfield. Tony Dinning is out, following his disgraceful sending off the week before, as is somewhat less fortuitously, Mike Flynn, the young Welshman, to be replaced by Paul Mitchell and Jason Jarrett. Mitchell is outstanding in the middle, he's not the most skilful but he is a young lad who will run and tackle all day, and he hasn't cost us a penny. It's a quality performance from a lad who, despite still only being 22 years old, never lets anyone down when selected. Oh, except when he got sent off on his debut at

Wrexham a few years ago! Both central midfielders play the full 90 minutes today as well, which I believe is another important factor in securing victory.

The midfield pairing have an excellent game and in the last minute it is Mitchell who puts a splendid diagonal ball down the right-hand side, which Liddell picks up. He sprints onto it, cuts into the box leaving a defender in his wake and fires a rasping shot into the far corner of the net. He turns to offer a dizzy grin to the crowd. An emphatic strike to seal a 3–0 victory. Liddell very nearly didn't play, due to the death of a close relative prior to the game, to whom he dedicated his two goals. He is also now this season's top goalscorer to date, not just for Latics but for the entire division. Not bad for a man who 'doesn't score enough goals'.

After the game I retire to The Pagefield to watch the England game and, apart from a brilliant Alan Smith headed goal, it wasn't half as good as the game I had just seen. Needless to say, moments before the goal I was heard to utter just loud enough for the entire pub to hear, 'What's he playing for – he's not international class!' One dickhead is claiming Andy Liddell could do a job for England. What a ridiculous notion! Don't you know he's played for Scotland U-21s and is therefore ineligible? Apart from that, yeah, he's right, I mean if Michael Ricketts can play for his country . . . Must lay off Kronenbourg.

Back to reality, and I consider the role of his strike partner, Nathan Ellington, in all this. At the start of the season, Andy Liddell proclaimed that he wasn't going to be playing second fiddle in the goalscoring stakes to anyone and welcomed the competition. The Duke has shown some great touches today, kept the Wycombe defence on their toes, but not got on the scoresheet. Not taking anything away from Liddell, but maybe now he has a big-name strike partner alongside him, opposing teams are worrying so much about The Duke that they are unwittingly giving more opportunities for Liddell to fill his boots. If Sir Andrew forges a name for himself as a danger man on that basis, and the opposition have got two forwards to worry about, it can only be a good thing for them and the rest of the team. Chuck a revitalised McCulloch playing on the left into the melting pot, and maybe the firepower is there after all. Another outstanding game from Lee today, including a goal and a man-of-the-match award, and it's fair to say that he is also causing his fair share of problems as well. Worth £700,000? Still debatable! Food for thought today, but at least it's *steak au poivre* rather than warmed up Sunday morning kebab.

IT'S GRIM UP NORTHAMPTON

10 September 2002, Northampton Town (a). Worthington Cup Round 1. Won 1–0.

The irony isn't lost on us: several hundred Cobblers' fans chanting 'You Dirty Northern Bastards' at our fans and our players. In the Northern Section of the Worthington Cup? I suppose it could have been worse, but only if Northampton themselves had drawn Carlisle away. I believe that Northampton were turfed out of the Southern Section of the draw to remove an imbalance created by Division One's Ipswich Town getting a bye into the third round due to their somehow getting into Europe in some other much less prestigious competition. As it is, it's a 300-mile round trip for us on a Tuesday night to play in a cup game which clearly isn't very high on anyone's agenda. Crowds are usually pitiful in this competition, and tonight is no exception as a mere 2,336 turn up for this thriller.

Two years ago a two-legged walloping of Scunthorpe set us up for a 'glamour' tie versus Wimbledon. The game at Wimbledon was a 0–0 draw watched by under 2,000 people. A slightly more respectable 5,500 turned up for the return leg at the JJB to watch Wimbledon win a slightly better game aided by the flailing elbows of big John Hartson. It's easy to knock a competition like this, but tell that to Blackburn Rovers fans, who have got into Europe on the back of winning it. I am fiercely critical however, the crowds and interest are minimal, we're not going to win it, so why bother entering it?

At least they're trying to improve the competition by reducing games to a single leg. Even the first-round minnows such as us stand only six wins away from a major final, and a one-off game increases the potential for upsets. Typically in the past, the smaller club would beat the bigger club in the first, usually home, leg only for the bigger club to knock five past them in the return leg, the exception being Everton, who seem to get walloped whoever they play. One step at a time though, so first we've got to conquer our fellow Northerners in a hotly contested local derby. Once again, in the absence of any serious alternatives, I am willing to drive, but my saviour arrives in the form of John Heeley, *Cockney Latic* Technical Executive, who offers to drive. A 4 p.m. departure from Wigan for myself, Statto and Stey Clandon. Clandon's a one-off in these days of Premier League armchair speccies. Not content with travelling halfway across the country to watch his second team at Northampton tonight, tomorrow night he will travel the full length of the country to watch his first team, Everton, at Southampton. I know plenty of folk have a second team, but going to Bournemouth and Cambridge to watch them last season on horrible Tuesday nights takes the biscuit.

Birmingham is navigated with ease. The radio reports on a Black Country fellow who has been fined for painting over a badger for a laugh when he was doing the white lines in the middle of the road. As it's 10 September, there's the 11 September anniversary stuff on the radio, and John mentions it's also his eighth wedding anniversary. 'Well I went to Darlington on the second, I think she's used to it by now!' 6 p.m. and we're at the Sixfields, parked up in TGI Friday's across the way from the ground. A quick hit on Burger King to get our tea and then we prop the bar up in TGI's paying a scandalous £2.75 for a pint of Stella. A little later on we are joined by a few off the Supporters' Coach, and Lee, a Bristol City fan who was born in Wigan whom I first met in Dublin at an England game in 1990. He always shows when we're playing down south. Or should that be up north?

There are a few complimentary tickets flying about outside the ground, but I manage to avoid them and pay £10 (reduced from £14, so well done to Northampton on that score) for a ticket from the Portakabin. Clandon, ever the Scouse blagger, purchases a kid's ticket for a fiver! So that's how he affords it. The home crowd are quite loud and partisan from the off, I think they sound even louder than they have done for previous league games, but that might be inaccurate because I've been blind drunk on my two previous visits to the Sixfields.

The first clear chance is registered by Tom Thumb, or is it Jamie Forrester, who curls one narrowly wide with John Filan beaten.

Probably the last action the Aussie sees of the game, backed up by the Wiganer behind the goal who offers to go and get him a pie and a Bovril in, which brings a smirk from the keeper. Wigan dictate and dominate in all areas, the tackles are flying in, which is good to see; we've all questioned their commitment at times, but it's not an issue tonight. 'Who's that in midfield for them, he looks like a bird?' I ask. Turns out it's Paul McGregor, who made a name for himself with Nottingham Forest as a youngster many years ago, and is as well known for being in a band as being a footballer these days. I didn't know he was still playing. He's getting murdered in the middle by Paul Mitchell, who I suspect doesn't play mellow indie pop in his recreational time.

On the half-hour, all is quiet so I make a call to a mate back in Wigan to check his availability for our game tomorrow. No sooner has he answered the phone than he is drowned out at my end by the deafening (well almost) sound of cheers from the away end! The ball has run free outside the box and Jason Jarrett slots it home with consummate ease to make it 1–0. The Cobblers' defence are as active as sleeping policemen. They're still waiting for a free kick which never came and are now accusing Andy Liddell of pulling a player back to create the goal. If you can imagine how much their players are fuming, you should see the state of the home fans, who are foaming at the mouth, although it's quite possible, judging by the state of some of them, that they were doing that before the goal went in. It's going to be a long night!

The home support are roaring their constant disapproval at the referee, they want him burnt at the stake. Unfortunately, the stand we are in is at pitch level and provides a poor view, so in true Wenger style, I can genuinely say that I 'didn't really see the incident'. They want blood and are chanting the hackneyed 'You don't know what you're doing' at the ref, despite the fact he's just given them a free kick and booked Greeny for nothing to try and curry their favour. He's public enemy number one; the home fans seem blissfully unaware that their team are getting completely outplayed both before and since the goal went in.

On 37 minutes, Lee McCulloch is stretchered off as a result of a vicious tackle, it doesn't look good. He's been one of the stars of the season this year and it's something we don't need, that's for sure. We also don't need Northampton fans calling him a cheat and booing him, but they are still fuming about the earlier incident. This does seem to fan the waves of discontent but both sides play out the remaining minutes of the first half at a much more even tempo.

The second half sees a renewed effort by Northampton to get into it as Wigan sit back for the first 15 minutes or so. We let them have it, but it becomes apparent that they haven't got a clue what to do with it, so we go on the offensive again, creating chances and moving the ball about efficiently. Within a matter of minutes, Andy Liddell hits two brilliant right-footed efforts from outside the box, and both look destined for the top corner, but the Northampton keeper Nathan Abbey manages to push them around the post. It's also great to see that when Northampton do have the ball, Latics are chasing them down, harassing them, forcing errors by refusing to give the Cobblers any time on the ball. I am pretty sure these are the qualities that have been lacking in our two previous defeats. Although, ever the pessimist, I am saying to anyone that will listen, 'You watch – all this possession, and they'll break away and score, extra time and we'll go out on penalties.' Nobody's listening to Suicidal Sid, including the players, thankfully.

The final score is 1–0 and if truth be known, we're never in danger. The Northampton lot are continuing their tirade at the ref long after the final whistle. I think it's just one of those places where they do it every week unless the home team is 5–0 up at half-time, and what the bloody hell is wrong with that? It's long been perceived that a crowd can influence a ref into making decisions, both positively (appealing along with the players for a decision) or negatively (by constantly whinging at the ref and claiming for everything – he's probably less likely to give a decision your way in this instance). Of course, any referee worth his salt would vehemently deny this and state, quite rightly, that they are merely upholding the law, but they are way outnumbered by fans who see it differently.

A very professional performance from the Latics, wearing their brand new white away kit, and perhaps the biggest surprise is that Paul Jewell played his strongest team and has resisted the temptation to throw in a few kids as in past seasons. I must admit that I came to this game expecting, I'd even go as far to say hoping, to see a few new faces as a lot of our younger players come and go without us even seeing them play. But I suppose, taking into consideration the distance we have travelled, I have few complaints about such a strong side turning out and giving a very professional performance to enthuse about.

An easy departure post-match, as you'd expect from a car illegally parked on a nearby restaurant-chain car park. Straight onto a dual carriageway, quick stop to fill up with petrol and provisions and we're on our way. We hit Birmingham at about 11 o'clock and, on searching for a decent radio station, we discover what I presume is a pirate radio station on frequency 92.0. It's bloody hilarious, I can't tell a word this fella's saying, he keeps butting in over the top of Bob Marley records, he's rapping away and a load of his posse are hollering away in the background.

It helps the journey pass a bit quicker. You're welcome to call us parochial northern white trash all you want for being so easily amused, and I've certainly no wish to offend any Afro-Caribbeans in the Birmingham area, who could be Yardies for all I know. Consider it a free plug for your station, which I, for one, will certainly be listening to again the next time I'm travelling through the West Midlands during the twilight hours. I wonder whether a radio station catering for alternative musical tastes could ever appear in the Wigan area. Perhaps some bloke speaking broad Wiganese over the airwaves of Lancashire. 'Eh up marrers, let's geet some Georgie Formby on,' while passing around the pies (as opposed to joints) from his second-floor flat in Beech Hill. Just to clear this one up: it's perfectly OK for Wiganers to take the piss out of Wigan, but when people from other towns start having a go at us, we reserve the right to have a go back.

IT'S BLOODY BALTI-C

14 September 2002, Chesterfield (a). Drew 0–0.

A good ten or so years ago, we played at Chesterfield in a night game, and as I was based in Nottingham I decided to hop on the train, as it was only a half an hour journey. On departing from the train I honestly didn't have a clue where the ground was and as there was only one other person who got off at this stop I followed him out of the station. I followed him through a load of parked cars, only for him to then get in his own car and drive off! I was in a big, long car park and the walk back to the station looked less than appealing on a cold November Tuesday night. I was surrounded by 8 foot-high mesh fencing on three sides, but there was a main road on the other side of it. There was also a gap in the fence where it had been pulled down to about shoulder height – problem solved. It was only when I had scampered over this fencing that I realised that it was covered in vandal grease, and so was my jacket. Chesterfield equals one ruined jacket and a 2–0 reversal. Don't climb fences, kids!

Initial plans for today indicate a train journey with a good dozen or so of my mob deciding to make a day of it. Half eleven and I'm driving around Wigan to pick up the other two. It's 12 o'clock before we get out of Wigan as one of our passengers is fast asleep in bed, oblivious to his prior engagement due to his general drunken state the previous evening. Abuse for me from Neil Goon for charging an extortionate £5 and suggesting a pint in lieu of petrol. This is in stark contrast to Tuesday at Northampton, when we all got John a pint, Stella shandy at that, mind, and willingly handed over the requested tenner apiece. Chesterfield, being roughly half as far as Northampton, and with one passenger less in transit, I hardly feel like I'm being a skinflint. Neither of my passengers has ever driven me to an away game, and both are unfamiliar with the concept of 'petrol money'. This could also extend to cover a bit of road tax, insurance, maintenance costs, depreciation, general wear and tear, and car parking fees where applicable. I also think that the long-suffering driver, whether it be me or someone else, shouldn't have to pay full whack themselves, as they are driving, and shouldn't have to go to the bar to get the ale in either. This cuts no ice with Neil Goon, who is incessantly calling me a tight bastard. 'Get a bloody taxi next time,' I retort, but the verbal assault continues all the way through the Peak District. Ian, on the other hand, is in far too much of a state from last night to consider his fiscal situation and wants us to turn around and go back home because he's had no sleep, having made it home via some woman's house.

We arrive in Chesterfield at about ten to two and get parked up in a council car park (charge 50p – all adds up you see, boys). The weather has changed dramatically since we left Wigan when we took the piss out of Ian for bringing his jacket. From glorious sunshine in Lancashire to cloudy, dull skies over this side of the Peak District, with a temperature of about minus 40. Never, ever trust the weather in Yorkshire. Or Derbyshire. It's fooled plenty more than me, as a quick scan of the away terrace reveals plenty of dickheads freezing to death in shorts and T-shirts.

In the absence of spotting any other boozers in the vicinity, we head for the Saltergate Social, a proper old-school supporters' club, a much-lamented feature of our old ground. A sporting venue such as this is sure to have coverage of this afternoon's Worthington Cup second-round draw, live on Sky? Well, it doesn't actually. I presume they simply don't have Sky and it's not down to the locals' ignorance of the draw being held this afternoon; they are still in the competition themselves, after all. I get on the mobile to a mate back in Wigan at half past two to get the SP – West Brom at home. Typical Wigan, even when we do pull a Premier League club, it's always the least attractive one. A home draw can't be sniffed at, though. I inform the Chesterfield lot we are sat near that they have got West Ham at home – ooh blimey missus, now there's a tie! They are good lads actually, having the craic, talking football, the way it should be.

I ask them if they're expecting a big crowd today because I have heard that they are opening a new stand. Unfortunately for them, it's nothing more than seats bolted onto the terrace, and second-hand seats from Leicester City's old ground at that – not much to get excited about really then! They tell us that due to financial irregularities from a year or two ago the club is on the bones of its backside and all intended redevelopment from when they had money in the bank has now been shelved as they are now £3m in the red. We can and do sympathise, as we nearly went out of business a few times ourselves in the last ten years before Dave Whelan came along. Nobody knows just how close either, but I suspect it could have been measured alongside an insect's genitals.

Onto the cold, blustery open terrace and at this point it would be usual to wax lyrical about the good old days when away fans got piss-wet in a crumbling, fenced-in animal pen, but as I am freezing it's difficult to get too sentimental about it. The bogs are vaguely familiar – a painted brick wall with half an upturned drain at the bottom and a geriatric hospital-ward odour. Chesterfield is clearly not the home of the urinal. My own major complaint is that the wall is about 8 ft high, thus preventing a view of the game while you take a leak. This was an endearing feature of the piss stones at our former home, Springfield Park, along with others such as at Rochdale, where they still might be, but I doubt it.

There is a small segregation area between home and away fans, which also doubles up as a deterrent from climbing the floodlights. It's another reminder of the good (bad?) old days as it is surrounded with loads of spiked fences, the sort which could be found at nearly every ground in the country a few years back. Brighton used to be particularly savage, as did Doncaster and Oldham. At some of the higher division grounds or abroad they used to put metal blades or broken glass on top or even devices capable of giving out electric shocks to deter would-be pitch invaders. From personal experience, I think the vandal grease would suffice for me. You still get daft buggers running on the pitch and it's rarely with malicious intent, but they know that their every move is being tracked by CCTV cameras, so the fun is very short-lived.

The game, like the weather, is unsettled with few bright spots. The only first-half incident of note is a very shallow penalty appeal from Wigan's Steve McMillan, which is turned down flat. There's a bit of discontent on the terraces around me, but I believe that we will have one good spell in the second half and steal it. Soak up the home pressure and counter, not that there is much home pressure.

Half-time and certainly no concourse selling overpriced lager at Saltergate, so a Chicken Balti pie will have to suffice. The highlight of the day. At the risk of getting serious, these crusty delights are right up my street. The first time I sampled one of these beauties was at Walsall a few seasons back and they now seem to have reproduced as far afield as Oldham and Colchester. Best enjoyed on an empty stomach, save three to six pints of lager, and priced towards the more expensive end of the market at £2 each, Egon Ronay would be swallowing his teeth in joy. Decent-sized portions of chicken, a tasty aromatic sauce, all enveloped in a gorgeous pie crust. Free transfer to the JJB please!

The remainder of the half-time interval is spent watching our substitutes knocking the ball about. Half-time seems to last about two minutes when you can get a beer, and about six hours when you can't. Roberts, Ashcroft and a youngster called Leighton Baines are curling pin-point balls into the top corner from 25 yards out. If they did that when they were on the pitch, they might actually be playing and not bench warming, but I think most spectators know though that there's a world of difference between warming up and doing it in a fast-flowing match. This emphasises why even the likes of David Beckham can blaze a free kick over the bar in a match when he's spent all week practising them to perfection.

The second half livens up with both sides coming out looking to create chances. Wigan are on top for the first 15 minutes, forcing several corners and having another penalty appeal but nothing comes of them. Our best chance comes from a break which ends in Andy Liddell failing to direct a header goalwards when clean through following a great cross from Nathan Ellington. Chesterfield are also doing their fair share of attacking and are causing more problems now that they have brought on one-time Wigan target Glynn Hurst up front. A Chesterfield attacker chases a ball which is going out of play and accidentally tackles the linesman in his attempts to retrieve it. The linesman falls flat on his arse and spends a couple of minutes hobbling about before receiving treatment and eventually retiring to be replaced by the fourth official. This isn't the end of it, though, as a request comes through the tannoy: 'If there is a qualified, fully affiliated FA referee in the ground could they please make themselves available at the main gate.' 'I'll do it!' is the cry from home and away end alike.

The 90 minutes are up, but there's another six to play due to the linesman's injury. Nathan Ellington finally gets a ball played to his feet, he runs at the Chesterfield defence and beats two men. He's clean through on goal and faced with a shot or a cross to a man coming in at the far side. He hits a tame (you've guessed it) cross-cum-shot which the keeper mops up with ease. We force a couple of corners, but Chesterfield have the lion's share of the late chances to steal it at the end – a ball whips across the face of our goal and is an outstretched boot away from giving them all three points.

A 0–0 draw away from home isn't a bad result, but it's the expectant away fans who are disgruntled, the home fans are delighted. I consider that it is the late events that shape a football fan's memory of a game, and as Chesterfield finished the game attacking, their fans are naturally more upbeat. Football fans have short memories and many a player or a team has got away with a bad first half by redeeming themselves in the second. It never works the other way around, though. Oh, and there is also the small matter of several million pounds that has been spent assembling our team, which means that we quite rightly have slightly higher expectations than the Chesterfield lot.

There is a muted round of applause for the players and the thousand or so travelling fans head for home and the tropics of Lancashire. Get the results on – the coupon must come up today. Three draws paying around £200 quid for a fiver stake. Only one comes in – Rochdale vs. Shrewsbury. The other two result in narrow away wins for Blackpool at Wycombe and Bradford at Walsall, suggesting I wasn't all that far off, but you get bugger all back from the bookies for getting it nearly right.

The other result of which I take note is Oldham whacking Mansfield 6–1. We have developed a serious dislike of Oldham in recent years, they seem to be a particularly bitter bunch, upset at their demise from the top flight (which they only got into due to their plastic pitch). Apparently we're not allowed to be called 'The Latics' because they are called 'The Latics'. They claim that we are insignificant to them, that we're not their rivals, that Manchester United are their rivals (yeah I bet they're really bothered by you as well), yet they are the first ones to come onto our website mouthing off when we get beat. I think they have a deep-rooted fear of us getting any success and exposure because we will start to become more recognised as 'The Latics' than they are.

Unfortunately, they seem to have put together a decent side this year and may well be up there challenging, and don't we know about it. Their latest stunt occurred on the Sunday night where some halfwit posted a story on our website about the Bristol Rovers chairman dying of a heart attack. When you read the story it was some kind of joke involving him laughing to death because we paid £1.2m for Nathan Ellington. It sufficiently offended many Rovers and (Wigan) Latics fans alike, and although I'm not the easily offended type, I still used the opportunity to get on my high horse and let these Oldham types know exactly what I thought of them. Tossers.

Our work for the day is done. I'm keen to bomb it back to Wigan, but the other two occupants are tactfully hinting at stopping at a chip shop. It's mentioned approximately 182 times between 5 p.m. and 6 p.m. I deliberately drive past one because they're winding me up; I don't even eat many chips, as my toned physique implies. We get as far as Hazel Grove before I eventually succumb to their culinary needs, but not before laying out the fundamental ground rule. 'No eating in the car, it'll bloody stink. I've got a job interview Monday, my suit'll stink of haddock by the time I get to work!' This proves to be a bad move as at least half of the travelling Wigan support passes by while we are sat on a wall scoffing chips by the A6 and, of course, it's me not the other two who receive the inevitable 'U FAT BASTARD' text messages. Cheers boys!

THERE'S NOTHING QUITE LIKE MEETING UP WITH OLD FRIENDS

17 September 2002, Tranmere Rovers (a). Won 2–0.

A quarter past one on the morning of Wednesday, 18 September and I am sat at my PC, eating cornflakes and laughing my tits off. What a game and what a night!

There's been a number of links between Tranmere and Wigan in recent years and this undoubtedly adds a little bit of spice to our clashes now that we are in the same division. There's not really any bad blood between the respective fans and players, with one notable exception. Arriving at the ground at ten to seven for this evening game, we decide to go into the official club car park. Without wishing to stereotype people from Merseyside, asked whether we're home or away, we gullibly answer 'away', to which the steward responds, '£4, mate'. Con artists! He does helpfully advise us to get rid of our cans and spliff 'cos the busies are on the blob at the minute', whatever that means.

The poor view from the Cowshed End is apparently worth £15 as opposed to the superior home Kop retailing at £12. Another case of away fans getting fleeced, methinks. Some very large kids decide to pay the much more reasonable sum of £3 to get through the juvenile turnstile instead. The bar's disappeared from inside the ground but the away end's packed solid with Wiganers as the 2,500-seater stand is completely full. Strange how Tranmere saw fit to announce an away following of 1,461 the next day. I'd like to have seen where they could have fitted the rest in. All I know is that however many are there, we give the boys great support on a high tempo evening, only matched by our abuse for one fellow in particular.

Simon Haworth. Where does one begin? When we paid £600,000 to Coventry in 1998 for a Welsh international, I think the majority of Latics fans were in a state of disbelief. His goalscoring record at Latics was very, very good: 44 goals from 99 starts must make it all the more baffling to the outsider as to why we hate the lazy Welshman so much. But Haworth became a symbol of everything that was going wrong at our club: a player who possessed skills that many of his predecessors could only dream of, but with the heart of a flea. The debates raged throughout last season – he was still our number 9, the man most likely to get a goal, and he could produce moments of wonderful individual skill from nowhere. He wasn't, by any means, the worst of the mercenaries who were bleeding our club dry, at least he made the effort to bugger off when he got the chance before his contract expired. You either loved him or hated him, but the manner in which he departed from the club ensured that 99 per cent of our fans ended up hating him.

It was apparent in the weeks leading up to his departure that he simply didn't want to play for Wigan Athletic any more, the club that had been, and still were, paying him a handsome salary. His performances deteriorated to a level where he found himself on the bench, and the final straw came when he came on as a sub against Cardiff City, his home-town club. With Latics already 4–0 up, he spent his time on the pitch gesturing to the Cardiff fans, 'Doing the Ayatollah'. Funny? Maybe. But to do this while still a Wigan Athletic player, was naive at best, and totally disrespectful of the club that were paying his wages. The gangly leek-eater never had the decency to apologise, so we'll never know what was in that head of his.

If Wiganers only have bad things to say about Haworth, I doubt anyone would ever say a cross word about Tranmere's current manager, Ray Mathias. Two very successful stints as manager of Latics ensures that he will remain an ever-popular figure, only denied an even greater prize by a cheating Shaun Goater and the lack of grace of Fathead Joe Royle in the play-offs against Manchester City. And did you hear the one about the centre-forward who scored 20 goals before Christmas and was then dropped barely to be seen again? Stuart Barlow's main crime was to ask for more money and an improved contract, hardly an act of treason, bearing in mind his goal tally. A few people accused him of being greedy, but I don't think you'll find too many people arguing that this dispute cost us promotion that season. Last year, when he returned with Tranmere, he scored the winner for them and many home fans actually clapped and cheered this! Indeed, his name is cheered tonight by the Wigan fans before the game when it's read out. Normal service is resumed later as when he takes a tumble he is called a 'diving Scouse bastard' and also receives some interesting hand signals when he has a goal disallowed for offside.

In contrast to this, the abuse of Simon Haworth is unabated. From the moment he steps onto the pitch, 'Simon Haworth is a wanker' comes booming out of the away end ad nauseam. Although we gave him some stick at home in March, the away support is always much more vociferous, and this is our first chance to show him exactly what we think of him. I feel a bit ashamed because there are a lot of kids in the crowd (real ones, not the thirty-somethings who have squeezed through the wrong turnstile) but it appears that they are joining in as well! It doesn't seem to be having the desired effect as the big Welshman is throwing himself about in the manner that we very occasionally saw when he was in a Wigan shirt. He's got a major point to prove and earns himself a first-half booking in the process, which inevitably delights the travelling contingent.

It's not a brilliant first half, the referee is giving Tranmere everything, and the linesmen must think they're at the Golden Jubilee judging by the way they're waving their flags about. This does work in our favour however, as Tranmere are piling it on and we are heartily relieved to see a Barlow goal disallowed for offside midway through the half. Rovers are playing the classic Mathias way that we are all so familiar with: three up front, getting behind the defence in wide positions and pumping crosses into the box. Ray is by no means a tactical genius, but he gets the best out of his teams attack-wise. Many feel that he would have had his limitations had he taken Latics into Division One but given the choice between his positive, passionate outlook and the dire, defensive style of someone like Bruce Rioch and there's only one winner.

Simon Haworth is doing his best to put one over his old club, but is being superbly shackled by Wigan captain, Jason De Vos. The threat is constant though, and we are quite fortunate that the game is still goalless. The Haworth-baiting has now reached epidemic proportions, as a group of individuals near the front have taken to chanting naughty stuff about Haworth's off-field activities during his time in a Wigan shirt. We can only speculate how pleased he is to hear the half-time whistle so that he can clear off up to the other end of the pitch for the second half.

The second half, not for the first time this season, springs the game into life, and it's good news . . . well, kind of. Andy Liddell makes a cracking run into the box and is felled crudely by a Tranmere defender, the referee points to the spot – PENALTY! The dust settles but Andy Liddell, the club's penalty taker, is sprinting towards the dressing-room, as disbelief hits the away support, 'He's been sent off!' Our player, not theirs! I reason that maybe he's bleeding, or his boot is split, surely he can't have been sent off for diving? The referee's gone too far this time! It's definitely a penalty, and Liddell heads straight down the tunnel while The Duke lines it up.

There are few protests at the sending off, mainly because it takes a while to register what has happened. No one boos the referee's decision because no one knows what it is. It turns out the Tranmere centre-half, Graham Allen, has lunged in, charged towards the prone Liddell, stuck his ugly mug into his face, and called him a 'cheating twat' to which Liddell has responded by pushing his face away with his hand. You can't raise your hand at an opponent in football, in any circumstances, so Liddell has to go. A three-match ban means he will miss games against fellow challengers Plymouth and Cardiff, along with the Worthington Cup tie against West Brom, all thanks to a mouthy Scouse git.

We still have the outstanding matter of a penalty kick to be taken, and with Andy Liddell sent off, the responsibility falls to Nathan Ellington. He hasn't scored in seven games, and I am seriously praying that he doesn't miss this penalty. Imagine what it could do to his confidence and our whole season if he does? With no exaggeration, he 'does a Beckham' – hands on hips then smacks it straight down the middle. Sometimes a penalty being converted only results in muted celebrations, as it is considered little more than a formality, half the celebration taking place when it is awarded in the first place. Not this time though, and the crowd goes daft when the ball hits the net, just like when Beckham banged that one in against the Argies. No shit. The Duke accepts the hugs and calmly walks back up the field, a sense of relief more than anything that he's back on the mark. A great booster.

A reality check: there's 35 minutes to go and we're down to ten men against a side that had us under the cosh when it was 11 vs. 11. I don't really do clockwatching as a rule, but I must be looking at my watch every single minute from here on in, muttering, 'There's no way we're going to hold out here,' with my arse flapping like a dustbin lid. It must be a great game for a neutral as Tranmere step up their efforts to get back in the game, but I am praying that we can somehow sneak another from somewhere. Rovers are coming at us in waves now, it's relentless, but tonight the Wigan team are lionhearts, every one of them tackling ferociously and leaping for every ball. Paul Mitchell, in particular, is hitting them with some crunching tackles and no one can touch the towering Jason De Vos in the air.

When we do break, we win a free kick. JDV steals a yard at the back post on his slack marker (a Mr S. Haworth of Cardiff, I believe) to flick a header across the face of goal, a further nod by Lee McCulloch and Nathan Ellington bundles it over the line! 2–0, it's two bloody nil! 'We've only got ten men!' rings out. It would be great to see The Duke bag a hat-trick, but I'll settle for this. Fortunes are about to get worse for Tranmere and especially for one duffel coat-wearing Welshman.

There's a few rough challenges going in on the edge of the Wigan penalty area; it's hard to see at the other end whether they are 30 yards out or on the goal line, which is no good at all for my nerves. I do see the ball land at a Wiganer's feet and then make out a Tranmere player go lunging in with both feet, sending the Latics player hurtling up into the air like he's on a trampoline. The away end erupts with rage, even from here we can see that the challenge was pure filth, whoever's done it must go. Leaving again, Simon?

Now, I could open up a moralistic debate about whether fans have the right to abuse players here, referencing such cases as Cantona at Selhurst Park or even the night prior to this game, when a Birmingham City fan ran onto the pitch to taunt the Aston Villa goalkeeper. But I won't, because if there's one little thing that every Wigan fan does know about Simon Haworth following his playing career with us, it is that no one knows exactly what goes on in that head of his. Yeah we might well have got to him abusing him all the way through the game, and I've heard on good authority that the Wigan players were winding him up too. You might consider all that a bit pathetic. But that tackle and attitude just typifies his time at Wigan Athletic: 2–0 down and he doesn't fancy it any more so he lashes out and exits via the coward's door rather than trying to help his team get back into the game. His final gesture as the abuse rings around shows him at his petulant best as he gives us his famous Cardiff 'Ayatollah' salute once more. I hope Matty fines him every last penny of his wages!

Tranmere rally at ten-a-side, but we're professional enough to hold them at bay and play out the remaining minutes. This is a big, big win, the three points earned are the difference between us remaining top or dropping to sixth, and both the fans and players know it. It takes a good 20 minutes to get off the car park, but this is probably a good thing as the Tranmere hard men are going around kicking in cars with normal fans inside, such as my mates known as the V100s, who were stuck on the main road. Now, like it or not, anyone present at this game would confirm that there was a large mob of Wigan present who wouldn't have been averse to a scrap with their opposing numbers, only police intervention preventing it. No need to go kicking off with innocent parties, though. That's lower than a snake's arsehole, and I know two wrongs don't make a right but I'd gladly have liked the Wigan mob to have met up with those Tranmere cowards and see how they'd have fared. A sour end to the day for the V100s, but knowing their resolve, by the time they had reached the Mersey tunnel they would have been laughing again at the actions of that silly Welsh bugger!

THE CHARGE IS COMPLACENCY. GUILTY AS CHARGED

21 September 2002, Peterborough United (h). Drew 2–2.

2–0 up and cruising with an hour gone, the cigars are lit as Peterborough are absolutely shite. A late sub who isn't on the team sheet comes on to spoil the day and cost us our top spot.

The first half isn't mindblowing football, but it's good enough. We create enough chances to go three or four up but no one's putting them away. After 38 minutes, Lee McCulloch has his shirt tugged in the box and the referee blows for a penalty. Andy Liddell, back on after Tuesday's early exit, steps up, performs a little shimmy (a new part of his routine) before sending the keeper the wrong way. I'd like to say the crowd goes wild, but it's all a bit expected and half the people near me use the goal as an excuse to bugger off for a half-time pint. Compared to the Tranmere goal in midweek, you would barely notice we'd scored.

Fanzine selling at half-time, sales are brisk, enabling me to sneak in a quick pint. This turns out not to be the best move of the day, however. That's because as I am finishing it off, Nathan Ellington is finishing off the best move of the day, sweeping the ball home from a corner to make it 2–0 at the start of the second half. First goal of the season missed, and I'm certainly not the only one, as half the stand is still downstairs supping up. Not really just after half-time either (53 minutes) and it looks well when a large percentage of the crowd miss probably ten minutes of every game due to having a pint. In my own defence, I only bought the pint a minute before half-time ended. Numerous wags offer to pay for my beer for the rest of the game on my return, they know full well the bar is shut, tight gits.

After an hour of the game, we appear to bring on an extra player called Complacency. I don't know why this Complacency fellow creeps into the side, but every now and again he turns up. No one likes him or rates him, but he looks to have a key role in today's events. Ideally, we'll get rid of him and we'll never see him again; he's not a popular player but I am quite aware that this might not be the last we see of Complacency in a Latics shirt. The fans are all as guilty as the players in this instance. It's hard to get worked up over this game, there's no doubt whatsoever that at 2–0 down, Peterborough will now roll over and die. I know it, all the other fans know it, the manager knows it and the players know it. Peterborough United evidently haven't read the script.

We're all slating the players after the game, but to be brutally honest, we're every bit as smug as they are. One minute I'm sat in my posh seat, looking at the players on display, thinking how great we are, and how we're going to romp this division, next stop Real Madrid at the Bernabeu in the Champions League. Quick as a flash it's two apiece and we've contrived to throw it away.

Talk about a smash and grab. They have two chances and score two goals. That's not to sound bitter, they take their chances and deserve a point every bit as much as we do. Both their goals are worthy of merit, too. The first one results from a cracking through ball by a Boro' midfielder which carves us open, and the lad takes his chance well. Their equaliser, 13 minutes later, is caused by the same player turning provider, chasing down a lost cause, to win the ball out wide. He whips a cross in, and with what looks like at least half the gleeful Peterborough team waiting in the box to fling themselves at it in a Red Arrows-style formation, there really is only going to be one outcome.

There's no doubt that this is two points lost: all we had to do was remain professional and shut up shop. What we actually did was invite Reg bloody Holdsworth around and instigate a grand opening of a Bettabuys superstore in the middle of our back four. Booing the players off isn't the answer, although it seems a realistic solution for some of the crowd. I think the players know that they have made a major cock-up on this occasion and don't need reminding of it.

Back to reality. A draw against Peterborough isn't as costly as a draw against Cardiff, whom we play in our next home game. There will be no complacency in that one, you can be sure of that. I'll forgive the team for today as long as they get it right for Cardiff. I'll also forgive Nathan for scoring when I wasn't watching, because I've put a tenner on a horse called 'Duke of Hearts' which romps home at 6/1. The boys on the pitch, like the fans in the stands, struggle to get hyped up for the likes of Peterborough at home. We all have our part to play and didn't perform. The next home game against Cardiff will be a totally different kettle of fish. Or sheep, if you prefer.

DREAMS CAN COME TRUE, BUT MINE NEVER DO

23 September 2002. Interlude.

It's not like Wigan Athletic rule my life. I guess I probably do think about them every day in a variety of ways, but there's probably a lot of fans who do exactly the same. Saturday was undoubtedly another kick in the teeth for us though, and there were a couple of incidents in the days after the game which had a very strange effect on me.

I didn't sleep very well on the Sunday night, it possibly had something to do with the fact that I had been out on the beer till daft o'clock (earthquake, what earthquake?), but I was very late leaving Wigan for work on Monday morning. I was stuck in traffic about nine o'clock, going through Goose Green, when I felt a pair of eyes burning in on me. It was a young man, driving a big Lexus-type car, with a gorgeous blonde sat alongside him. He was staring intently at the Latics team mini-kit hanging from the front of my car, and this stare was only broken when I caught his eye. The driver of the car was Gary Teale, Wigan Athletic winger, signed from Ayr United last season.

In his first few games, he was a truly fantastic player. He played against the league champions, Brighton, and tore them apart with his pace down the wing and accuracy when whipping the ball in. 'He can catch pigeons, this lad,' exclaimed Paul Jewell. This season, he's been largely inconsistent. Why? I wish I knew, as he still must possess that pace and ability. He just tends to stop and pass the ball now rather than having a run with it. If it's a confidence thing then I just can't understand why – he must have landed a good wage increase since moving from Ayr to Wigan. If that doesn't show that someone's got confidence in you, then what does? Since his early days, he's been in and out of the team, and he can have little complaint about that due to his inconsistent performances.

It was just a surreal moment in my eyes; he was staring with great determination at the team kit. He didn't look intimidating, quite meek in fact, sat there behind the wheel of a luxury 40-grand car, looking back at the ordinary Joe on his way to the office in his M reg Golf. I have driven a Lexus myself in the past, not mine, obviously, and they are a class car. I am 29, have a degree, professional qualifications and I am a country mile away from being able to afford a car like that. This is why the expectancy is on the players to perform, their trade gives them the lifestyle that the ordinary fan can only dream of, so are we wrong to expect them to keep playing for the full 90 minutes? I'm not having a go at Tealey, I really rate and like him. But I liked the Gary Teale I saw last season much better and can't wait for him to return.

On Tuesday night I had a terrible night's sleep and a bizarre dream. I dreamt that I was in my 'den', nothing to do with Millwall but a secret den which all kids used to have before PlayStations took over. My den was my pride of place, well hidden in a local park, and I might well have been laying out the carpet which I had recently procured from the council tip on Frog Lane, but I can never remember the detail in dreams. On this occasion there were loads of kids passing by outside, shouting and making noise. Some were just the local kids, whereas others were older, rougher kids. None of them came into my den, it was too well hidden. But they were lurking about outside, and would undoubtedly wreck it if they found it – it was all a bit scary for me, and I awoke in one of those cold sweats, as seen in episodes of *Dynasty*.

I thought about contacting one of those dream psychoanalysts about this but I think I know what they'd say. Apart from, 'Go away you fucking freak!' No, you see, thanks to our draw with Peterborough, and Cardiff's draw with Plymouth earlier on Tuesday night, we had now slipped to third in the league on 20 points. It was all getting too close for comfort, and the vultures were circling: Cardiff 21 pts, QPR 20 pts, Oldham 20 pts, Crewe 19 pts, Blackpool 18 pts, Brentford 18 pts. Ah yes, it was all clear now: these were the kids who were trying to destroy my dream, and 'the den' was the club that I loved. Come on, I'm 29, I don't really have a secret den, do I? Or maybe you just haven't found it yet.

The dreams continue. I once read an article about football dreams in a Gillingham fanzine entitled *Brian Moore's Head Looks Uncannily Like London Planetarium*. Some time later, when I had dropped off, there I was, at the Priestfield Stadium, home of the Gills. Not on the terraces though, but on the pitch, which was sunken like a Roman amphitheatre, playing! My fellow Latics team-mates, were, in fact, my former workmates, mostly women at the time. Not that I'm complaining about the service as they set me up twice!

Next minute, I find myself travelling on a local train from Swansea to Cardiff, through the Valleys, and at every stop there's hordes of Welshmen on the platform hurling abuse at us. The train was packed full of a mob of Wiganers, and I was only concerned because I was trapped in the aisle by a window and thought a brick was going to come through at any point. The travelling Wiganers didn't seem too bothered by this though, as they were too busy humming the theme tune to *Van Der Valk* on kazoos with the 'oohs' inserted at relevant points. I also recall a little Asian chap manning the trolley service, which had the usual overpriced pop and crisps, but also a mile-high stash of pies and pasties, all with red foil trays. I'm cracking up. Our last away game of the season is at Cardiff, and could be a promotion decider. It is a hostile place to go at the best of times, but I know I'll be there regardless. I also had a dream about a beautiful maiden with fair hair and heaving bosoms, but I will leave describing that one for my follow-up book *Let's Get in the Nack*.

ARISE SIR ANDREW LIDDELL

28 September 2002, Barnsley (a). Won 3–1.

Barnsley away has been earmarked early doors as a major turnout. Ex-Premier League club versus little Wigan, and I knew before the game, when I was walking down the hill at Oakwell and the 'Mudhuts' chants were ringing out, that there was only going to be one winner today. Feel a bit for Barnsley's current plight but not so much as I don't want us to take all three points off them.

Wakefield RUFC is the pre-match venue, and a severe hammering of the £75 jackpot bandit for myself. Five-pence-a-go fruit machines are a cop-out, bandits for girls in fact. They are cheap because they don't pay out, although it's got to be said that 'Casino Crazy' is one of the better bandits I have found in a lifetime spent in arcades and pubs. I have fond memories of one of my mates taking one for £250 in a snooker hall in Wigan and filling a pint pot up with golden nuggets. The rugby union club is an amicable enough venue and the food smells great. However, they don't have Sky, so after a swift pint we get itchy feet and venture into Wakefield. When we ask for directions to 'Boland's Bar', the bloke we ask says 'WEEE-IIIRRR?' as opposed to 'where' in just about the broadest Yorkshire accent I've ever heard. We always drop on the village idiot when asking for directions.

We do eventually find Boland's Bar and I settle down for a few pints of Guinness and the noon kick-off of Leeds vs. Arsenal. This pub is a big old place, and it's as rough as buggery but there's enough of us in here not to be budged. It's Wakefield's version of Harry's Bar, full of Leeds fans, and I wouldn't like to tar all Wakefield folk with the same brush, but I've never seen such a public display of ugliness before. Arsenal are a class above and Leeds can have no complaints about the 4–1 drubbing they receive. I soon get into this fascinating football and am only distracted by a comedy text message from my mate Naylor back in Wigan asking me, 'HAVE U TWATTED ANY FAT MINERS YET?'

Back to the rugby club before the coach leaves at two, where I have another pint and a takeaway chicken chasseur, which miraculously manages to refrain from landing on my clothes. The traffic's very slow-moving and it takes most of the hour until kick-off to reach Barnsley. On approaching the ground there's a mob of lads spilled all over the road, at least 100 of them. I recognise a few familiar faces and they're all Wigan. Closely flanked by a load of coppers, some of this lot scare the living daylights out of me, so God knows what Barnsley think. As our own contingent comes bouncing off our two coaches, there must be 250-plus lads parading down the hill to Oakwell, in what resembles a scene from *Zulu*. Add these to another thousand or so in the ground, and it's a strong and drunken away following of the highest order.

We're in the ground for all of two seconds when we score. Andy Liddell, former Barnsley player, has turned in the box and planted one in the far corner. Plenty missed it, still outside queuing to get in, I just catch the ball nestling in the net. No better sight, apart from loads of Wiganers jumping about with glee. Barnsley are very lacklustre, a team disastrously low on morale. They still haven't really come to terms with being relegated, and apart from the lad called Betsy on the wing, don't look dangerous at all. The lad stood behind us IS Ron Manager, barking orders at the players in deadly serious fashion, 'Keep it tight . . . Push it out . . . Mark them up . . . Push them up.' Sadly not 'Shut Up' but there's no harm in him and I have a tendency to do this myself at times, so I'm keeping quiet. It's 2–0 before half-time as Matt Jackson thumps home a header off a Scott Green corner. It's a bit sad, really, to come to a proud old place like this and take the piss but you can't get sentimental about the opposition. They'd be doing the same to us if they could.

There's all sorts of half-time entertainment going on, including the standard penalty shoot-out and a game of touch rugby, all very dull though, and no bar means we're forced to watch it. The stewards at the front of our stand are all happy, cheery-looking sorts, defying the notion that all Barnsley folk are typical, miserable, tight Yorkshiremen. Rumour has it they are only so welcoming towards visitors because it gives them someone else to moan at. They're soon to fall out with us, though.

Five minutes into the second half, Barnsley and ex-Everton midfielder Mitch Ward, who doesn't even vaguely resemble David Hasselhoff, lunges in on Lee McCulloch to earn himself a red card. The fifth one we've seen in 12 games, and I often find it takes the shine off a win, because neutrals will look at the game and say 'yeah, but they only had ten men' even though the game was already wrapped up before the red card. The third goal isn't too far away, and a cracking ball in from Ellington is met with a thumping header from Scott Green. This one is down our end, and when Greeny comes charging over to the away support waving his shirt about over his head, there's a stream of Colin Jackson impersonators hurdling over the perimeter, led by my mate and newly redundant postman, Mushy. I stay out of this one as I'm four or five rows back, but the poor stewards haven't got a clue. As they force the Wiganers back off the turf, a bloke with a horrible brown suit on comes charging over, and attempts a few WWF moves on some of our number. There's a bit of human tug-of-war, but everyone gets back off the pitch without ejection or arrest. I'm quite open-minded on the subject of pitch invasions: whereas I would never condone someone going on with the intention of intimidating a player, I fail to see the harm in fans jumping on to celebrate with players when a goal is scored.

The players seem to be caught up in the mayhem, as straight from the kick-off Barnsley pull one back, through their one impressive player, the boy named Betsy. That's as close as it gets, there's no way that the ten of Barnsley are going to pull two more back, and that's the way it stays.

The noise from the away end is now deafening, and it was pretty loud prior to this. Everyone is singing Andy Liddell's name just to let Barnsley know how silly they were to sell him to us – it took him all of two minutes to prove that today and we're really going to miss him when he starts his three-match ban. We've done a real job on them today, and I can't see their fans putting up with this kind of performance for much longer, finding a way out of their current troubles will be another story of course. From the Wigan point of view, it's a great day and a great result. I know that it will count for nothing if we don't manage to get promoted at the end of the season but it certainly doesn't stop us toasting a great victory. The players' tunnel is right next to the away end and the team gratefully accept the plaudits of the fans as they make their way off. The Duke hobbles off with a slight knock, and as he receives a standing ovation, I swear blind that he's blushing! The Barnsley fans, by contrast, are booing and baying for the blood of their team. Amazingly, this emphatic win has resulted in a drop down to fourth place, as the other teams around us (Cardiff, QPR and Oldham) all record better results than 3–1. As we leave Oakwell, we see a mob of their fans coming charging around the corner. Hello, looks like it's going to be lively. It's not us they're after, though, it's their manager and board: 'We want Parkin out' is their chant.

The coach goes straight home this time, due to another ridiculously over-zealous police escort. Now, I'm not saying there should be a booze stop to help soothe the journey home, but when you don't have anything at all to drink and you've just spent the previous 90 minutes shouting and bawling your head off, it does get quite painful. A few cans to lubricate the vocal chords wouldn't go amiss, especially for those of us who, like me, find it completely impossible to fall asleep on any form of transport. We amuse ourselves by laughing at clusters of red-faced Blackpool fans overtaking our sluggish coach, gesticulating wildly. One fat freak is more or less hanging out of his car window, kissing the badge on his horrid tangerine shirt. As we've just won, and they had just lost 1–0 at Chesterfield, I've no idea how this ferocious fatty's actions are meant to do anything other than create mirth. You can see his chubby chops reddening further as he desperately tries to convey exactly what a bunch of pie-eating wankers he thinks we are. Must try harder, obese Blackpool muppet. Hilarious.

Drinking is resumed as a party atmosphere prevails in Rik's Bar. I've bumped into one of the team and brought him in with me, and the poor bloke gets mithered to death. He'd probably prefer fit birds to fat alcoholics, but you can't have everything. On to the Aussie Bar where I do my usual trick of hurling abuse when they play 'Delilah', 'No Stoke songs in Wigan pubs, you tossers!' Drunker than Alex Higgins on a Bank Holiday weekend. I'm up early Sunday thanks to some Cockney geezer who has taken to ringing my mobile throughout the night and asking for 'Marie'. After being told on several occasions that Marie isn't here, he changes his tack to asking 'What are you doing with Marie's phone, then?' I inform him that Marie probably doesn't want to see him again and that's why she's thoughtfully given him a bogus number (MINE!) which quietens him down for a few hours.

Sunday's big bet is determined in honour of Saturday's goalscorers, as the Ladbrokes' inhabitants all pile on Scott's View at 5/1, which funds yet another day on the beer. I sleep like a baby when I get home at midnight. Well, until 4 a.m. when abusive Cockney bloke is on the phone again . . .

OCTOBER

THOSE GLORIOUS EUROPEAN NIGHTS ARE NOT TOO FAR AWAY (20 MILES AWAY IN MANCHESTER, ACTUALLY)

1 October 2002, Manchester United 4 Olympiakos 0 (Champions League).

I KNOW PEOPLE WHO WATCH UNITED; SOME ARE FROM MANCHESTER, SOME ARE FROM Wigan. It's not a big deal. Many people seem dismissive of the fact that there are a hell of a lot of people who actually do go watching United every fortnight, more than any other club in the country. The major problem is that they are outnumbered ten-to-one by sad lard-arsed tossers countrywide. All through my student days exiled from the North-west, I had to put up with little rich kids with their shitty, plummy accents that a lot of students seem to acquire, even if they are originally from Barnsley or Newcastle, talking of their love for 'Man-Yew Noi-Tid' while I was following a club who were not far off the bottom of the entire league. Bitter? You bet, but I won't be piping up too much during tonight's trip to Old Trafford because if Home Counties boy overhears me, he might get his mates from Salford to kick my arse.

It may give an Oldham fan an instant hard-on when I say this but there is nothing that upsets me more than seeing 18,000 spare seats in our ground every other Saturday when there's probably that same amount of people who claim to be United fans in Wigan who could fill them. However, as most of them don't even watch their 'own' team (except on telly) we've got a real fight on our hands getting them to come down to the JJB to watch ours. They have historically justified their non-participation in following the sporting fortunes of their local club by hypothesising that 'Latics are shit'. I even hate the enthusiastic ones who try and show an interest, but then say something like, 'Oh that Norman Etherington's scoring a few goals, isn't he? And Jim Farnham's doing a great job between the sticks' I make no apology for being a football nut, and can't give these muppets any leeway, I'm afraid.

Why are Manchester United a big enough draw to make people want to associate themselves with a city to which they have no allegiance? I decided to venture to Old Trafford to find out. Yes, Old Trafford, not my local, The Pagefield, where Wiganers will congregate and sup cheap ale at £1.50 a pint to cheer on 'their' heroes, along with thousands of other pubs nationwide, but Old Trafford, Theatre of Dreams.

Hopefully this isn't going to be an ABU (Anyone But United) review of the evening: there are a lot of wonderful qualities about Manchester United which set them apart from the other 91 league clubs. I'm going along to enjoy the game and make a few comparisons between them and the rest, including Wigan Athletic. I'd also like to apologise to many of the decent United fans out there for having a go at your fellow fans, but I know from reading their fine fanzines that the diehards despise the 'day trippers' as much as the rest of the country does. And, yes, a lot of the decent ones do actually come from Manchester. From what I've seen over the years, the split in Manchester is roughly 50/50, end of story. It must be hard work for all the loyal Manchester United fans to have to constantly justify their support. Is it any wonder that they have developed a siege 'us versus the rest of the world' mentality? But, anyway that's their problem and not mine.

It takes a five-minute conversation with a mate to get hold of a ticket for this near-67,000 sell out game. So much for the 'can't get a ticket' brigade. The ticket costs £27 (ouch!) but then again this is the cream of European football, so maybe not too bad when you consider that Swindon are charging a mere £6 less than this to get into their ground this season to watch a Second Division game. Not impossible, not even difficult to get a ticket, use of eyes and ears should seal the deal. I've not been to Old Trafford since I was a kid, except when watching New Order at the cricket ground over the summer where I was so wasted I could have been in Hawaii for all I knew, so it's almost a new experience. As we near the ground, the body of people making their way to the ground builds up, but only when we turn into one of the official car parks (cost – £100 per season), does it get anything like overwhelming as we struggle to nudge through.

Darren points out that we will be leaving five minutes before the end, as otherwise they will shut the gates and we will be stuck inside the car park for an hour due to the volume of people coming out. Fair enough, he's the expert – but I ponder that he's missed many a late goal due to this policy over the years. We get a burger each and I take in the atmosphere on the concourse surrounding the ground. There are a few chants of 'United' but very little of that hostility that I dare say is evident when the Scousers or West Ham are in town. Our tickets are for the North Stand, the biggest and newest stand, and despite the near-capacity crowd and it being 15 minutes until kick-off, there is barely a queue to get in. Even for the food and beer stalls, it's only a five-minute wait – and people are queuing in an orderly manner despite the lack of queue rails! The 'invisible' rails are merely some yellow markings on the floor which are directing people, but they certainly stick to them. The JJB pre-match, and especially half-time, rush for food and refreshment is basically a rabble of pushing and shoving. Can we learn something from our Premier League neighbours here? Definitely!

Up a couple of flights of steps to the middle tier and we're out there. The view is exemplary and the sheer size of the stands is breathtaking. The next thing I notice is the away support – 4,000 or so noisy Greeks, or, more likely, UK citizens of Greek extraction, singing bizarre songs and banging drums, determined to get behind their team.

My initial concerns before attending the game were whether or not I'd stick out not being a United fan, not knowing the songs or the little quirks of people who sit in the same area of the ground for every game. I also feel a little bit guilty for probably stealing the seat of a genuine United fan, but at least I'm not some celebrity tosser. I'm a genuine football fan, I've paid my money to watch the event and I intend to enjoy. The spectators around me aren't the most vociferous I've ever sat amongst, a bit of a mixed bag really, whereas at Latics you can basically pigeonhole the fans into a handful of categories: muppet, drunkard, hooligan, or old-timer. My worries about not jumping up or singing aren't realised because no one around me seems to be doing this either, the more giddy types I presume can be found at the ends behind the goals where the greater noise is coming from. There's a wide variety of accents within earshot, but most of the fans are at least in possession of a 25-mile-radius-around-Manchester accent; sorry to shatter the illusion. It's just another night at the football for them, whereas I'm getting a bit excited about seeing world-class players such as Beckham, Veron and Christian Karembeu (ex-Middlesbrough and now of Olympiakos) in the flesh.

There's a few expected boorish comments about the Greek support, 'You'll not be able to get a kebab for love nor money tonight,' but my neighbours seem to know their football, applauding moves from both sides. There's also a bloke behind me calling someone 'Cheesehead' throughout the game and, although I manage to narrow it down, I can't for the life of me work out whether he's referring to Beckham, Silvestre or Veron. Could be me for all I know, but it's pissing me off big style!

Back to the football and United create more chances in the first fifteen minutes than I've seen in two months of watching Latics this season. I like the look of Veron and can't understand the bad press he's been receiving. He's a real class act, he can pass first time better than most people can after taking a touch, and delivers accurate balls with every single part of his foot. Far from being a disappointment, he's running the show – involved in nearly every move with some exhibition passing and ball skills. If he's got a fault, apart from not being a tackler, it is that he is just too fancy at times. The Greek side make the fatal mistake throughout the night of allowing him time to elaborate, time which he is scarcely afforded in the Premier League. The closest that the early exchanges come to producing a goal comes from the unlikeliest of sources – Gary Neville having a long-range rasper tipped around the post by the Greek goalie.

I am wondering whether Giggs is playing 15 minutes in, as I haven't seen him do anything at all thus far – a quick look around and, yes indeed, there he is. No sooner than acknowledged, Giggs runs through to tuck away the ball and put United 1–0 up.

The singing is picking up a bit, not so much around me, but at either end of the ground, the familiar 'Pride of all Europe' and that other one which no one outside of United understands. The noise mainly emanates from what used to be the Stretford End and pockets of the other, the sound's not deafening, but there's probably three or four areas where it's coming from.

The Greek singing is typically European – very well coordinated and very aggressive chanting, coupled with a bit of Cozy Powell-esque drumming, scarf waving and bouncing up and down. As no one can understand a word of it, I speculate that perhaps they are protesting at the sacking of my good friend Mushy from Royal Mail last week. The home crowd give them a pleasant round of applause for protesting against this blatant injustice.

The Greeks do have a few chances, but it's mainly breakaway stuff, whereas United are starting to dominate, with the usual suspects, Beckham, Scholes and Butt coming to the fore. The second United goal isn't too far away, and has me up cheering with the Mancs: the ball falls to Veron in the centre-circle, he turns and moves towards goal only to find the Olympiakos defenders pushing out along with Solskjaer and Scholes, leaving no forward pass on. He knocks it square to Beckham, and carries on his forward run. Beckham one-twos it, catching the Greek defence completely flat footed and leaving Veron clean through on goal. Rather than go around he produces a moment of class by lofting a delicate yet perfect chip over the advancing keeper. Nearly as good as Paul Jewell's opener versus Rotherham at home in 1987!

The finish looks pretty good on TV later but really doesn't do it justice – I was sitting directly behind it and as opposed to being a chip, it was a swerving flick with the outside of the boot. Nice one, Ali G! This is undoubtedly the highlight of the game, and starts the United fans singing their own anthem 'Veron, Veron' to the tune of a certain Gary Glitter number. As we approach half-time, the game enters a niggly phase as the frustration creeps into Olympiakos's game and the referee isn't shy of producing a flurry of yellow cards. After a series of bad challenges, De Elias goes in on Veron two-footed and is sent off for his troubles. The game is effectively over as a contest on the stroke of half-time.

Half-time with the home side 2–0 up and there's little euphoria, just expectation that more goals will come against one of the weaker sides in the Champions League. It's also reassuring to know that, wherever you go, half-time 'entertainment' is truly naff. Tonight we have Fred the Red, a half-time draw and a marriage proposal. 'Should she say yes?' asks the Tannoy announcer. 'No' is the reply from 67,000 voices. She says yes. He must be very brave or very confident to propose in the first place in front of such a crowd. Best of luck, mate, whoever you are. I have gone bucks in the half-time draw, a pound apiece for a chance for a 50/50 split of £2,000 with Daz. In fact, I've negotiated a 60/40 split in my favour, on the condition that if our number gets called out I have to go on the pitch to claim our winnings and indulge in the formalities: 'What's your name and where d'yer come from, mate?'

'Err, it's Mickey here from Liverpool, cheers for da cash, la, I'm off to buy a shell suit wid it!'

The second half is burdened with all the expectations you'd expect, everyone is waiting for the floodgates to open, but United have taken the foot off the pedal. That's not to say it's dull, the football is crisp and superb throughout, no doubt aided by a splendid pitch seasoned with light drizzle. Normally, when I watch Wigan Athletic I like to bark orders as to where the ball should be passed. From my lofty position high up in the South Stand, I can see the moves that are on and bawl instructions accordingly. Tonight it's on its way there before I even have time to open my mouth. The woman who was sat next to me in the first half strangely hasn't returned for the second – Christ luv, £27 for 45 minutes' football! There's now two dodgy geezers there and I swear blind one is Bez of Happy Mondays fame, though he doesn't quite look gaunt enough. Keep shtum just in case, although I've probably heard every accent in the country tonight, including some Cockney whining about getting to Old Trafford taking him 'five hours to get up the M1'. I consider helpfully telling him that he could have taken in Tottenham vs. Cardiff that same evening and saved his expense and travelling costs, but decide to refrain.

The third goal arrives and it comes from another pass from that man Veron, feeding Giggs, who whips a low ball in, and the outstretched boot of an Olympiakos defender sends it spinning past the hapless keeper into the net. Giggs is surprisingly then taken off without the opportunity to go for a hat-trick. The Greek fans are getting a bit frisky, and I can quite clearly see it kicking off near the segregation point with all the fluorescent jackets running in to tidy it up as soon as possible. The stewards and police have probably seen this many times before and deal with it with the minimum of fuss, and it's barely acknowledged elsewhere and definitely wasn't picked up by the TV cameras. Lessons to be learnt again.

Forlan and Fortune come on and look like lost little boys. When Fortune gets the ball, he stands there and looks around as if to say, 'What do I do with it now?' The fourth goal is a typical, clinical Solskjaer finish and I'm pretty certain that Veron had a hand in this one as well. I feel more at home as the crowd salute Ole Gunnar with their own version of 'You Are My Sunshine' (a big Wigan anthem) except here it's 'You Are My Solskjaer' and good use of the 'And Alan Shearer, comes nowhere near ya!' line. The United fans are very proud of their ability to produce an original song for each member of their squad, although they are currently struggling with a pretty lame 'Rio, Rio' for their expensive summer signing. Undoubtedly, though, the biggest song of the night is when they are singing Roy Keane's name, even though he isn't playing. Loathed by the rest of the nation and loved by United. I probably fall into the 'loathe' category if I'm honest, but I'm bold enough to admit I'd love him in my team.

We do, as suggested, leave five minutes before the end to avoid getting stuck for hours, and it proves to be a good move as we get back to Wigan for half past ten for a pint. Time to reflect, as I consider how Wigan Athletic could ever achieve that same level of interest even in our own town. We never will: sad but true. We don't have a season-ticket waiting list. We don't have a Torquay/Penrith/Singapore Blues fan club. We don't have world-class stars. That doesn't mean that the local people shouldn't want to express pride in their local club by actively supporting them and contributing to their future. Some of our fans don't want a load of know-nothing Johnny-come-lately's turning up, sitting in our seats, and making the half-time beer queue longer – they haven't been through the suffering we have, so why should they share our future successes? However, if we are ever to develop our crowd, then these are the people we need to attract, drag them away from the MUFC-noon-live-on-Sky-kick-off, and make them feel part of their local club at the JJB.'

BAGGIES BOING-BOING OUT

2 October 2002, West Bromwich Albion (h). Worthington Cup Round 2. Won 3–1.

Not exactly a plum tie, it was only a few years ago that we were playing West Brom in the league. Meanwhile, those jammy buggers down the road at Bury get the draw we've been crying out for against Bolton Wanderers (Scumderers!). The noises coming from West Brom fans on our website aren't very promising either. It's too expensive, they are expecting US to reduce our ticket prices because THEY aren't sending a full side. They've got Blackburn at home two days before on the Monday and Newcastle away three days after on the Saturday, and therefore this game isn't a high priority for them. Well, those issues are all their problems, I'm afraid; if they want to get in on the cheap, they should get the money off their own club, as they are the ones who are cheating them. Expensive? They will wonder what's hit them when they get charged close to £40 at Stamford Bridge or White Hart Lane later in the season! And as for their decision to rest a few players, well we've got a scratch side playing as well, as Andy Liddell's suspended!

Gutted that a certain WBA player isn't on the field, as my mate Naylor was looking forward to giving him some serious abuse, and has been sending me text messages indicating that the chap concerned is a kerb crawler. Now, this game is on a Wednesday and Wigan Athletic don't normally play on a Wednesday. However, I do play on a Wednesday, for Cockney Latic FC. We've written the grovelling letter asking for a 6.30 kick-off switch from 9.30 so we could play first and then leg it across the road to the JJB Stadium, but to no avail. Talk about running about, with the team consisting of 100 per cent Latics fans on the day of the game, we have a total of four who are willing to play. Carl H, proper manager not Phil Neal-type yes man like me, states, 'We'll just have to leg it across afterwards.'

Big queues to get in and a missed kick-off. I get in just in time to see Jason Koumas pull out a Mach 3 and shave the post with a cracking free kick which has Filan beaten. Wigan start to get involved and take the game to the Baggies. Gary Teale is giving his full-back a torrid time. Tony Dinning is relishing the big game, he's running the show in midfield, a million miles away from Colchester. The Duke is twisting and turning, terrifying the WBA defence. They are all tackling like tigers – if only they had been up for it like this against Port Vale and Colchester we might still be top. Ouch, old wounds being opened.

Neil Roberts, the £450,000 signing from Wrexham, has taken Lidds' place up front. I've never seen a footballer with such a phenomenal workrate, but unfortunately he plays back to goal feeding others, in a position where he will always be judged on goals. He holds it up very well tonight and deflects a lot of the physical stuff away from The Duke; the two seem to work well together, perhaps a better contrast than The Duke and Lidds partnership. On the half hour, Latics are pressing forward. They get a corner and it's cleared, it falls to Matt Jackson who heads back into the box, Nathan Ellington then thumps it home with the West Brom defence looking distinctly Division Two-ish. 1–0 in our favour and deservedly so. Another great Koumas free kick hits the base of the post and bounces away to safety with Filan again beaten; he must have his lucky underpants on tonight!

We hold on until half-time. 1–0 up against a Premier League side and outplaying them, mustn't grumble. They will of course point out that West Brom have got an understrength team on display, but the likes of Lee Hughes, Daniele Dichio, Jason Koumas and Neil Clements are no slouches. What a shame Fatboy Gregan isn't playing! Half-time sees an opera singer take to the field for a musical interlude, all very awe-inspiring but I think I preferred Fred the Red at Old Trafford. Both the mascots are taking pot shots, and unbelievably, they have both got their birds with them as well. (At Wigan, long-standing mascot JJ, formerly known as Springy, suddenly found his ideal partner one close season, called 'B'. She must be his soul mate because just like him, she's got polystyrene legs and a three foot tall foam head. What's the odds on that? She's also rumoured to be a right goer.) Wonder if Brighton have two male mascots with furry muzzies and leather pants in keeping with the town's more liberal image? The penalty shoot-out is clearly rigged as the Baggies mascots are using underhand tactics by having proper football boots on, whereas the luv'd up Wiganers have size-42 foam clogs on.

Bury winning at Bolton raises a cheer at half-time, but also a bit of green eye because if there's one team we do want to play more than anyone in this competition it's those horrors from the Reebok. What will actually happen is that Bury will beat them and we'll go and get Bury in the next round. The second half is underway and Latics now seem even more up for it. Within five minutes of the restart, we score again. Tony Dinning drives a shot across goal, The Duke gets a touch while the Albion defence remains static. He stops the ball with one foot and turns on a sixpence to fire it into the corner with the other. It looks suspiciously offside, but watching the replay later, it wasn't – it was quick thinking by a striker in form. 2–0 and West Brom want their mummies.

The Baggies create chances aplenty, but then again we could, and should, have half a dozen ourselves. Neil Roberts misses two very good chances, Jarrett has an effort with which he perhaps could have done better and Ellington also comes close on more than one occasion. Gary Teale's getting a bit of shite off some idiots near me, because he has pulled out of a tackle and also passed the ball when he had a great chance to get clean through on goal. I sympathise, and always try to stick up for Teale. As a former winger before the pace disappeared, I recognise that we're a bunch of isolated weirdos who do strange things. That's why they shove us out on the wing in the first place!

Nathan Ellington has had a storming game, but going into the last quarter he appears to be limping slightly. Take him off please, Jewell! Save him for Saturday, he looks knackered. Teale, speak of the devil, chases a lost ball down the wing, and pressures the defender who is attempting to clear. He steals it off him, looks up and puts an inch-perfect ball onto The Duke's head with only one consequence – 3–0. This is much too easy. NOW The Duke is coming off. He'll be back for the match ball in ten or so minutes and receives a standing ovation for a virtuoso hat-trick.

It takes 88 minutes for WBA to register on the scoresheet, when Lee Hughes manages to pull one back for the Baggies with a fine volley. A quick nervous glance at the watch, surely it's wrapped up by now? It would take something special for them to get back in this game, not to mention some comedy defending. It's not going to happen, the boys are jubilant and we all hope that they can all continue this same form and spirit into Saturday's game with Cardiff. There's no pitch invasion, as most of us big kids can't be bothered going down to the front and getting our trainers dirty. Actually that's not strictly true, as there is a solo pitch invasion by someone who shall remain known as 'Bolton R Scum'. Nathan Ellington is off into the night with the match ball, it's not the first time he's turned it on like this. Last season, he hit a stunning hat-trick for Bristol Rovers to send then Premier League Derby County crashing out of the FA Cup. It's clear to see why he is so highly rated – he really is an unstoppable talent when he's in the mood. Performances like this emphasise exactly why Paul Jewell parted with £1.2m for his services. A true match winner on his day, and let's hope he has plenty more before the season is out.

Best get to the Soccer Dome! Around the back of the North Stand towards the away end, some Wigan kiddies are singing at the West Brom lot. The only words I hear back off the Brummies are 'Well done Wigan' while bemoaning their own side's inadequacies; very sporting of them and for that reason I hope they stay up, especially if it's at the expense of Bolton going down! Just as well I'm not playing, because by the time I have legged it to the Soccer Dome I am a sweaty mess. The game is five minutes old and we have somehow mustered up a squad of eight players who despatch our opponents 8–4. Should have been a lot more were it not for one of our players kicking an opponent and attempting to throttle the ref, earning himself a red card and a lengthy ban for his troubles! Seven wins out of seven for Cockney Latic FC for this season, putting us well on our way to a second successive Division One title. A good night all round, and at half past ten I finally have time to sit down with a beer or two and reflect on an eventful evening. Arriving home in the early hours I spend at least half an hour flicking through the various sports channels to read all the Teletext pages and the name of young Nathan Ellington is prominent in the headlines of every one. I feel so proud and pleased to be a Latics fan. A great win, but I'd swap it now for victory over Cardiff on Saturday.

TAFF LUCK FOR THE LATICS

5 October 2002, Cardiff City (h). Drew 2–2.

A game against Cardiff is never complete without the preceding scaremongering, usually along the lines of 'Oh yeah, there's 5,000 of them coming,' or 'They're bringing six coachfuls of lads to cause mayhem because some of their lot got battered last year outside Champions Bar.' The Family Stand is always sparsely populated when Cardiff come to town, suggesting a lot of parents keep their kids away. It's never really happened in the ground, perhaps a minor scuffle when a few of them were sat in the home end during our first season at the JJB, but I blame that almost entirely on the police making the game all-ticket for away fans in the first place. It's a pretty poor state of affairs, however, when a home fan is intimidated from attending a game because of the away fans' reputation.

No need for it really, if people just want to go and watch the game, but it's fair to say that there are certain factions from Cardiff and Wigan who are keen to dance, so for that reason half the pubs of Wigan are shut. I go to my usual pre-match boozer for a pint only to find it's a 'knock on window' job, but even so there's a few more faces in than usual because other places have closed completely. Despite having no active involvement, myself and a thousand others are ear-wigging on the constant updates of the pre-match battlefield. 'Two coachloads of Cardiff stopped at Marus Bridge . . . Sixty Wigan in Worsley Mesnes, heading to Newtown to meet up with them.' The Old Bill have all this kind of stuff sewn up now though, and successfully prevent physical contact between those parties wishing to do their bit for Anglo–Welsh relations. There might be mindless violence on the agenda, but it's more like a game of chess these days, hours of waiting and watching and precious little action.

Make no mistake though, on the pitch, today is a big game between two of the sides who have been tipped as favourites for promotion, it has all the makings of a cracker. Once again, Andy Liddell is suspended so Neil Roberts will deputise. I've done an about-turn on Roberts, I feel that if he's given a regular run in the team, he will get goals. I've decided that, bearing in mind my bets normally duck anyway, that I'm going to have a tenner on Neil Roberts. I go into the Ladbrokes on Park Road, only to find they don't have a price on him. I can have Ellington for 3/1 though, I'm tempted to do Earnshaw as cover – a cracking player. I'll try later in the ground to see if they've got more faith in our own Welsh Wizard.

Many pages of magazine articles and webspace have been devoted to the Roberts debate and I doubt I'd cover any new ground by opening it up again here. Let's just say he is one of the friendliest and most down-to-earth players at the club and you can't fail to like his enthusiasm. His attitude is spot on, and I've never once heard him complain when he's not in the team, but on goal return alone he doesn't warrant a permanent place up front. He'll score the first goal today and make me eat those words, because I'm putting my money where my mouth is.

Time to find out our reward for knocking West Bromwich Albion out of the Worthington Cup. We're in The Brick, which does have a telly with Sky on so we can join in the anticipation of watching our team's name coming out of the bag. This is a surreal scene that happens probably about half a dozen times over the course of the season. The home team gets drawn out and if it's 'Gillingham' then it's, 'Oh God, please, no not us' (simply too far for a night fixture) or if it's Bolton Wanderers then, 'Come on, let's have it', and then this is repeated until your team comes out. It's a common event for football fans worldwide, I should imagine. Everyone wants a big club or local rival but everyone can't have one, and we seem to suffer more than most when it comes to crap cup draws, so the optimism is a little muted.

Everyone seems to be anticipating an away tie, but after six balls have been pulled out, and we've managed to dodge West Ham away, 'Wigan Athletic' are the seventh: a home game. Not bad, it'll save on expense. What we need now is a big club to make a big evening. Many mouths are muttering, 'Come on, come on . . . Arsenal . . . United . . .' whatever their preferred outcome. 'Wigan Athletic will play Manchester City.' The place erupts! What a draw, everyone is buzzing about this one and chanting 'Blue Army, Blue Army'. City at home, that'll do us, thank you very much. We asked for a big club, and we've only gone and drawn the MASSIVE club! The remainder of the draw fades into oblivion. There's none of the usual 'why couldn't we have had that draw' moans, just smiling faces, this time we've hit the jackpot. A chance to pull in a really decent crowd on a great occasion. Who knows, we might even beat the bastards who cheated us in the play-off finals three years ago. At long last, someone has smiled upon us in a cup draw.

We move on to the ground to have a beer under the stand, as it's a bit chocker in the pub, to say the least. We've realised by now that the City game will take place on bonfire night and that it will also probably be earmarked for a live on Sky spot, but neither of these factors can diminish our interest in the game. An opportunity to stick my bet on, £10 on Neil Roberts to score the first goal at 7/1, not very generous considering his 1 in 5 record. Yeah, you're laughing now luv, but you'll be cadging ale off me tonight when I'm 80 quid richer! I'm tempted to change it to Robert Earnshaw or The Duke, as even she thinks I'm crackers, but maybe using reverse logic and putting on a bet that I know won't come in will actually bag me some cash, a tidy £80. Does it bollocks!

Pre-match and they've got the opera on again; fair enough if it helps gee the crowd up, but the atmosphere is hostile enough. It's all well and good having a pint with the opposing fans before and after the game, but it's not going to be like that today. Both sets of fans are up for it, making plenty of noise and directing verbals, as much as the segregation will allow for. Cardiff are giving it a wonderful rendition of the Welsh national anthem, while the home support are singing 'Eng-er-land', despite Wigan having several Welsh players, and Cardiff having several English players, on their books. Cardiff's following isn't very large by their standards; although they are one of the better supported clubs, they've brought fewer fans than last season. They always bring a hell of a lot more to Wigan than we ever take to Cardiff, but then again it's not the friendliest place and we always seem to play them on a Friday night. They travelled in numbers to Tottenham for a Worthington Cup tie in midweek, so there are mitigating circumstances as to why numbers are down. They've still brought three times more to the JJB than anyone else has so far this season, so deserve a round of applause for that.

Right from the kick-off, the game matches the highly charged atmosphere. Some of the players seem to be losing their footing slightly as the pitch has cut up a bit following last night's chubsters' game, but apart from that, Latics are carrying on from where they left off on Wednesday against West Brom. Both sides are knocking it about in a great advert for Division Two in a match between those the bookies predict will be the two top sides come the end of the season. Let's hope so!

It's Cardiff who draw first blood. The ball is pumped into the Wigan penalty area; it needs clearing first time, but that doesn't happen. A couple of bounces and flicks and it falls at the feet of Robert Earnshaw, back to goal. He turns and plants it in the top corner in one lightning-quick move, a great opportunist goal. I'm fuming with our defence for not clearing the ball, but I do recognise a class striker and this lad certainly looks the part. Oh, and my bet's down the pan. Wigan's response is equal to, and as swift as, Earnshaw's goal. A series of fast-flowing passes down the left sees Neil Roberts step over the ball and Tony Dinning charge through from midfield to the edge of the box to finish a fine move with a blistering left-foot screamer. The keeper has no chance, and Wigan are level. The home fans are on their feet with this one: have some of that, sheepshaggers! Only a month ago we were questioning whether Tony Dinning should kick a ball for the club again after his petulant sending off. Today, as on Wednesday, he is excelling himself, outshining his equally expensive opposite number in midfield, Graham Kavanagh.

Latics are rampant, and a few minutes later a ball in from Tony Dinning bounces about in the box and that man Nathan Ellington steals in to poke it home: 2–1 and utter mayhem! It's unbelievable just how quickly our fortunes have turned, from devastation to delirium in a matter of minutes. Cardiff are shell-shocked, like a boxer on the ropes who has just taken the mother of all sucker punches. The favourites to win the Second Division title are looking distinctly second best, we are completely dominant and Lennie Lawrence admits as much afterwards. Alas, my bladder won't hold out, so with 38 minutes on the clock I go down to the concourse to relieve myself. While down there, it would be rude not to have a pint. There's a ridiculous amount of lads already down there. These games against the likes of Cardiff seem to bring all the home faces out, unfortunately many of them spend more time at the bar than actually watching the game. I hear a few oohs and aahs coming from the crowd, but there are no further goals and the score is 2–1 at half-time. We'll settle for that.

My early departure from the first half at least means I manage to catch the start of the second. The pace of the game continues, and it's still Wigan in the ascendancy. We're creating all the play and all the chances, but this game needs to be wrapped up. Jason Jarrett runs through from midfield, and blazes over with the goal at his mercy, The Duke also has a couple more chances. Steve McMillan, overlapping from left-back, gets to the angle of the six-yard box to fire a shot in, but the Cardiff keeper, Neil Alexander, manages to pull off a fine one-handed save to tip it around the post from point-blank range. Gary Teale fails to shoot when he has a great opportunity to do so.

Anyone familiar with watching Latics over the last few years will be fully aware of what happens when we fail to put away our chances. We once drew 15 games in one season, and I swear that in at least 11 of them we conceded a late equaliser after being in front for most of the game. As the game enters the last few minutes, Cardiff are now starting to knock it about very well, stretching the Wigan back four and pushing onto them.

A sickener: in the very last minute Cardiff get an equaliser. It's very similar to their first goal: a ball into the box isn't cleared, former Wigan loan star Peter Thorne flicks it on and little Robert Earnshaw pounces again. John Filan calls his defence 'flaming galahs' or something. Earnshaw is absolutely deadly, imagine him and The Duke up front together. There's only a few minutes of injury time left, and it's the home support's turn to feel numb. It's a common emotion, whether you support Burnley or Boavista, that horrible, sinking feeling when you've been leading and dominating a game for long periods of time, only to let it slip. One minute you're buzzing, the next minute your stomach is churning over, and it's definitely not the chunky steak pie you had at half-time playing up. The game peters out, neither side wants to lose a valuable point, both a little half-hearted in pushing for a winner. We've been the better side but the scoreline doesn't reflect this. Nevertheless, a point isn't a disaster.

The whistle blows and there's no booing this time, it has been a classic game. I dare say that's not the best that Cardiff have played but they've managed to sneak a point out of it, and we've managed to hang on to one. On leaving the stadium, there's another military style operation to keep the fans apart, but there's no trouble. Serious surveying of the tables in the pub after the game shows the two points dropped have cost us second place, as we're now in third. Oldham are now sitting on top of the table by a single point. It's all very tight up there, but as long as we're in the leading pack that'll do me. Consistency will be the key in the coming weeks, lack of it has been our Achilles heel in the past, but it could be our passport to Division One.

DUNCAN SHARPE – AN OBITUARY

7 October 2002.

Every now and then something occurs which puts personal problems and moans about football into complete perspective. The tragic and sudden death of Duncan Sharpe was one such event. On 7 October 2002, the Chief Executive of JJB Sports and Vice Chairman of Wigan Athletic committed suicide near his home in the Ribble Valley. He was a former professional golfer and was married with four children. My sentiments are firstly with his family, as they have suffered the greatest loss. They were and still are a wealthy family, but they have had something so precious that money cannot buy taken away from them. Unbeknown to many, Duncan had struggled with illness and depression for some time, but it was still a tragic shame that he chose to take his own life.

He was a very successful businessman who had a real passion for Wigan Athletic, and many people thought that, as son and heir to Dave Whelan, Duncan Sharpe *was* the future of Wigan Athletic. The story always went that it was Duncan who persuaded the JJB chairman to invest his millions in his local football club in the first place.

Without Duncan Sharpe and his influence, there might not have even been a Wigan Athletic in 2002. Now we have to get used to a Wigan Athletic without Duncan Sharpe.

Rest in peace, Duncan.

HELLO SAILORS

12 October 2002, Plymouth Argyle (a). Won 3–1.

What a complete farce. Plymouth may as well be Pluto such is the complexity of trying to organise this one. Minibus, car, plane, train, one night, two nights, on the day, numbers coming, hotels, B&B, 'mate who lives down there', Friday night in Bristol anyone, Newquay, Torquay? Needless to say, a sum total of two of us end up going. We've heard the train tickets are only £36, excellent! None of that driving home dog rough on a Sunday for us: put your feet up, read the Sunday papers, crack open a beer and let the train take the strain, as they once said! However, we and others have done that much fannying about that they've put the price up and we're forced to book our extortionate £70 each 'three day advances' before they go up to the even more incredible price of £96 each on the day. Bloody hell, you could get to New York and back for that!

Trains are great. Venues have been largely inaccessible so far this season due to the state of the lines and strikes, but you can't whack them for comfort and general giddiness, for the London trips in particular. The journey will be five hours there and six hours back. A bit of a nightmare but we'll probably either be drunk, getting drunk or blind drunk and fast asleep, so not too much to worry about. The next step is to sort the digs out, should be easy enough in October.

At first I try the hotels in the centre of Plymouth, as our train only gets in at 10 p.m., thereby facilitating a quick drop-the-bags-off-and-hit-the-town manoeuvre. The first ten hotels I ring up all have available rooms for the Friday but are full for the Saturday night. I then start to ring up a few hotels in The Hoe area of the town, which I am led to believe is genteel enough and only a short walk from the station. Same story. 'So just what is going on in Plymouth on Saturday night?' is my secondary query. No one can elaborate, but being optimistic I reason that it must be an International Netball Tournament and not the return of a thousand drunken sailors. Eventually I get a result from the Grosvenor Hotel, costing £45 a night for the room, so £22.50 each. We're ready to rock.

Friday afternoon and I'm having a few beers waiting for Canny in The Swan and Railway. I am somewhat bemused by the complete lack of fellow Wiganers, but presume that the 3,000-strong travelling support must have made their way down this morning. The train is ten minutes late, which might cause uproar in Tokyo rush hour, but is a pleasant surprise (if anything) in this country. We pick up our outbound tickets and are told to get our returns from Plymouth on Sunday.

The five-hour journey is slightly arduous, but we speak to a couple of others who are already down there and learn that they were put on a coach at Bristol, so maybe we should be grateful for avoiding that. A lad gets on at Crewe on his way to Manchester; he realises about an hour after getting on that he is on his way to Birmingham. We laugh out loud at the dozy bastard. We're getting text messages through of the rugby score. Wigan Warriors, lodgers at our JJB Stadium, are playing St Helens for a place in the Super League Grand Final, and Saints are winning. I hold no shame in admitting that this gives us immense pleasure. It's no longer cool to hate the town's rugby club, a lot of our younger and (probably) more sensible fans now watch both. Many fans who have watched Latics for any length of time hate the bastards with a passion, though. There's too much bad blood, going back to the 1980s when the rugby club watched idly as football in the town was in danger of becoming extinct. 'Always a rugby town,' they said – not any more and those who go around with their eyes closed eventually walk down a dead end.

We're seen by the rugby lot as a bitter bunch but if someone wants to tell me exactly what they have ever done for Wigan Athletic over the years then I'll gladly listen. Silence. I thought so. How can we possibly support each other: put simply, it's us versus them in this day and age. We compete for the public's finite disposable income. How many people in Wigan can afford to spend £15 for two nights running, plus all the associated expense? If they enjoy a great deal of success then the local people will be more inclined to watch rugby league rather than their local football club. So how can I wish them well when their success would be to the detriment of my football club?

We arrive at Plymouth at 10 p.m. All attempts to walk it to our digs are thwarted by a downpour of Niagara Falls proportions, so we have to wait ten minutes for a taxi. They say it's grim up north, but it's absolutely bucketing it down here, not the mildest of evenings in

Devon. As the Stella takes hold, Canny has to talk me out of lamping some prick who has jumped the taxi queue. The taxi drops us off and we hastily do the aforementioned unpacking and freshening up. Another poor show by me, as some women have just asked us if we would like to share their taxi back into town, but I can't work out how to lock the hotel door so they bugger off without us while the attractive hotel receptionist shows Mr BA (Hons)-and-professional-accountancy-qualification-thicko how to close a door properly. We get walking and are drenched within a matter of yards, taking refuge in the nearest boozer (The Walrus) which becomes HQ for the weekend.

We trudge into town and immediately end up on Union Street, the area we've been told to avoid. We don't see any trouble, but if looks could kill, then there'd be two empty seats on the train journey home. The natives aren't over-friendly, so we're pleased to bump into some fellow Wiganers. They tell us about some 1970s-themed nightclub next door called Flares, which looks like a viable option bearing in mind we aren't going to be walking too far in this atrocious weather. It's not too bad, as it happens, and certainly not as unpleasant as the previous atmosphere we encountered. The ratio of women to men indicates that we can't fail in here, even though some of them are clearly lesbians. No, they really are, they're kissing and groping and everything! There are a few decent-looking birds, but more importantly, a surplus of rough-looking ones. Despite confidently giving and getting the eye off a few of the better sorts, I am getting mauled by a little blonde bird who must be 40. I try to brush her away (some would say I did a runner) but it's too late and I've been spotted by far too many of the Wiganers present. Ridicule will ensue for the rest of the weekend. It's only half past eleven so I scarper to the bar to anaesthetise myself, ready to finish the job in an hour when the alcopops have numbed the worries about nailing this horror. We up the ante as Canny homes in on a Myleene Klass lookalike (so he says!) and I pester her mate. They attempt to cadge a drink and leave. Can't fail, we said!

9 a.m. on match day, at least four hours kip, we reckon, so head downstairs to polish off a full English. We are highly amused by some posh Chinese bloke on the next table who is demanding 'crispy bacon'. He must repeat himself at least eight times: 'I want my bacon crispy.'

'Did you order poached eggs, m'darling?' asks the harassed waitress.

'No, no I asked for crispy bacon, which is the one with the crispy bacon? It has to be crispy bacon.

'I only DO crispy bacon!' he elaborates.

'Is he after shagging it or eating it?' says bad head here, just out of earshot of someone having their breakfast 30 miles away in Exeter. 'Did you hear that prick? What the bloody hell does he want for £22 a night?' Strange as our sense of humour is, myself and Canny spend the rest of the weekend doing passable impersonations of him. We love you, fussy Chinaman.

We stroll into Plymouth with the intention of having a look around the shops and going to the bookies. The weather is better and the sun is shining. I give 'Malc' Barnes a ring, who has travelled down with a dozen-strong mob from Springfield, to find their whereabouts. 'I'm in The Walrus,' says he, sounding only remotely like John Lennon. There go good intentions. The Springfield mob have been drinking more or less straight through since their train left Wigan at 9 a.m. yesterday and are looking decidedly worse for wear. There is also, quite surreally, a young lad and his family sat down at the next table with a 'Ban the Bomb' placard. What the hell is that about then? The Walrus is elevated over a main road, and we're just about to discover the solution to the riddle of the Saturday night hotel room shortage.

The Springfield mob leave the pub to head to another but seem to have been halted in the beer garden, leaning over the main road, so I have a nosey outside to see what's happening. 'Canny, come here!'

'Why?'

'Just bloody come here!'

At least 10,000 people marching down the street all chanting, 'WHO LET THE BOMBS OUT? BUSH, BUSH, BUSH, BUSH!' The CND are in town, mobbed up, complete with banners stating 'Don't let Plymouth become the next Chernobyl'. With our vastly inferior numbers, you'd think perhaps we'd support them and be sympathetic to their cause. More likely, 'Acid', Howard, Griff and Co. are compassionately shouting, 'Have a wash, you scruffy gits,' and 'Get a bloody job.'

We move around the corner to a pub called The Bank and the Springfield lot are throwing it back, Aftershocks at 12.30 p.m.

They've met up with Derby, a lad who I grew up with who's now in the Marines. They all seem a little too cosy in here, so we decide to disperse, but not before Canny relieves the bandit of £63. We flag a taxi to the ground as, according to Derby, it's up some 'big bastard hills' and at a quarter to three are dropped off in front of the stadium.

Now I knew in advance it was being redeveloped, but nevertheless, it does look very impressive both from the inside and out. Loads of coaches here, so it looks like a top following from Wigan, until someone points out that most are actually ferrying Plymouth fans in from the far reaches of Cornwall. I'd guess there's only around 400 from Wigan who made the journey here today, and no bloody wonder, bearing in mind the horrendous 600-mile round trip. We're also missing a good few who are probably getting baton charged around Slovakia at this very minute while watching England.

We've got half an end and, although not a patch on the JJB (of course), it's a bonny ground, the view's not bad and the £15 entrance seems quite reasonable. Beer on the concourse too, always a welcome sight for the thirsty traveller. There's a minute's silence in memory of Duncan Sharpe and this is impeccably observed by the Plymouth fans. Massive respect is due to them for this, bearing in mind most of them probably weren't even aware of who Duncan Sharpe was or his great influence on the development of Wigan Athletic.

The Springfield crew bounce in just as the game kicks off to witness a tight opening 15. After 18 minutes, Plymouth are pressing down at the far end: I can't fully see what's happening, but it's a familiar, dangerous sight, the situation from which Cardiff scored two the previous week, as the ball is pumped into the box and it's bouncing about and no one from Wigan clears it. It falls at the feet of Plymouth's Ian Stonebridge who fires home to give them the lead. Bugger! I get that sinking feeling once more, 300 miles away from home just to watch my team get stuffed. The Plymouth fans and players are buoyant. Their fans attempt to rile us further with a chorus of 'St Helens, St Helens, St Helens', but, of course, what they don't expect is for us to join in! Must try harder!

On another day in another season, well, last season in fact, Wigan would have folded at this point, and when Plymouth continue to attack and push for a second they would have got it. Today, their lead only lasts seven minutes. Gary Teale puts in a fine ball to tee up Tony

Dinning, who crashes home a volley in front of the travelling support. We're level. Great goal, Tony; he's matured more in a few months than Paul Gascoigne did in 20 years.

Both teams have a go at taking the wheel in this game, Gary Teale and Jason Jarrett go close for Latics, but neither can apply the finish. Half-time and yet more beer, and why not? Because there isn't a great travelling support it means that the usual bedlam to get served isn't applicable today, so we can double up, have a balti pie and utilise the public conveniences. The second half gets underway and we are amusing our feeble minds by engaging in a spot of banter with one of the stewards, who is having the piss taken out of him by both home and away fans. He's got slicked-back, heavily gelled hair, earrings, a gold chain worn outside his well-unbuttoned shirt and a luminous-green steward's jacket, teamed up with a set of Blues Brothers market-stall shades and a pair of Hush Puppies. Nice! He thinks he is the dog's bollocks and seems to be lapping up the chorus of Wham's 'Freedom' we are serenading him with. George Michael he is not, he's a bit skinny and looks more like a poor man's Billy from *EastEnders*; in fact he reminds me more of a greasy weasel, but we don't know any pop songs about greasy weasels. Wham it is then.

An early second-half chance for Plymouth is foiled by the, once again, outstanding John Filan, and from that point on Wigan begin to get a real grip on the game. Nathan Ellington comes more into it, firing one effort wide and then being thwarted in a one-on-one by Plymouth's French keeper, the wonderfully named Romain Larrieu. The pressure tells on 58 minutes, and we're in the lead with the same combination as earlier. A Teale shot is only parried and there's that man again, Tony Dinning, to follow it up to score his second of the game. 1–0 down, 2–1 up, it's always the best way and we're looking good value for it as well. The remaining half an hour sees Wigan dominate, we have plenty of opportunities to score even more but only in the last minute do we add to our tally when Nathan Ellington goes charging through from the halfway line, to slot a low finish past the unfortunate Argyle keeper.

So it's now six out of seven Away Day victories for Wigan Athletic, which is great form. A word of praise for the Argyle fans as well, who backed their team throughout the game. Their crowds have dipped somewhat as the euphoria of last year's Third Division Championship has worn off, but they haven't got on their team's back too much and appreciate that they have simply been beaten by the better side. Great to see Tony Dinning coming over at the end, fist in the air, mouthing something which looks remarkably like 'Fucking get in!' My sentiments exactly, Tony!

There's a contented air as we walk down back into town through the park. We cruise through a few quiet pubs where the locals call us 'Matlows', a term of offence, not endearment, for Naval folk, I presume, before settling in one to watch the England game. This pub is full of Plymouth's firm so we initially keep quiet as there's two of us and forty of them, but as the game heats up they are left in no doubt as to our allegiance as northern accents are bawling at the telly. The locals are very patriotic, so we're hoping to play the old 'we're all English together' card as it isn't the friendliest pub in Plymouth, especially after they've just seen their mighty Greens get dicked by us northern upstarts at Home Park. Thankfully, England, just like Latics, turn a 1–0 deficit around into a victory so everyone is jubilant and they abstain from kicking our heads in. I am flagging badly at this stage, wondering if I'm going to see the night out, but manage to fight it off and get my second wind following a quick visit to the traps.

We return to the hotel to get changed and then back out to the Barbican area of Plymouth, which we have been told is much friendlier than Union Street. We bump into the Supporters' Club party and a few of the other Wiganers who are stopping over, and discuss the day's events. The streets are narrow and the pubs are old-fashioned, a world away from the tacky theme pubs which dominate Wigan town centre. We give one of them a miss as it's full of the Stone Island brigade and find another little pub to settle in further down on the left. Now, please remember that we've been back to the hotel and now look more 'Disco Dave' than football hoolie and are trying to look inconspicuous, but before we've even opened our mouths, our eyes and ears are burning again. Are they all 'local pubs' around here or what? Inevitably, five minutes later, all the lads who had been giving it large in the previous pub have now walked down to this one! The phrase 'having a quick pint' is often over-used in my opinion.

We skulk away from these tossers, away from the Barbican area and drop on a pub which is full of Rotherham rugby union players who have also played in Plymouth that day. They are all singing and dancing on the tables, and before long we are lambadaing with the players' wives on the tables. Blimey, we've just escaped one undue kicking, we don't want some prop forward jumping on our heads for touching his missus up, thank you very much. Have we got a death wish tonight or what? Enough is enough for the two of us, so we head back to Union Street to find the Springfield mob. They're nearly all in bed drunk, at 10.30 on a Saturday night! We manage to contact one of their number who is sober enough to answer his phone to get a number for one of the others who is still out. After numerous brief phone calls involving many repetitions of the word 'WHAT?', we ascertain their location as being a nightclub called Destiny's and flag down a taxi.

There's a big queue for Destiny's, but we find what's left of the Wiganers and they are all trolleyed, whereas I've found what is probably my third wind and am knocking back Smirnoff Ices at the slightly steep price of £3.40 a go. Some lad at the bar clocks my accent and offers some helpful advice: 'You'll be alright in here – just don't open your mouths. Some people'll smack you if they hear a northern accent, not me, like,' and puts his finger over his mouth, in a 'keep it shut' motion for comedy effect. Needless to say, we see our guardian angel getting scragged out by the bouncers for fighting a mere ten minutes later. The next fight we witness takes place when the bouncers start fighting with each other, rolling about on the floor while the onlookers nervously watch and form a large circle like in a school playground. What is it with this town?

The club is open until 4 a.m. and I reckon we manage until about 3.30 with Canny's two bob of justice calling the shots. I don't mind '70s music, but I much prefer dance music, which they are playing in here, and am just bouncing away in a world of my own, totally arseholed. We somehow manage to locate our hotel in the early hours and, before we know it, it's Sunday morning and time to weigh in a quick full English and get packing. No Crispy Bacon fella today.

Now, I wouldn't normally feel the need to overelaborate on a journey home, but believe me this one is an epic. Here goes:

11.30 a.m. – Attempt to leave hotel. Pissing down, go back inside to ring a cab.

11.40 a.m. – Taxi arrives to take us to train station.

11.50 a.m. – Go to ticket office to pick up return tickets. Told that we should have picked our tickets up at Wigan and they 'can't get them off the system'. So despite paying £70 each and engaging in a 20-minute slanging match with some docile cow behind the counter, we end up effectively jumping the train with a 'note from our mother'.

12.15 p.m. – Train arrives. It's one of those brand new ones and it's on time. Excellent!

1.00 p.m. – Train arrives at Newton Abbot. The announcer says that we must wait here for an hour while the tide goes out at Dawlish. So much for newfangled trains.

2.30 p.m. – After an hour and half wait, we are told that no trains can leave the station until six o'clock and a coach will be provided to take us to Bristol. A two-hour journey on a coach with a leaky roof that is pissing in on us every time it slows down or turns a corner. A message to the foul-mouthed, aggressive teenage Welsh lad sat behind us: shouting 'fuck' loudly to yourself every 30 seconds does not make a coach move faster. He's definitely Cardiff.

4.30 p.m. – Arrive at Bristol Temple Meads. Fat coach driver is abused by Welsh lad. I would like to grab this little bastard by the scruff of the neck and ask him how it can be the coach driver's fault that the trains are shit, but I'm much too weary. The mouthy sod has only got to go Cardiff, unlike some of us.

5.00 p.m. – After purchasing basic provisions – a bottle of water, a Mars Bar and some Wheat Crunchies (crispy bacon flavour, obviously!) – we await the 5.15 to Glasgow Central on platform 3. Although the Welsh lad has buggered off, we are left with his legacy as we have now started to mouth obscenities about Virgin Trains ourselves.

5.15 p.m. – A train arrives. First of all we are told that it terminates here, and then we get another message through the Tannoy and on the screens that it is the 5.15 to Glasgow. We get on, as do many others, a previously packed platform starts to empty. And then the doors lock and it moves slightly. It's not going anywhere though, an announcer states that two trains will be connected to one and the doors must be locked for security purposes while this takes place. Fair enough.

6.30 p.m. – The train hasn't moved. Nobody actually knows where this train is going except that it is definitely calling at Birmingham New Street. Or maybe Penzance. The buffet is most definitely not open and you can't get to the bogs or even get up to have a stretch because there are bodies everywhere. We decide that if they open the doors we will get off and stop overnight in Bristol. The cheeky (bar) stewards then have the cheek to blame a woman who has pulled the cord for the delay as her five-year-old son is stuck on the platform when the train starts to move off with her locked on the train.

6.45 p.m. – Train(s) eventually move off from Bristol. Journey time thus far is seven hours. It's a living hell, but there's relief as at least we're now moving.

7.00 p.m. – Bristol to Birmingham, and everyone is sat around, joking and laughing about it, while mumbling about the appalling service, in that oh-so-British way. Ho hum, mustn't grumble, there's plenty in Gidlaw cemetery who'd swap places with us. We're chatting to some nice bird sat across from us. She's not taking us on too much, though, because we both look and feel like we've just done 40 days in Tenko.

8.00 p.m. – Another announcement from the train manager, who has remained safely locked away in fear of his life throughout the journey. This announcement is equally as useful as his previous ones. This train is in fact two trains and will split into two on arrival in Birmingham, with coaches A, B and C going to Newcastle via Leicester and Sheffield, and coaches X, Y and Z going to Glasgow Central via Crewe. As they have already told us, though, that 'the signage on the train is incorrect' we aren't sure which coaches are which without jumping off the train in mid-motion and checking from the outside. Wow, a game of Russian roulette. Great fun!

8.33 p.m. – On arrival at Birmingham, we conduct a great deal of gesticulating and interrogation of people getting on:

'Where are you going, mate?'

'Why do you need to know that, you're not a conductor.'

'Look, just bloody tell us where you're going!'

We are miraculously on the right part of the train and have managed to retain our seats, despite bouncing up and down the train to find its destination. However, the fit piece has departed and we now have Swampy and his missus sat with us. They are drinking home-made cider.

8.45 p.m. – The train is in motion again and the buffet car is finally open. It's well stocked with at least three bags of crisps, two cans of cider, some Virgin cola and a bowl of repulsive-looking couscous, ample provisions to keep the munchies away from Kate Moss for at least twenty minutes.

9.45 p.m. – The ticket inspector finally surfaces just before we get to Crewe. Swampy and missus show a Teale-esque turn of pace and leg it to the bogs! Isn't that supposed to be our trick?

10.00 p.m. – I've never considered the bar at Crewe station to be some kind of Utopia, but I am delirious with joy to have made it this far. To have a pint of Caffreys, a game of 'Millionaire' and throw all our money into the bandit is like two weeks in Hedonism III. Of course, we've missed the connecting train from Crewe, we now have to wait for a bus service to Wigan because 'the lines are down'. Damn right they are!

10.30 p.m. – A Hurst's of Wigan coach turns up and is greeted with scenes of wild jubilation from the four people waiting for it.

11.30 p.m. – After a brief (piss) stop at Warrington Bank Quay we eventually arrive in God's own country. Today's honorary knighthood goes to Canny's stepdad Tony, who picks us up from the station and takes us for a Chinese supper. A top bloke for a Nob End (Preston North End) fan.

11.42 p.m. – Arrive home completely shagged. Stick needles in my Branson voodoo doll. Three trains, two buses and an eleven-and-a-half-hour journey. What a bloody shambles.

I'm still in a grumpy mood all day Monday because I have missed out on a Sunday night turnout so set about writing a foul letter to Richard Branson. I then stroll down to the bookies to collect my winnings. Yes, I've won on a football coupon! However, even this little result turns into something of a bollocks-up. A Euro qualifier treble has been placed – £5 for three aways: Austria at Belarus 6/4, Norway – a dodgy 7/2, but they are stubborn buggers who I predict will bore an ageing Romanian side into a draw before poaching a late winner. Both in. However, my 4/5 banker – Russia at Georgia, gets postponed (twice) due to floodlight failure and the weather. So, rather than collecting a £100 treble I am forced to settle for a £55 double, not bad, I suppose, my first return of the season on the football betting front, and some recompense for the

£300-plus I have shelled out this weekend. I put these winnings to one side, to go towards my latest venture of a new club night in Wigan, entitled 'Guru Rogan Josh', featuring the best of seminal acid house music and flaming hot curries . . .

THE YOUTH OF TODAY

15 October 2002, Wigan Athletic 0 Wrexham 1. FA Youth Cup Round 1.

Found out about this one 20 minutes before kick-off. At 6.45 p.m. I get my coat on and set off walking until the phone goes, and it's Vaughanie asking for a lift because it's going to piss down. Oh yeah – the car! Forgot I had one on matchdays, I've got that used to walking it to the JJB out of habit, but I'm hardly likely to get drunk tonight, and there should be adequate parking and no congestion afterwards.

I suspect that the majority of the crowd, save the mums and dads, have just come to see one player in particular. A couple of years ago, Jairzinho, the Brazilian World Cup legend, came over to meet Dave Whelan and Co. and set up a Brazilian Soccer School in Wigan. Well, it's a bit like Rio de Janeiro, as we live in mudhuts, or so the song goes. Jairzinho brought with him a Brazilian kid called Mauro Viera Silva as a sample of what could be produced, and he has been playing for our youth team ever since. From all reports, he's something special. Just the thorny issue of work permits to resolve and we've got ourselves a young Ronaldo playing up front in a year or two. Magic!

Although he is working and earning a living in this country, I believe that there are specific rules governing football transfers whereby a non-EU national cannot get a work permit unless he is playing a certain percentage of international games for his own country. Whether football is different to any other form of employment has been tried, tested and broken before with the now infamous Bosman ruling, but this may take considerable cost and effort just to open the floodgates for another deluge of foreigners into the British game. Some of the more base ideas include marrying him off to a local girl or finding a relative who is eligible for a Portuguese passport. The lad just wants to play football! Although I doubt that a sham marriage to a Platt Waz single mum will aid his footballing temperament, we're selfish buggers and want to see the lad play.

In order to take a look at the Brazilian, all I have to do is turn around, as he's sat behind me in the West Stand, shivering away with his hood up. A disappointment, is it down to injury or eligibility? I don't know, some say he is now too old for this competition as he turns 19 this year, in which case he should be a first-year professional. Or is it the blasted work permit? All very mysterious. I've also come to see how Greg Traynor is developing, who played in the first team at 16, and also a lad called David Moore whom I have noticed had quite a prolific goalscoring record in the youth team last season.

We settle down to watch the game with a coffee. Very necessary as it is the first game of the season so far where the phrase 'It's bastard freezing!' has been used. Fail to acquire a teamsheet, so I only recognise a handful of those on display for Latics. In nets is Ryan Yeomans, who has been our second-choice keeper for most of the season, as the rest have retired or fired off and no one else wants to take a chance on trying to dislodge the magnificent John Filan. The aforementioned Greg Traynor and David Moore are playing in midfield and up front respectively. The other familiar name is the captain and left-back, Leighton Baines, who has also seen action with the first team this year. I remember the warm-up at half-time at Northampton and thinking 'he's a skilful little bugger' so I'm a little surprised to find out that he's a left-back.

Wrexham, on first impressions, look slightly more skilful and stronger and that proves to be the case when they take the lead after seven minutes. This launches Latics on the offensive and they create a bagful of chances, but no one converts. Baines is taking all the set pieces and his delivery is excellent. He whips in a great free kick onto Joey Roberts' head, which just goes narrowly wide, and Moore also sees a couple of chances either thwarted by the keeper or go wide.

1–0 at half-time and we go down to the West Stand concourse. No one at the bar, yet most of the 341 crowd are queuing for a pie or Bovril. Pint for us then! The second half begins as the first ended, with Wigan pressing. The young lad Traynor is knocking some delightful balls about but the Wigan boys, for me, lack a bit of cutting edge. The player who stands out for Wrexham is a little ginger winger who looks about 12. A crafty little bugger, who has the Wigan full-back on his arse a few times. They also have two huge centre-halves who are dealing appropriately with any aerial threat that comes their way.

Nothing is going the young Latics' way tonight. On several occasions they string together some great passes, but the final one lets them down. Thompson, the right winger, is heavily involved, he's got skill but I don't think even he knows what he's going to do next. On one occasion, he takes delivery of a brilliant crossfield ball, drifts inside, turns in and out to beat his man, gets into the box and he's done the hard work, only to fire narrowly wide with the goal at his mercy. Although I never want to see Latics lose at any level, it's got to be said I don't fancy extra time much, as it's freezing. The better, more composed team wins. As we leave, Vaughanie is on one of his rants, 'Bloody hate Wrexham, they're complete twats, no matter which team they're playing against, they always bloody beat us!' He's got a point as they beat us three times last season, despite getting relegated.

My verdict on the youth team isn't a particularly enthusiastic one. I predict that maybe one or two will make it through the ranks, but it is so much more difficult now that we've got readies. The days of the production line of great young players Wigan Athletic used to have to play and then sell now look to have past, but everyone I speak to says how important it is that we continue to invest in a youth policy. And still the questions remain about our young Brazilian: is he a future star of Wigan Athletic, or just a publicity stunt?

OH NO IT'S SATURDAY AGAIN!

19 October 2002, Stockport County (h). Won 2–1.

Plymouth took it out of me big time, so I pass on a pre-match pint and am listening to the banter on our local radio station. Shame on the DJ who confuses Andy Roberts with Neil Liddell, but the legend that is Matt McCann is always good value. Some good fayre on offer this afternoon, and it's great to hear Matt laying into Carlton Palmer, as a totally unconnected debate about 'Who is England's worst ever player?' is being held. This is backed up by the ongoing and escalating Roberts vs. Liddell debate so you can shove your Premier League nonsense on other stations.

The return of Andy Liddell from suspension has got everyone talking. Liddell is a recent player of the year, a legend amongst Latics fans. After all, not many players are given the prefix 'Sir' without even meeting the queen. However, his deputy, Neil Roberts, has played exceptionally in Liddell's absence, and although he hasn't scored, the team as a whole have been creating and scoring plenty. The news filters through on WISH FM at about half past two: Andy Liddell is on the bench! Brave move! Despite Liddell's comment that he 'doesn't expect to get straight back in', it's a tremendous boost for Neil Roberts to keep the star player out of the side. If Liddell slaps in a transfer request, though, Jewell will get sacked!

Matt confidently predicts a 5–1 drubbing for Stockport. If we were playing Juventus he'd predict the same, such is the lad's unwavering optimism. The question everyone is asking, though, is, 'Where are all the Stockport fans?' I mean, come on, I travel further than that to work every day and only 500 of them can be arsed travelling to Wigan? I know they've suffered a few hard times lately, last season's relegation must have been depressing and they've hardly been setting this division alight, emphasised by a 4–1 home defeat suffered to Crewe last weekend. Considering they've never played at our new ground it is a very poor away following. We get a lot of bad press for our perceived lack of support, but there's no way we'd ever take fewer than 1,200–1,500 to any game in the North-west area regardless of our league position.

In the first couple of minutes The Duke is well onto them, frightening the life out of the Stockport defence by creating two early half-chances. However, three minutes in disaster strikes. A long punt forward by Stockport isn't dealt with by Nicky Eaden, two Stockport forwards come charging through, and it's no surprise when their top goalscorer, Luke Beckett, wins the race to the ball. He takes it on and coolly slots it through John Filan's legs. Shit! The massive travelling army from Stockport go wild!

We're not totally convincing, but slowly creep back into the game without actually scoring. The most notable and unsavoury incident happens midway through the first half when an aerial Stockport ball is heading out for a goalkick. Ali Gibb of Stockport goes up for the ball with Wigan's captain Jason de Vos – CRACK! An almighty clash of heads that makes half the South Stand wince. Both players are flat out and no bloody wonder. De Vos is up first, bleeding from the forehead, he leaves the field for treatment. The Stockport lad is out cold and has to be stretchered from the pitch – I think he is moving when the match eventually resumes, but that's the last he'll see of this particular game. Glad to hear there is no permanent damage to either player as no one takes pleasure in seeing a player get carried off in that manner. It's a shame really for Stockport, as he seemed to be causing quite a few problems for us down their right wing, but I make a mental note never to accept a head-butt off Jason De Vos.

Stockport bring on a sub whereas, for Wigan, Tony Dinning drops to centre-half while Latics play with ten men for a spell. De Vos then returns, heavily bandaged, Terry Butcher-style, to a great ovation. Somewhat inevitably, his first task is to go up for a header, which he wins! Stockport aren't brilliant but possess a real livewire in Luke Beckett who is causing problems with his pace. He's got bags of confidence, no surprise that he's the division's top scorer. Now that their dangerous winger has gone off, though, he's not getting the service. They are defending their one-goal lead stoutly as we are restricted to a few half-chances, with Carlton Palmer 'marshalling' County at the back. The best first-half opportunity for Latics comes just before the break when a ball is played in and Lee McCulloch comes charging in to meet it with a side-footed volley which flies over the bar.

Half-time and I pass on the beer and get a coffee because it's getting a bit chilly. As we pass through autumn into winter, the queue for the beer diminishes and the queue for hot drinks gets longer so I spend the whole of the half-time break queuing for a cup of Kenco. The queue is bedlam; the kids (for that's what they are) behind the counter are doing their best, but haven't got a clue. There's a terrified little kid who can only be eight years old at best stuck in the middle of it, getting shoved left, right and centre in this six-deep mess. Sensing an opening, I barge the little bugger out of the way and push in front of him. Nah, only kidding. I push him to the front and tell the youth behind the counter that 'this little un's next'.

Four minutes into the second half and a cracking ball in from in-form

Gary Teale is met by Nathan Ellington stealing a yard in front of the defence. His firm header just creeps in below the bar to give us a valuable equaliser. A great poacher's goal. That's six in four games now for The Duke, bang in form. The Duke's burst of goalscoring has come at just the right time, with Andy Liddell being suspended for the previous three games. Neil Roberts has performed brilliantly and the team as a whole have gelled. For all Neil Roberts' endeavour, his inability to score goals like Liddell can, especially crucial ones, means that he is on borrowed time. Even more so when he misses two second-half sitters, one with the goal gaping at his mercy, and the score tied at 1–1.

Andy Liddell by now is warming up in front of the South Stand, who are chanting his name. This winds me up a bit, the crowd quite rightly idolise him, but it isn't going to help Roberts' game while he's still on the pitch. It can't be easy for Roberts knowing that Jewell's going to haul him off any minute. He's never been barracked by the crowd, ever. Nor has he had a bad game today, but it's one apiece and Liddell is the man to pull something special out of the drawer and the whole stadium knows it.

And then a moment to cherish: a loose ball in the box is only half headed clear by Stockport, the ball falls to Roberts, who hits a corking volley into the top corner. A fantastic goal, and no one deserves it more. Made up for him. He turns to punch the air in the direction of the South Stand when making his way back for kick-off. I wonder whether the gesture is an attempt to say to the Liddell-chanters 'have some of that' but knowing the lad, he's not got a bad bone in his body and is just genuinely savouring his strike. Go on, Robbo lad!

The final half-hour is nervy at best. Our last two home games have ended 2–2, and on both occasions we have let in a late equaliser. It looks for a while as if that could happen again as Latics adopt their familiar stance of sitting back and hoofing it forward, rarely committing men towards attack. It has cost us in the past, but it doesn't today. The substitutions are made – three in all, all separately as well to slow the game up and eat up time. Only one is forced, as Tony Dinning goes off and appears to be holding his wrist and limping, not a good sign. Jewell is in the wars himself as he attempts to kick a wayward ball back into play and falls over. Andy Liddell comes on for Gary Teale and looks distinctly off the pace – justification of the manager's decision perhaps?

Stockport do actually get the ball in the net after 75 minutes, when Beckett races through one-on-one to slot home a carbon copy of his first goal. Thankfully, the linesman's flag is up, and we all explode with relief. The 90 minutes are up and the fourth official indicates that three extra minutes will be played. Lee McCulloch spends at least two and a half of these showboating by the left-hand corner. He wins about four throw-ins on the bounce, all within a few yards of the corner flag. This sort of stuff is great fun to watch when you are winning, but must be very frustrating when you are trailing. It does the trick, and the ref blows for full-time. As we are leaving the stadium, the news filters through about our rivals: Cardiff – lost, Oldham – lost, Crewe – lost, QPR – drew. This can only mean one thing: WE ARE TOP OF THE LEAGUE! We are now in a position where we can afford to draw next week and still retain our top spot. It would be great to win, but we face a team with even better recent form than ourselves. Luton Town's last five results are an emphatic WWWWW.

MY OLD MAN SAID FOLLOW THE VAN

22 October 2002, Notts County (a). LDV Vans Trophy. Won 3–2.

Welcome to LDV World! A world where sub-thousand crowds watch sub-standard teams playing sub-standard football in sub-freezing temperatures. Maybe that's a little bit harsh here, it has been pretty good to us over the years, as during its 17-year existence in all manner of guises, we've managed to win the thing twice. It is a much maligned competition which clogs up the fixture lists of lower division clubs, but at least they have the sense to regionalise it, and it does of course offer the finalists a jaunt to the Millennium Stadium. Sadly no European place on offer.

I arrange to get picked up at Knutsford services at five o'clock. I am a little dubious about leaving my own car at a service station for six hours, firstly because I am concerned about theft, but more importantly, because the thieving gits are asking £6 for me to leave it there. When Heeley and Clandon arrive in John's car, I laugh off the scandalous fee adding that, 'They can shove their six quid up their arses, I'd rather get clamped.' Also, as it's pissing down, I reason that 'No stupid bastard's gonna go around clamping cars in this bloody weather!' Famous last words? No. What softarse had actually done, and didn't tell them, was pay up and display my dirty ticket. A possible fine of £60 means that, unless the odds of clamp avoidance were less than 10/1, it was probably more cost effective to begrudgingly buy a ticket.

Fearful downpours as we bomb down the M6, and I'm questioning whether this game will actually go ahead. It wouldn't be ideal to get there and find it's off, as Notts County is a trek for a Tuesday night. Mind you, in the southern draw of the same competition, Chester are at home to Plymouth; are they taking the piss or what? How can Chester be in the southern draw when Notts County are in the northern draw? I suppose every away game is a trek for Plymouth fans, but what the hell are Chester doing in the southern draw? Unless that well-known Lancashire mining town, Plymouth, have been put in the northern draw. Surreal.

Still, I prefer away games in this contest as the JJB Stadium looks even sillier than Notts County's ground when there's just a couple of thousand rattling around in it. We arrive in good time and park up in the yard across from the away end. I wonder whether we should be paying someone for this prized spot, but as it's ten past seven and there's only two other cars on there I doubt it. We nip to the pub called The Navigation around the other side of the ground. This was the one from Boxing Day a couple of years ago, a load of lads came charging out when our coach arrived looking for a scuffle, only to be faced with Adolf Hitler, Spiderman and a gang of cavemen on our annual fancy-dress outing. The look on their faces was a picture and they scarpered without a punch being thrown.

I decide to buy a programme, as we have tended in the past to field much weakened teams in this competition so at least I'll be able to identify some of our youth team starlets by their squad numbers. I part with £1 for a weighty affair only to find out that I have just purchased a bloody fold-out Notts County 2003 calendar, with the teamsheet on the back! Hmmm, shall I put it on the wall of my bedroom or keep it pristine in its folded-up state to maximise future earnings when it's a collectors' item?

Entrance to the ground is a mere fiver, one can only speculate how low the crowd would be if it were full whack. Clandon, true to form, gets in for two quid, I hear him reciting his date of birth to the operative on the next turnstile: 'Fifth of the second 1987'. Two minutes later the 'juvenile' is supping lager! We make our way out into the stand, and despite expectations of an abysmal crowd, we are still taken aback by the sheer emptiness of the ground. I'd be amazed if there's more than 600 in, they've only actually bothered to open two sides of the ground. The atmosphere is null and void and there's very much of a reserve game feel about the evening, the players are simply going through the motions.

The Wigan side are slightly stronger than I had anticipated and could be best described as a mixed bag. Curiously, Richard Edghill, ex-Man City, has signed on a non-contract basis and is making his debut at right-back. At left-back is Leighton Baines, a highly rated 17-year-old making his full debut. And on the bench are some slightly more familiar first teamers and young Greg Traynor. A bit makeshift, but nevertheless quite a decent side. Notts County seem to be fielding quite a strong team from what I can gather, although Allsopp and Caskey are on the bench.

With just nine minutes gone, Latics are ahead. Gary Teale, playing up front, receives the ball on the far side, cuts inside the Notts County right-back (Preston-born Nick Fenton) and fires a low shot past the Notts County goalkeeper, Stephen Mildenhall, Age 24, Height 6ft 5ins. Look, I've bought a programme, I'm using it! To say the goal is greeted with muted celebrations would be a mild understatement. I settle for a barely audible 'yes' and clap twice. This is in stark contrast to the other 63 Wigan Athletic fans present who are conga-ing around the away end with their underpants on their head.

After 22 minutes, Teale is in again following an Andy Liddell flick, which he calmly slots past the advancing keeper. A weakened Wigan Athletic side with seven changes from Saturday are pulling Notts County apart and playing delightful football. Thirty-six minutes in and we're now 3–0 to the good. I see a ball into the box and a head rise to plant it in the corner. I thought at the time it was Scott Green, but it turns out that Scott Green put the ball in for Jason Jarrett to head home. How inconsiderate of them to keep scoring at the far end of the ground.

This is too easy – one of the most impressive first-half displays so far this season, although I concede that County are diabolical. Most importantly, the golden rule of LDV Vans games looks unlikely to be breached: that there shall not, never, ever, be, under any circumstances, any extra time, be it golden goal, or penalty shoot-out, especially when it's bloody freezing and we're miles away from home. I am a fan of the golden goal rule, but it often means that teams just play for penalties even more and are petrified of risking going forward or making a mistake. I have already asked whether that rule still applies where 'each side takes a player off for each five minutes of extra time until it's 7-a-side' and people look at me as if I am mad. They did apply this one season, I'm sure of it, but no one believes me.

3–0 is the score at half-time and, although I intend buying a hot drink during the break, the decision is made for me when Clandon gets the beer in. The turnout is strictly hardcore tonight, the real diehards who rarely miss a game. I shouldn't really classify myself amongst that number because I know full well that if it wasn't for this book I'd be tucked up at home in bed watching *The Bill* or some other shite. There's probably another 20 or so like me, who are just making a big effort this season and the rest are probably locally based Wigan exiles. I'd guess the 100 per cent records amongst the fans have been whittled down to a handful after tonight, and more remarkably I still have one of them.

It's got noticeably colder during the break as the lager filters through, so it's gloves and cap on and back up to our seats for the second half. We arrive just in time to see Gary Teale blast wide to spurn a hat-trick opportunity, but the second half carries on in much the same vein to begin with then, on the hour mark, Notts pull one back through a header from Ian Richardson (Favourite Food: Pasta; Hobbies: Fishing) which creeps into the far corner. The County fans, all situated in the same stand, immediately perk up a bit. 'We're gonna win 4–3' is their chant.

This goal changes the whole pattern of the game, as rejuvenated County go on the offensive while Latics look edgy. A nervous finish is suggested as County bring on a series of substitutes, including Danny Allsopp. He crashes a shot against the post and, with Filan still floored, the rebound is slammed home to pull it back to 3–2 with ten minutes left. Oh dear.

Twenty minutes ago I was calling out for subtitutes such as Traynor and the young reserve keeper to be given a blooding. Surely this low-priority competition would represent an ideal opportunity to give them a run-out. Now, though, I'm glad that Filan is still between the sticks and we have a strong side still out there as they hang on, but not without the odd scare. The crowd isn't announced, but on checking Teletext later it is given as a generous 1,020.

After the game you will be amazed to hear that we don't get kept in the ground for 20 minutes. It doesn't take us half an hour to get off the car park, nor do we get stuck in traffic in Nottingham city centre, or escorted by the police to the M1. At 10.50, we are at Keele Services for a quick piss stop. My rants about motorway service station pricing policies bore everyone half to death. And for that matter has anyone else noticed that those 'Tiredness kills – Take a break' signs are always situated a mere mile and a half before the next services? Thieving gits.

We arrive at Knutsford at 11.20, where I am pleased to see my car still intact, imagine paying £6 to get it robbed. I'm in bed for midnight, watching the Champions League highlights and then reading the Teletext, laughing at all the other paltry crowds and wondering why this competition is still in existence. The next riveting exercise is to work out who's won and in the next round draw. Will it be Crewe, or Blackpool or Shrewsbury, or maybe even a pulsating local derby against our illustrious Conference neighbours Leigh Railway Mechanics Institute? Nah, it'll be Carlisle away!

'SIT DARRRN, SHAAAATTT AAAPP' WHAT DOES THAT MEAN, THEN?

26 October 2002, Luton Town (a). Drew 1–1.

I hate Luton. Even more so after today's game, it's those fans more than anything. A bunch of annoying, mouthy, plastic Cockneys from a shithole of a town. Whoever implied that there is a North–South divide clearly has never visited Luton. Not a great turnout from Wigan, admittedly, as our next away game is at Blackpool. Blackpool or Luton – no contest!

Still, at 8 a.m., I find myself boarding the coach at its usual departure point along with the usual faces. By using the 'it's not raining at the moment so I won't need a coat' school of thought I'm soaked to the skin already from the walk into town. A video of last season's Wigan vs. Stoke game is put on. Showing a tape of a 6–1 victory certainly gets you in the mood but is also a little dangerous as it could make today's game a bit of an anti-climax. Still it certainly passes the time. A text comes through, it's the LDV draw from *Soccer AM* addict Ian back in Wigan: Doncaster at home. Fascinating! For them, I suppose.

At five to eleven we arrive in Toddington, just outside Luton, for pre-match drinks. What a great place this is, there are about eight pubs all spaced out across a village green. Sadly, due to the actions of forty coaches of Birmingham fans a few years ago, there's only one of them willing to accept us, so thanks to The Sow and Pigs for their hospitality. The initial queue for the bar is bedlam, so I sneak off to a bakery to get some food inside me. The crowd slowly drifts away to The Griffin past the 'No football or rugby supporters allowed in here' signs. Rugby supporters? I thought they were all angels? At £2.30 a pint I feel that they are charging us danger money anyway, and having looked in an estate agent's window at the scandalous price of houses around here I can't really see the great appeal of this place.

Off to Luton through the illustrious parish of Beech Hill, which is highly amusing to some of the simpler minds on board. I am merely speculating about the quality of curry that is on offer in the area. Pass through the local's back passages to gain access to the away end, as is the way at Luton, one of its few endearing qualities, I suppose. Luton's a funny-looking ground, the way the houses envelop the stands on all four sides means that they can't expand anywhere. There's been talk of them moving for several years, but they're still here. The stand to our left is a strange affair as it consists solely of executive boxes – it was probably converted this way when Luton were in the top flight and football first caught the eye of cash-rich yuppies looking for an alternative way to entertain their clients. They obviously saw this as a way of making a fast buck, but it's backfired now as all the other home sections sell out regularly while the exec boxes remain half empty.

The fans in the stand to our right include some of the biggest muppets known to man. Now I've been to some scary grounds in my time, and you learn not to give it back at certain places as the nutter who is giving you verbals may well decide to attack you with a machete after the game. This ridiculous bunch of clowns are not threatening in the slightest. There's one animated lad at the front in particular conducting them all. He's all jewellery and shell suit, and he keeps us amused from the first minute to the last, without having any idea at all what a tit he looks. They have a fine array of songs, to give them credit, searching deep within their vocabulary to try to find exactly the right combination of words to describe what a bunch of northern scumbags we are. Their repetitive chants of 'Who are you?' are met with a dismissive 'We are top of the league!'

However, there is a football match going on amidst all this, it doesn't appear any of the Luton lot are watching it mind. Just before kick-off, Joe Kinnear comes out onto the pitch and is greeted with a rousing chant of 'You fat bastard' from the travelling supporters, whereupon he opens his jacket and playfully pats his expanse of girth. Top geezer, respect Joe. We've started off looking a little bit rusty, our shooting and passing is somewhat wayward and we're relying on long balls too much against quite a large Luton side. The Luton fans treat us to a three-verse chorus which begins with 'You're not very good'; defies logic when you consider they are ten or so places lower than us in the league. They're right though, today at least, we aren't very good at all.

The referee constantly gives in to their mindless braying, much to the frustration of the Wigan players. And it's got to be said that frustration is the main theme running through most of the afternoon for us. There are chances aplenty, with Lee McCulloch and Nathan Ellington both squandering opportunities. One of my mates delivered some new boots to The Duke at the JJB yesterday and they don't seem to be doing him any favours, as he is misfiring. There is a very poor atmosphere in the away end, no one seems to be arsed about singing, in stark contrast to some of our previous fixtures, and I end up in a slanging match with one woman. Luton have fallen into the Plymouth trap of chanting at us 'You can shove your fucking rugby up your arse' which always raises a giggle and gets a few dozen of us sat to the right responding with 'We only hate Wigan Rugby'. One woman in the away end is shouting abuse at *us*, 'Why don't you watch the *football* game, tossers?'

You're right about the tosser bit in my case, love. But at least this tosser is singing, supporting his team, and generally joining in the banter with rival fans, while you sit there fucking moaning because we've sung a little ditty having a go at our local rugby club. I'm sure Paul Jewell will come over and thank you after the game for sitting there in silence, only opening your gob to shout down your fellow fans who are trying to get a bit of atmosphere going. Accept that the vast majority of Latics fans hate Wigan Rugby, and accept that there are many, many valid reasons for this.

Luton, as the home side, are taking the game to Wigan, as their front two of Aaron Skelton and Steve Howard are proving a handful for the Wigan centre-halves. Howard in particular is having a rare old tussle with Matt Jackson, who receives a yellow card for his troubles. They've won all of their last five games, so the Hatters have no shortage of confidence. After 24 minutes, they take the lead when a ball is fired into the box from the left wing. John Filan, who has been wonderfully consistent this season, neither comes for the ball nor holds his position on the line and gets stuck in no man's land. A far-post header is sent back across the goal over him and Aaron Skelton nips in to slide it home. The ball nestles in the net a matter of yards away from me, a horrible, sickly sight under the circumstances. The Luton fans to our right, if not annoying before, are positively infuriating by now, and no amount of hand gestures will soothe the pain.

We come back into the game a bit more, several chances fall to Neil Roberts and Lee McCulloch, but none are converted. It's an open contest, though, and if Filan was at fault for the goal he more than makes amends for it towards the end of the first half with a really special save. Luton's top scorer, Steve Howard, hits a fierce low shot towards the far corner from only a few yards out and the whole crowd, including the away fans, are convinced it's a goal. Filan's reactions from near point-blank range are to make a brilliant full length save to tip it around the post for a corner. I can only liken it to Gordon Banks's save from Pelé in the 1970 World Cup. No kidding, he had no right to save it.

The second half continues, Wigan attack well but just aren't getting the rub of the green in front of goal. To say that Wigan are the stronger in the second half would be true, but even so, Filan is called upon on a number of occasions, and is having a brilliant game, making several world-class saves to keep us in the game. If he's not the No. 1 in the PFA Division Two team of the year this season, my name's Rik Waller. Five minutes left and Jackson again clatters Steve Howard, who drops like a sack of shite. Was it a foul or was it a dive, I don't know, due to the crappy view on offer from the Luton away end. The referee has made his mind up and sends Jackson off for a second yellow card offence – we're down to ten men.

With a couple of minutes on the clock, Wigan push forward again. A free kick is awarded which is swung in by Steve McMillan. It's met by the colossal Jason De Vos, who powers in a header. He heads it down so hard that it comes back up and hits the roof of the net. We go ballistic, I am jumping about like a loon, gurning away at all the Luton lot. Everyone has charged down to the front and is just bouncing up and down with joy, awwww – look at diddums' faces! If there was another 15 minutes to play then I think we're all convinced that we would go on to win this game, but there isn't, so we take the draw.

After the game the players look very pleased with themselves, and so do we. In truth, both players and fans were a bit lacklustre today, but I guess that a lot of people would have taken a point before the game and that is how it has turned out. Everyone knows that it's much more enjoyable to come from behind, and I say that without even the faintest hint of innuendo. We cheer them off, and Paul Jewell shows us his clenched fist in approval, and then we leave the ground, complimenting the locals on the cleanliness of their whites hung out to dry in their back yards. We get on the coach and clear off back up the M1.

It's turning into a day full of draws and the next one is always one of the highlights of the season – the FA Cup First Round draw. Actually, the Third Round draw used to be the highlight, but we've rarely made it that far recently. A heady mix of excitement and dread fills the coach. As usual the local derbies against local league and non-league clubs are high on everyone's wish list, and the familiar ooh-ing and aah-ing commences as the balls are drawn out. Tiverton Town are one of the first names out ('Please no, it's bastard miles away,' are my words, but some of our lot actually *want* a daft draw like that) and will play Crawley – phew! I am heartily and understandably relieved to see Plymouth drawn at Bury. The likes of York and Hull provide a bit of a buzz, along with Team Bath, who I am pretty sure I once played against. Oldham raises a big 'Come on!' because we hate those bastards and like whacking them, but they get Burton Albion. When Southend are drawn out, I wince slightly but, no fear, as we escape again. The next ball out is Hereford (Ronnie Radford token mention), who will play Wigan Athletic. A mix of jubilation and apprehension as the draw fades, save the cries of 'bastards' when Notts County draw Southport away and startled 'oohs' when Tranmere vs. Cardiff is pulled out.

Traffic is gridlocked at Birmingham, so we end up taking a daft detour via Leicester and Nottingham. One lad in particular, who missed the game in favour of Luton's hostelries, doesn't realise this as on at least three occasions he goes stumbling down the coach as the others have told him that we're at Haydock Island when we're actually somewhere in the East Midlands. The traffic delay just gives many of the coach occupants time to get their vocal chords into action with a few karaoke numbers and daft drinking songs, even managing a bit of East 17 for the scrote at the front of the Luton end. Back in Wigan, and it's The Swan and Railway, Rik's, jump the queue for the Aussie Bar, behave like a prick, stumble back to some woman's house at 3 a.m. pissed out of my brains, no away win there either, end up sat on The Pagefield wall at 5 a.m. waiting for it to open! Sunday morning memo: must give up drinking.

THE REFEREE'S AN R'S HOLE

29 October 2002, Queens Park Rangers (h). Drew 1–1.

October's a long month, but just one more to go versus the jolly Cockneys from Queens Park Rangers. I arrive at the ground inconspicuously, fully aware that I may have made an arse of myself at the weekend. Now I've slagged off a few teams for their paltry away following so far, I will however always give credit where it's due and the QPR support is excellent. Seven hundred and twenty-seven for a midweek game is a great turnout from London and they are very, very noisy throughout, easily outsinging the home support for large parts of the game.

Andy Liddell finally forces his way back into the team on the right wing at the expense of Gary Teale. Teale doesn't deserve to be dropped in my opinion, the change has been made simply to fit Liddell in as we need him in the team somewhere, he's a class act. I'm not keen on him playing on the right wing, but it's the only way that the other two strikers can be accommodated. He's played there before and looked hopeless, but at the time the whole team was hopeless, so let's give it a go and wait and see.

Eight minutes in and QPR forward Andy Thomson chases a through ball into the box and looks to be suspiciously upended by John Filan. The fans around me are calling the QPR player for diving, but I definitely think there was some contact. A very close call, and I don't think too many of the home fans or John Filan could have had too much cause for complaint if QPR had been awarded a penalty. 'We've not had a bad ref at all yet this season, have we?' Famous last words!

The referee, it turns out, is a complete rookie, in his first season as a league referee and reffing only his eighth league game. He awards us a free kick on the left-hand side just outside the box, and Liddell steps up to take it. Quick as a flash he fires the ball straight across the goal and plants it perfectly in the top corner. He catches the QPR keeper and defenders completely unawares and it is a fantastic finish from a player who has quite a collection of stunning goals in his locker. The ball seems to take about 20 minutes to land in the net, almost in slow motion, but there's nothing anyone can do about it thanks to the superb placement. Eventually it hits home that it's a goal and the crowd celebrate. 1–0 Wigan.

Jarrett loops a tame header at goal but it has the keeper flapping as he tips it over for a corner. From the corner, Jason De Vos smacks the ball against the foot of the post – I actually hear the 'ping' noise as it happens, despite it being down the other end of the ground. A slick passing move ends with McCulloch charging into the box only to be clearly upended by a QPR defender – a certain penalty is waved away by the referee. One each, I suppose, at least he is consistently bad for both sides! McCulloch gets to his feet with the ball still loose and tries to launch it goalwards but the QPR defence are now back in numbers. No more goals but this is fun – we're well on top and we're going to get at least half a dozen here as QPR don't know what day it is!

Approaching half-time and it's around about 'that time' when we usually concede. And from a situation where we never really looked in any danger that is exactly what happens. A QPR forward is chasing a nothing ball towards the Wigan goal line near the corner flag, John Filan comes to meet him but gets nowhere near the ball as the QPR player heads it harmlessly into touch. Both sets of players about turn and head up the pitch to face the resulting goalkick. The referee, on the other hand, has different ideas and mysteriously blows for a corner. Where this decision comes from I don't know. The Wigan fans, the players, the management, and even the QPR players are all scratching their heads, but QPR decide to take the corner.

The resulting QPR goal happens solely because the Wigan players are still fuming about the decision. The corner is whipped over and cleared – phew! Unfortunately it's not cleared very well and the clearance is pushed out wide to QPR porn-a-like, Richard Langley. He whips in a dangerous low ball across goal and Matt Jackson and Thomson both touch the ball past John Filan. For me, it looks like Jackson's goal but Thomson claims it, as Jackson I'm sure would also prefer. While the QPR fans celebrate, the Wigan crowd are going bloody mental at the ref. The ground is reverberating to 'The referee's a wanker'. The poor bugger is going to end up atop of a Marsh Green bonfire if he doesn't run for his life after the game. I don't sit in the West Stand, but as the half-time whistle goes a minute or two later I can clearly see that the ref is getting serious abuse as he tentatively makes his way down the tunnel. Wigan manager Paul Jewell is letting rip at the incompetent git as well for good measure.

As we all know, psychologically the best time to score a goal is just before half-time, so this gives QPR a lift, whereas Latics are dejected. If the players are anything like any team I've ever played for, the half-time break would have been spent taking turns to slag off the ref, rather than spent getting their heads around second-half tactics. The game resumes with Wigan pressing, but QPR are now much more stubborn in defence. Perhaps a repeat of last season, where we took a first-half lead only for QPR to equalise undeservedly bang on half-time. They then went on to steal a win with the last kick of the game despite barely troubling us throughout. Wigan continue to press after the break, but chances are squandered by Latics and blocked by resolute defenders.

As the game progresses, we resort more and more to aerial attacks which QPR's huge centre-halves Clarke Carlisle and, victim of a thousand playground giggles, Danny Shittu, easily mop up. Hit them on the floor, for God's sake, they can't live with you! The next clear chance is created from a corner as De Vos wins a header which The Duke follows up with a fierce shot but now it's his turn to nearly smash the post in half. The more the game goes on, the more likely that the scenario from last year could repeat itself, as we just cannot seem to score. QPR bring on Jerome Thomas, on loan from Arsenal, midway through the second half and he looks very tricky. He beats the first man with ridiculous ease every time he is prompted to run with it, but as soon as he stops to think about his next move someone gets a foot in to curb his enthusiasm – certainly an interesting one for the future though. Thankfully, he and QPR are playing very deep and I don't think he realises his own ability yet. Late on and QPR win a free kick which looks in all the way, here we go again! Filan belies his inactivity on a quiet night to expertly tip over the bar and the resulting corner is cleared.

One final chance occurs as The Duke takes on and beats the entire QPR defence. They manage to direct him out to the far side of the box, from where he cracks a tame shot wide. And that's it, whistle blown and the 90 minutes are up. The two points dropped have just cost us our spot at the top of the table and we drop down to fourth to emphasise how tight it is. Four teams are jostling away with no one stealing any clear ground. All of us Latics fans are of the belief (or at least hope) that we can sustain the pace and pull away from the pack forming at the top, and I'm sure the fans of the other clubs up there feel the same. If it doesn't happen then there's going to be some serious heart conditions knocking about come May.

NOVEMBER

SO SOLID CREWE (ACTUALLY THEY WERE A BIT SHITE)

2 November 2002, Crewe Alexandra (h). Won 2–0.

CREWE MAKE MY BLOOD BOIL. ALL THIS NONSENSE ABOUT THE LEGENDARY 'footballing philosophy'. 'We like to knock it around a bit . . . Crewe intend playing their way out of trouble . . . Dario's boys play football as it should be played . . . The Crewe philosophy is to play football the beautiful way.' WHAT A LOAD OF BOLLOCKS! Are the other 91 league clubs playing lacrosse or something? As far as I am aware, there are 92 clubs in the league, all of whom play football: why should Crewe get all the credit? Is their team packed with Brazilians? Is every ball inch perfect, played to feet? Does their right-back never hoof or slice the ball into touch and do their centre-halves never have to launch the ball forward or perform a wild defensive header? Do their forwards never get caught offside? Do their wingers never run the ball into the corner flag and do a few keepy-uppies when they are hanging on grimly to a 1–0 lead in the dying minutes? Of course they bloody do, every team does! It's Gresty Road in Crewe, behind the railway station, not the Copacabana beach, so pack it in!

I've seen Latics play some exquisite football this season, which they haven't got any credit for nationally, they've also played poorly in parts, which hasn't been reported either. But at least that's consistent. We hear about Crewe's wonderful football, why don't we hear about them playing shit? They must play badly sometimes, otherwise they'd be on top of the Premier League. But then no one reports about that, do they, because the football media much prefers to praise them. To suggest that Crewe 'play football the right way' is clearly insinuating that the other Division Two teams play the wrong way, so you can't blame them for wanting to whack the bastards. Which obviously gives rise to a lazy journo script of 'Crewe never gave up on their footballing philosophy despite the rough, dirty physical presence of their evil, bullying bastard opponents.'

There is little difference between Crewe and everyone else. You see: football is football, and it is 99 per cent spontaneous. You can set formations, arrange marking zones and practise set pieces but you cannot rehearse passing the ball about. The only two points during the game where you can actually predict where the ball is going to be is at 0 minutes and 46 minutes. The rest of the time, unless you're part of an illegal betting syndicate, you have no idea whereabouts on the pitch the ball is going to be. And even if you have such empathy that you can anticipate where your own players will be, you certainly can't dictate where the opposition is going to be, the blighters might just want to get in the way and interrupt your slick passing. Oh, you get the picture!

Today's a new fanzine day, so I'm up at nine sorting that out. By two o'clock I've parked up by the Red Robin and nip in to shift a few, and perhaps have a pint, depending who's in. I find it to be full of obnoxious Crewe nobheads, there are a few Wiganers in who stop me and buy one, but I don't know everyone's face so wave one in the direction of a few lads at the bar (they fit the customer profile) and shout '*Cockney Latic*, mate?' One of them pulls out a lighter and brandishes it. 'Is it a Wigan fanzine, I'll fucking burn it, your fanzine's shit, your team's shit and your town's shit.' 'Is that a no, then?' I ask, still keen to push the sale, but Mr Mouth and his chums break into a rousing chorus of 'Shit on the Wigan' followed by 'No Surrender to the IRA'.

A survey of the mildly intimidating situation I now find myself in: there are about 20 of them and I am centre stage. Scanning around, most are aged late teens/early 20s, they don't look particularly hard or well dressed. This is the 'Kevin and Perry' of football mobs. Ooh, you bad, bad boys, 20 odd of you, surrounding and attempting to threaten a lone fanzine editor who is just going about his business. Without getting drawn in to a detailed explanation of hooligan etiquette, it goes without saying that real lads wouldn't do this. I've seen some frightening characters at football matches, including some of our own lot, but these lot are all mouth. I once had a bad experience at Crewe as a 16-year-old which I still get ribbed about so now I'm standing my ground. Four doormen enter the pub in response to their singing and ask them to leave. Shit on the Wigan? Shit scared of bouncers more like it, as they quietly file out and head towards the ground, no doubt keen to go and graffiti the bogs in our ground with fabricated tales of how they've 'done Wigan'.

On to the ground and my *Cockney Latic* crowd prediction of 7,100 doesn't look far off the mark. The away following is pitiful: fewer than a thousand fetched from a place which is a mere thirty minutes away by train. I don't like harping on about this but let's face it, there's no club in the country who gets as much stick as Wigan for crowds, most of it for no other reason than our ground is so big. If we had a crowd of over 7,000 in a 10,000-seater stadium, no one would bat an eyelid, but because it's a state of the art 25,000 seater spanker, this somehow makes us an object of ridicule – for daring to think big?

Consider as well that three days after today we will play Manchester City in a cup tie for which 11,000 tickets have already been sold, it does work in our favour sometimes. The stadium wasn't built to host Second Division football and hopefully it won't do for much longer. It does mean that, unlike Crewe, when we draw City in a cup we can satisfy the demand for all those extra glory hunters, er, I mean floating fans.

Nevertheless, it's time to put one of the most tiresome football myths to bed. The Latics take the field with a similar team to Tuesday, except Kennedy's in for the injured McCulloch. We start off much the more creative and inventive of the two sides, completely outplaying Crewe. Surely not? Ellington narrowly heads over early on in the game, and following that, Wigan pass their way into the Crewe box but it seems to be skidding through for a goalkick. Tony Dinning doesn't give up on the ball on a wet surface, and nearly gets to it but is shoulder to shoulder with Crewe defender, Richard Walker. At that point, Walker appears to lash out at Dinning, or at the very least obstruct him. It's not clear cut, but there is a strong penalty appeal. A split second of uncertainty from players, fans and referee alike, and he points to the spot – penalty!

That's the decision we wanted but the Crewe fans aren't half kicking up a bit of a fuss. And if they're not too happy about that decision then they're absolutely livid 30 seconds later as the ref calls over their centre-half and brandishes a red card at him. Was it harsh? Maybe. It has similarities with Andy Liddell's sending off at Tranmere – there didn't look to be malicious intent, but an arm was raised, and that is a sending off in most people's eyes. Liddell is the man who steps up to take the ninth-minute penalty. The now familiar shimmy, and he dispatches it low into the right-hand corner.

Now I know I've had a right old whinge at Tuesday night's ref, but I am unsurprisingly quite content with today's man in black. He has incurred the wrath of the away fans, however, who have established him as some sort of baby murderer and persist with a simple, ingenious chant of 'wanker, wanker' throughout the first half. Crewe, I have to concede, are playing some good stuff in parts, and their fans, those that have bothered to come that is, are all the more vociferous as a consequence of their perceived injustice. Crybabies aside though, Wigan are dictating, as you'd expect with the advantage of an extra man, or two extra men from the Crewe perspective. Ellington could and should have bagged a hat-trick by half-time. The weather is foul, though, and the pitch is obviously hampering Crewe's attempts to play beautiful football unlike 'Route One' Wigan.

In contrast to the midweek QPR game, this time we manage to extend our lead in spectacularly bizarre fashion, following a hopeful punt into the area which causes confusion. The sort of ball which one of Crewe's Adonis-like footballing artistes wouldn't dream of resorting to is crudely nodded home by one of their defenders, following a textbook chest down (which flies up into the air) by Jarratt. Straight past his own keeper, tremendous! Did they work it out on the training ground or was it straight from Dario's golden coaching manual? The Crewe fans are again screaming blue murder, claiming that Jarratt handled it when he brought it down. I suppose they are now adopting the 'if we appeal for everything, eventually we'll get something, because he obviously feels guilty about unjustly sending our man off' notion, but it ain't working. 2–0 up at half-time.

More of the same from Wigan second half, as chance after chance is created but not converted. Peter Kennedy finds himself at the back post in space with an ideal opportunity, but lashes a swerving volley against the post, and Ellington again is guilty of the odd miss. After the game we find that our win has moved us back up a place to third and, more importantly, put some distance between ourselves and Crewe. There are the usual mutterings which are raised periodically about 'not scoring from open play', but the only statistic that really counts is the three precious points that we have taken from the game.

REVENGE IS SWEET

5 November 2002, Manchester City (h). Worthington Cup Round 3. Won 1–0.

Now, what was that I was saying about this competition being a waste of time?

There is a lot of recent history between Wigan and Manchester City. It's been airbrushed from their side, as have all their memories of their 1998–99 season spent slumming it in Division Two, but some of us have slightly longer memories than that. Certain people should still be doing time for fraud after what many of us witnessed in the Second Division play-off games. They handled the ball in the first leg to aid an equalising goal, the referee waved away the most blatant penalty appeal I have ever seen at Maine Road because he was shit scared of upsetting 30,000 City fans and then Shaun Goater used his arm to score the winner. The bastards robbed us, and then went on to do the same to Gillingham in the final, who, if they'd gone up, wouldn't have been able to rob us in a play-off final the year after.

It was the now sadly deceased Duncan Sharpe who put the City directors to the sword when they came to our old ground, Springfield Park, and spent the day complaining about the facilities not coming up to scratch. The story goes that he reminded them that they were in this division on merit and therefore shouldn't have such a condescending attitude to smaller clubs, as their results on the field suggested that they were no better than the opposition that were facing them.

Now City have regained their rightful place in the Premier League (?), they are admittedly quite a big draw for us, and tonight heralds a cracking occasion which every Latics fan has been buzzing about for weeks. The talk is of how many tickets have been sold, whether City will be playing their strongest team, and how we are going to make amends for when they robbed us in the play-offs. The local radio station are even replaying commentary from the play-off first leg with the rabid commentary of Matt McCann, screaming down the mike, 'Stuart Barlow, YYYYEESSSSSSS! It's 1–0 after 22 seconds!'

We're live on Sky and it's also Bonfire Night but it doesn't seem to have dampened the enthusiasm of the fans for this. A 6 p.m. start in The Pagefield, where we witness an impromptu firework display in the car park. Not really the sort of thing I can get excited about; as far as I'm concerned when you've seen one firework you've seen them all, but it adds a touch of seasonality to the evening. The pub is filling up like it used to in the days when we played at Springfield Park. In fact, I well remember being in here after the last game at Springfield, the aforementioned play-off semi-final against City. It was absolutely chocker that night, you simply couldn't move, and it's a huge pub. It was physically impossible for many to get to the bar and they sold out of ale completely in the space of an hour, so people were just going to the off-licence across the road for top-ups.

It's pleasing to see that most of the people in here are actually going to the game and resisting the temptation to watch it on Sky. Landlord Dave is bobbing about selling raffle tickets for an autographed Latics shirt in aid of charity, so I duly oblige, despite never winning at these types of things. There are quite a few unfamiliar faces, but from the accents most appear to be Wiganers, probably the first game of the season for many of them, but we shouldn't really grumble. If our crowds are going to increase then we need these people and everyone starts off somewhere, perhaps as an occasional fan, before the football bug bites when all is said and done.

More and more of my mates arrive and I distribute tickets. Naylor tells us of two van loads of stereotypical Mancs pulling up outside the Bottle and Basket up the road. Every one of them a fat bastard wearing their horrible Le Coq Sportifs and asking, 'Ee are, our kid, d'ya know where the ground is? Do they sell Stella in 'ere, our kid?'

'It's a fucking off-licence, our kid, so I should imagine so,' he replies and sends them off in the direction of Bolton, as is the tradition of the friendly locals in Wigan. Well that's what he tells us he says anyway!

Off to the ground with the sound of fireworks ringing in our ears. As the trickle of fans gets thicker there's a real buzz building up. There are coppers in vans and on horses, there's singing from various little groups and dodgy burger vans parked up everywhere, along with the sound of all the locals chattering away discussing the forthcoming game. Just as we get inside there is an announcement stating that the kick-off will be delayed by 15 minutes for 'security reasons'. This sends us in the general direction of the bar to force down a quick pint and find a spot in the packed concourse. I hear the good old opera singer performing out on the pitch, he is singing something that sounds like Johnny Mathis's 'When a Child is Born'. It isn't of course, but you can't expect an ignoramus like me to know anything about opera. I wonder if he does more modern numbers for the youngsters – I'd love to hear an opera singer doing a rendition of a nice Prodigy number, 'Smack My Bitch Up' or 'Firestarter' perhaps. Pavarotti sings Eminem?

At about five minutes before kick-off we make our way out into the stand, which is a struggle in itself due to the sheer volume of people. The sight of the packed ground is a wonderful thing. My mood is then slightly inflamed, because we cannot get anywhere near our usual seats and have to sit about three rows back from the pitch in the corner as it is the only place where there is any space. We normally sit towards the back of the stand where the elevation enables a much finer view, but it's jam-packed up there. I immediately assess that there's going to be a problem here, as there are certain people amongst our little mob who like nothing better than a spot of abuse and player baiting. Normally not a problem, as even the loudest mouth on the quietest day from our usual spot doesn't travel all the way to the front of the stand.

Not too many families near us, just as well really, as it's a football match not a trip to the theatre and abuse of a certain centre-forward is the order of the day. We've also established that there is a small group of City fans sat near us; we struggle to identify them at first, but one of them is cunningly sporting an 'Ediots' jacket, which kind of gives it away somewhat. Now, trying to play devil's advocate here:

they aren't doing any harm, they are in fact looking very sheepish and are only watching their team. But there is no reason for them to be in here, especially when there's only 4,000 City fans sat in an 8,000-seater stand, it's just asking for trouble. Yeah, I know rival fans should be able to mix, but football wouldn't be football if we could all happily sit together in some big love-in. Reverse the situation and consider what would happen to me if I went in the home end at Maine Road. I have no sympathy for them at all, not even when they are noticeably shifting buttocks on their seat as a naughty Harold Shipman ditty starts up behind me. If they've got a problem, then they should have brought one of the still available tickets for their own stand. There's no hiding our allegiances, though, as we're up on our feet and singing from the off.

'You Are My Sunshine' is reverberating around the ground as the teams enter the arena and City are giving that rendition of 'We Love You, City' which always sounds almost robotic to me when they repeat it for the second verse. The game finally kicks off at 8 p.m. and isn't exactly one for the football purist. Latics are playing with determination and purpose, dogged but not spectacular. City are having quite a few chances, their Premiership class enables them to cut through us, but they seem to be lacking in the ability to kill off their moves with a decent final ball. Their front two of Anelka and Goater are getting some fearful and fully justified abuse off the home support. I've heard Goater when he's been interviewed on the telly on occasions since that night in May 1999 and he seems a pleasant enough chap, with a softly spoken Bermudan accent, but I'm sorry, you reap what you sow. I'm sure that had a Wigan player put the ball into the net with his arm on that fateful night, he would have claimed it and felt no remorse about doing it either. But once again, that's all hypothetical. The facts are that Shaun Goater used his arm to put the ball into the net, which is cheating, therefore Shaun Goater is a cheat or, indeed, a wanker, as the crowd are insinuating: end of story.

The weird thing is that Goater has been linked with Wigan since the summer, and most concur that he could do a really good job for us, and perhaps be the man to get us out of the division. Where the debate really flares up is whether or not we would accept him after we had suffered such a major injustice against us in the past at his hands (literally). It's a wet night and the surface is very slippy, with tackles flying and the City lot are dropping like flies as both of their centre-halves, Sachin Distin (isn't he a singer?) and Steve Howie, are forced to go off injured within a matter of minutes on the half-hour mark.

This disruption and reorganisation works against City as Sun Jihai concedes a free kick near the corner of the box. Andy Liddell swings it in and City fail to clear the hard, low cross which skids and bounces and Neil Roberts slides in to put the ball in the net. 1–0 to Wigan! Watching it later on the telly, it was a great, instinctive finish from a player many don't consider to be a goalscorer. I've eaten so many words already tonight that I should be throwing up the content of *Lord of the Rings* in alphabet-soup vomit. Thirty-four minutes gone and 1–0 up at home against a full-strength Premier League side, it's just a little bit early to camp out in our own half. I have just stated that I'd be happy with 0–0 at half-time, but the boys are going one better. For a competition I don't like, I'm getting well into it.

The match resumes in similar mode as before: City are tidy in patches but slightly ineffective up front, Matt Jackson is having the game of his life minimising the threat of Nicolas Anelka. Yeah, that's right – Nicolas bloody Anelka, not some scrote from Chesterfield! There is a mini-crisis as Andy Liddell has to go off with what is later diagnosed as a calf injury. Gary Teale comes on, and although we worship Lidds, Tealey is a more orthodox right winger (are wingers ever orthodox?) and will undoubtedly relish the opportunity to have a run at Premier League defenders. Wigan carry on in their industrious but not spectacular vein and retain their lead until half-time.

It's started raining, which isn't good for those of us who have been forced out of our usual seats and are right near the front. Thankfully, it's not blowing our way, so we remain dry. Forty-five minutes for City to get back into the game and 45 minutes for us to hold on to our lead. The crowd are belting out that old favourite 'Let's Hang On', the Frankie Valli number, usually much more prevalent at away games, but the words have never been so apt as tonight.

I'm not sure about City, they are having a bit of a go, but they are either having an off night or not busting their balls to get back into it. I wouldn't like to insinuate they aren't trying, though, as it would take a lot away from a really stubborn, hard-working performance from the Wigan side. After all, this competition probably represents City's best chance of winning a trophy and getting into Europe next season.

City's Chinese star Sun Jihai, who in the first half looked a very major threat in midfield, has now been moved to fill one of the gaps at centre-half and is given a torrid time by Nathan Ellington, more fuel for Premier League scouts, I fear. City do seem to have stepped up a gear and are finding a bit more space, but every time they do, it is closed up by tight defending, as Latics get bodies in the way and hoof the ball to safety. Ellington is running himself into the ground, and is subbed midway through the first half. Up next, a Wigan corner creates havoc in the City defence and Matt Jackson blazes over a close range opportunity to seal the game.

We are 'enjoying' some banter with Darren Huckerby, who is warming up in the corner in front of us. It goes roughly along the lines of 'Get your hair cut, you posing twat, you're not in a boy band y'know.' or 'Huckerby, you rent boy, didn't you play for England once, they must have been bloody desperate.' Hardly cutting edge, but he takes our abuse in good heart and gestures a spot of mock laughter with his hands on his sides in our direction. On the pitch, however, he scares us, he's lightning quick and an excellent crosser of a ball. As City have used two subs already, it's the last throw of the dice for them, but he's a bloody good player to be able to throw on and is certainly liable to threaten our slender lead.

The last 15 minutes are like a scene from Rorke's Drift in what Kevin Keegan describes as a 'proper cup tie'. We are familiar with the concept of holding on to a one-goal lead, we must have been in this situation at least ten times already, but not against Premier League opposition with a place in the last 16 in this fine, highly prestigious competition at stake. Who, me, two-faced? Once again, John Filan is producing some breathtaking saves: firstly he diverts an Ali Benarbia free kick and he also stops a point-blank-range Huckerby effort. As the minutes tick by, the crowd get more and more upbeat, and we see the familiar sight of all the youngsters, and some not so young, congregating at the front of the stand and banging on the advertising hoardings.

At the final whistle, pandemonium breaks out, as hundreds stream onto the pitch – there was none of this against West Brom, and I guess it shows the strength of feeling against City. I feel obliged to join them and make my way across, patting Nicky Eaden and Tony Dinning on the back as they leg it off the pitch. It's perhaps a bit unfair on the players who do not get the opportunity to milk the occasion, but it's our club and we want to celebrate. After this, the inevitable happens and the Wiganers on the pitch turn to taunt the City fans. It starts off with kids, who for all their posturing, soon run off when they discover that a small number of the City crowd are more than up for running back at them, by which time some of the older lot are steaming over and a major incident looks on the cards. There's bottles and coins flying at us from the City lot, and apparently, handcuffs and padlocks too, as the two groups try to get at each other.

Now I'm not one to condone this behaviour, but it flashes me back to 1999, when thousands of City fans tried to attack disconsolate Wigan fans, who had just seen their team robbed, by charging towards the away stand, and chucking coins, amongst other stuff, at families and children. Maybe two wrongs don't make a right, but that's about as sympathetic as I get, I'm afraid, towards City's cause. There must have been the entire 30,000 home crowd on the pitch on that night, and it only took the intervention of mounted police to prevent a lot of innocent people getting hurt. At least Wigan fans didn't respond by chucking coins at them, but then I like to think we've more class about us than City. The hostilities continue outside, and if any City got scared, as they did by all accounts, then tough shit. Taste that medicine, it's yours I believe.

We get back to the pub and drink an inordinate amount of beer until we get booted out at about one in the morning. Everyone is buzzing, as justice has finally been done over the cheating City scum. The draw is made for the autographed Wigan Athletic shirt, and whose ticket comes out but mine! Har Har!

The next day, and the plaudits for Latics are outweighed by the extensive whinging from City. To be fair, their fans have taken their defeat on the chin, although some still call us a 'tinpot club'. Don't they ever learn? Kevin Keegan, on the other hand, is full of his usual shit. 'I wish I'd have played kids now' is his first attempt at an excuse. He then moves on to blaming their lack of a police escort making their coach late. Well, I'm very sorry Kevin, I know that you don't get to our little footballing backwater very often, but it's only 20 miles away and you should be able to work out how long it takes. They had travelled from a hotel in Worsley, which isn't even that far, so I really don't know what their problem was. Not to knock him too much though, as he wishes us well for the next round and hopes that we can go all the way to the Millennium Stadium. Only three games to go. And why not!

BEST TO LEAVE EARLY, DON'T WANT TO MISS KICK-OFF

9 November 2002, Blackpool (a). Won 2–0.

A 5.35 p.m. kick-off away at Blackpool is always going to end in tears, there's no disguising that one. It's great of Sky to do us a favour for once, as a Blackpool vs. Wigan fixture is traditionally a noon kick-off to avoid the usual mayhem. A large group of my chums (names to be withheld for the duration of this report for their own sakes!) catch the 9.20 a.m. train. I decide on a scandalously late one, the 11.20, a mere six hours before kick-off, arriving just in time to watch the Manchester derby. Now you can say what you like about Blackpool, but until Ajax elect to join Nationwide Division Two, then Blackpool is as good as it gets as far as away trips go. And as away trips go, this was as good as it gets! One of the daftest days out I've had in ages, and needless to say all sorts of stuff has to remain out of print for other people's sake, not mine. Honest.

The day gets off to a bad start when my intentions to jump the train are foiled by a dozen coppers on Wigan North Western station. I still have outstanding debts owed to me from Virgin Trains following the appalling service on the way back from Plymouth, and therefore felt that they should be the ones with the guilty conscience for having the cheek to charge me, when they do in fact owe me money. I've had one letter from them saying 'we are looking at your case' which is an admission of guilt, as far as I'm concerned. Wigan station is buzzing on Saturday morning, packed full of lads. I feel a bit sorry for the young Chinese lad, who on pulling into the station has a carriage all to himself, only to soon find himself surrounded by 100 Stella-swigging lads when the train pulls out! It's a rogues' gallery and no mistake. A friendly officer from British Transport Police estimates

Wigan's travelling train mob at 600 plus, although just how many of them will actually make it to the game is highly debatable. It's a given at Blackpool, I'm afraid, that a lot of our 'support' just go for a piss-up. Add the TV factor and later kick-off and it's going to be even worse than usual. Personally, I'd like the Old Bill to round them up and force them to watch the game, as they can scream at the telly all they like, but none of the players will hear them. It's not for me to call though, it's only Blackpool where people fire the game off in such large numbers, there's just so much other stuff to do around there. Saturday afternoon in Blackpool is like a Saturday night anywhere else.

On arrival at Blackpool North we are the first off the train, managing to avoid the repulsive sight of Mad Mary, the Wigan Rugby fan who looks like an extra from the set of *The League of Gentlemen*, milling about in the foyer. We bypass the first couple of pubs and head off to the Sports Bar around the corner, a good move actually, avoiding the obvious targets when the other train occupants pile in. We meet up with the lads who have arrived on the earlier train who greet us with a bit of Shania's 'Gonna Get You'.They've definitely been in The Flying Handbag from the sounds of it! All done while banging their hands on the table and racking them up. Game of pool anyone? We settle down to watch the Maine Road derby. Cheating twat, still not forgiven him, scores two to give City a well deserved win. From our point of view, this obviously means that, on current form, because City have beaten United, and Latics have beaten City, then Wigan Athletic are better than Manchester United.

From there we make a couple of calls and move on to The Hop, a much livelier place. It's packed full of Wigan, probably at least a hundred or so. The police are parked up outside and the word's going around that '40 Blackpool are on their way'. Needless to say, they aren't, and as there's now a Blackpool face with us, he confirms that this story about Blackpool fans attacking some Cardiff a few weeks ago was also bollocks. Our numbers increase and, after watching the end of the Derby, we then await the draw for the next round of the Worthington Cup. We get Fulham at home, not the greatest draw, but to be honest, there's not that many good draws left. I'm happy with a home draw, as today represents the first of three Saturdays on the bounce where we will travel away. I thought we were destined to get a Tuesday night away game at Crystal Palace or Ipswich.

It's now about three o'clock and most are pissed as farts already. An impressive number of Wiganers walk through the centre of Blackpool to get to Yates', followed by Brannigan's across the road. There's a stag party in from Manchester, a couple of whom are making a nuisance of themselves, but they soon clear off when they see that the numbers aren't in their favour. From here, we move on to the Tower Lounge, which is like a nightclub, despite it only being teatime. There's a rugby team in here from Workington and for a while it looks like it's going to kick off with them, but our lot are very restrained. It's no wonder there's so much bother in Blackpool though, it's just one mob of drunken lads after another. I think our lot are too stoned to care about any of that sort of business anyway. As with previous years, the size of our gathering means that we are all but untouchable anyway.

From here I decide to make my way to the ground, on my tod as well, as the lure of a lapdancing club proves more enticing than Bloomfield Road for others amongst my group. Full marks go to some of the chaps, who go in armed with some iffy fivers, the lack of adequate lighting in these places does work to the punter's advantage sometimes I presume! It's gone five o'clock so I saunter, or should that be stagger, along the prom towards Bloomfield. I make haste in the direction of The Manchester for a final swift one pre-match.

Now, for many years, Blackpool were insignificant to us. Even when they were doing better than us, there was never any animosity between the two clubs. I could never really understand their intense rivalry with Preston and Burnley. I always considered the latter two to be big old clubs with a large fan base and strong tradition. I know Blackpool have an equally proud tradition, and indeed much more history than a club like ours, but whereas a trip to Deepdale, or certainly Turf Moor, may bring about the odd moment of arse-twitching, a trip to Blackpool is never intimidating in the slightest because we rarely see a Blackpool fan, let alone the local hoolies, and frequently outnumber them in their own ground. Since getting relegated and coming back up though, they've rebuilt two sides of their ground and there's a new cockiness about them. I'd say bloody good luck to them, but as they seem to have taken a strong dislike to us, I can't and won't bring myself to do it.

They've started calling us Plucky Little Wigan on the Internet, which emphasises what sad, bitter souls they are. Since their team and ground have improved, their crowds are now up on a par with ours again, and on the approach to the ground I actually see three Blackpool fans, possibly the first time I've ever seen any Blackpool fans outside the ground. I've still never seen any in the pubs, but I think they steer clear of the touristy places anyway, as they're usually full of drunks from elsewhere whether there's a football match on or not. Losing to them today would be unbearable though, they're still crowing about beating us three times last year, and if the players have anything about them they won't let it happen once this year.

The end we are in used to be the home end, and as they have moved the pitch 50 yards further away, the view isn't the best, but at least the seats afford a bit of elevation and shelter. There's a big away following of around 2,000, plus another several hundred in the pubs of Blackpool. There is a bit of noise coming from the Blackpool fans all the way at the other end of the ground, but the travelling contingent is very, very loud. I miss the kick-off but don't miss much from a Wigan point of view. Former Wigan player (son of Kenny and reputed Jordan shagger) Paul Dalglish goes close, by all accounts.

Blackpool have two danger men; one is John Murphy, their tall centre-forward who is causing all manner of problems with his height, even against Jason De Vos. The other is the aforementioned Paul Dalglish. He was crap when he played for us, but really looks up for it today. Whether it's his new boy-band haircut or the fine coaching skills of Steve McMahon that's propelling him to new heights, I don't know, but he is outplaying the man who effectively replaced him, Gary Teale. Most of Blackpool's early chances fall to Dalglish. I count three early chances, I don't think he had that many during all his time at Wigan. He does well to hit the target, one of them in particular is a rocket, but Filan is equal to him on all three occasions. Dalglish even has a go with his head, I didn't even realise he had one, as he certainly ran around like a headless chicken during his time at Latics.

Just as Blackpool are starting to dominate, a Wigan break finds Tony Dinning on the edge of the box, who fires home a fantastic drive to send the masses barmy. There's a pause before it registers, because the far end is a long way away, but there's no mistaking the sight of the net bulging when it does. Excellent, this'll shut them Blackpool Internet muppets up! When we score this early, the opposition come at us, we end up suicide defending and clinging on to a point for dear life at the end. But it doesn't happen; throughout the first half and for most of the second, Blackpool completely outplay us, not unlike us last year, when we were doing everything but score. There are chances for us to extend our lead, The Duke never gives up and his nuisance factor keeps the Blackpool defence on their toes.

It's not clear why, but the fourth official is brought on and he's from Preston, which is enough on its own to enrage the Tangomen. The Wiganers are in good voice and are serenading Blackpool with a rousing but not very politically correct chorus of 'You're just a town full of faggots'. Just for the Sky cameras that one, I guess. The other one doing the rounds I'm not quite sure about is 'Are you City in disguise' following our midweek victory.

The major incident in the second half has the Blackpool fans going absolutely ballistic. Paul Dalglish has a header saved on the line on 67 minutes, but Filan has only one hand on it, not over the line. However, when John Murphy follows it up and toepokes it, the replays shows that it goes a yard over, and the Blackpool lot are rightly up in arms about it. Tough shit, Blackpool, this day just gets funnier!! We get text messages from our mates back in the pub telling us that the ball went over, so I reckon we may well have got lucky there.

Blackpool are camped in our half. They deserve an equaliser, you'll find no argument there, but it doesn't happen. What does happen, though, is they get caught on the break. Mike Flynn closes down the Blackpool keeper Phil Barnes, who comes rushing out of the box to attempt to clear a through ball, but only succeeds in hitting Flynn's midriff. Faced with an empty net, he rounds on goal and gleefully plants it in. It's his first goal for the club and he cannot resist coming over to celebrate with the Wigan fans, the look on his face as he realises that they are charging over the pitch towards him is quite a sight. He gets booked for allegedly 'signing autographs', top geezer!

The excitable away crowd are soon joined on the pitch by the Blackpool fans from the other end. I'm not sure whether it's an attempt at confrontation or whether they want to get at the ref for the earlier incident, but it's soon tidied up. Nothing left to do now but play out the final few minutes and applaud the boys off. An unconvincing performance, but a very precious three points.

After the game, there are hundreds of Wigan lads and lasses walking down the main road back into Blackpool centre, singing away; the Blackpool fans disappear almost as quickly as they arrived. I get as far as The Manchester and nip in to have a pint while I try and find the rest of them. The cheeky buggers on the door are now charging a pound to get in, but it's worth it for the quality Old Skool being knocked out by the DJ. The lads whom I've come with are holed-up in some boozer on the outskirts. I say I'll come up, but can't be arsed in reality, their selling point that they've been 'chasing Blackpool's lads all the way around the town' doesn't really appeal at this point. Plus, drinking time is at a premium as the train is at 9 p.m. and I've bumped into the Springfield boys for the first time since Plymouth, so I stay put and have a couple more scoops. I'm reunited with my 'non-matchgoing' crew amongst the bedlam that is the nine o'clock train back to Wigan.

The train home is a complete mess, there are several incidents happening around me which I'd rather not report on because there's nowt big or clever about it in the sober light of day, let's just say it got pretty dark in there. I could lecture about treating people like animals by herding them about and they'll inevitably misbehave, but there's some seriously drunk people on board. A Nob End fan on the platform at Preston station gets fearful abuse and the Old Bill have to back down from trying to arrest someone when 30-odd people 'liberate' their target. It's all just getting a bit silly.

Arrival back in Wigan sees a mass of bodies marching up Wallgate, a wonderful sight as everyone is singing merrily, everyone knows that the lads are back in town with the points in the bank. Another night disintegrates into a drunken haze in Rik's at the end of an excellent day out.

BOTHERED

12 November 2002, Doncaster Rovers (h). LDV Vans Trophy Round 2. Lost 0–1.

The club have followed Notts County's lead and are charging a fiver. We are late for the kick-off, not due to the massive crowds descending on the ground, but because, I'm afraid, we simply can't be arsed attending this chore of a fixture. It has taken a superhuman effort to drag us away from a warm pub with cheap beer and Basle vs. Liverpool on the telly. A quick Bovril, and the Uncle Joe's are passed around. We find a decent spot and settle in the West Stand, the only stand open. The travelling Donny fans number a few hundred, tucked away in the East Stand, and are a lively bunch. The chants of 'Lancashire-la-la-la' which I heard while coming over the bridge, were in fact chants of 'Doncaster-la-la-la' and if a singing War of the Roses competition were taking place tonight, then we'd be retreating into the Irish Sea by now.

For some reason, Donny used to always have the Indian sign over us in the mid-1980s, and used to regularly cost us valuable promotion points. Dave Cusack, Donny player-manager and Chuckle Brother lookalike, was one of my first genuine hate figures. And who could forget Tony 'The Belly' Kelly blasting a penalty way over the bar and into orbit, along with our promotion hopes, on Easter Saturday 1986 when we'd done all the hard work by beating our promotion rivals, Plymouth and Reading, in the previous weeks.

Tonight, at the ripe old age of 43, Dave Beasant is making his debut between the sticks for Wigan Athletic in the LDV Vans Trophy. Now, I don't actually mind this myself. It's raised a few giggles at rival clubs, but then they don't have the splendid problem of possessing John Filan, the best keeper outside the Premiership, as their first choice goalie, so they can't fully appreciate our predicament. There aren't many keepers knocking about willing to play reserve-team football, and this is why we have had a 17-year-old keeper on the bench for most of the season. The story going around is that Beasant has been playfully leaping around in the mud in training the day before this game in great anticipation of playing once more, so bloody good luck to him. Certainly a useful character to have around the place.

The first half is evenly matched. We pass it well and Donny look to counter, Beasant deals with whatever comes his way comfortably. The clearest chance of the half occurs when a ball is whipped over and falls to Wigan right-back Nicky Eaden, who finds himself in acres of space at the back post but completely misses his shot. The likes of Kennedy, Teale and Flynn start off brightly enough, but after a couple of mistakes apiece their heads go down a bit. Doncaster also create a few chances of note. They have a lad of mixed race in the middle. Don't know his name, but he looks the part and forces a save out of Beasant just before the break, putting a stop to our bid to christen him 'Dodgy Dave'. All in all, 0–0 at half-time looks accurate enough to me.

During the break, Jewell signals his intentions to take the LDV Vans Trophy seriously by putting The Duke on. Jason Jarrett is the next one to come on, but it's turning into a very frustrating night, with little going right for the home side. The Donny team, who really aren't very good, smell blood and start to step it up a gear, while Wigan stick to lazy passing and half-heartedly going in for the 50/50s. Quite a large section of the home crowd are turning against them fast, mostly for these reasons. As we have moved down to the other end of the ground, there are now a set of particularly loud-mouthed idiots sat behind us. Fair enough, I suppose, as that's exactly what I was this time last week against City. But then again, I wasn't abusing my own team's players and there were no kids sat around me at the time.

After we have taken our seats, a bloke whose face looks familiar from somewhere either in the football world, or maybe he's a rugby player but we can't place it, sits in front with his missus and a little 'un who can only be about four or five years old. The nipper is a worry to me as he is climbing under and over his seat, and jumping about and I've got a Bovril in my hands. I have to steer him in the right direction and sit him back down with a pat on the head and a 'watch yourself little fella' as he nearly falls right over the top of the seat and onto the concrete terrace beneath. I presume the group of fans sat two rows behind me can see this little 'un as well, but it doesn't stop them letting rip with their abuse at the players, our *own* players, that is.

We have one chance of note in the second half, a stunning 30-yard strike from The Duke which bounces down off the underside of the bar. He's just not having the rub of the green at the minute. Soon after, a free kick for Doncaster is swung in and the Doncaster centre-half lashes it past Beasant. A probably deserved goal and the Rovers fans go mad. So our long unbeaten run has been breached. Who cares? Much better to lose out in this competition than to let it affect our league form. If we have to lose a game though, and no one, not even Arsène Wenger, expects to win every game, then I'd rather it be this one than a league game. Sadly, this doesn't stop a group behind me letting rip with one of the most pathetic displays of abuse of our own players that I have ever heard all the way through the second half.

By the time 90 minutes are up, Beasant is going up for corners and most of the home support is booing. Whereas I'm not exactly ecstatic with the performance, if it's just an off-day then they picked the right day to have one. Doncaster's reward is a plum away tie at Crewe in the next round. Bothered.

A LOAD OF BULLOCKS

16 November 2002, Hereford United (a). FA Cup Round 1. Won 1–0.

FA Cup first round day 2001 was a very embarrassing and painful day for me. While perched at my usual spot in my usual Saturday night haunt, a small dark-haired girl approached me. She told me that her friend liked the look of me and asked if I was single, while pointing to a gorgeous-looking blonde. What was my response? Due to the large combination of alcohol I had consumed and a couple of mates nearby grinning mischievously, I simply told her to sling her hook and assumed it to be a wind up. It wasn't. 'You'll never see her again,' remarked Moore at the time, and he was right, I didn't. Oh yeah, and non-league Canvey Island dumped us out of the FA Cup on our own ground, causing the biggest shock of the day. I've had better days.

Naturally, I usually enjoy much more success with women than that, I would just hate this manuscript to turn into a Mills & Boon, that's all. Honest. A whole year later, we are paired up with Hereford, the game is immediately moved to a 5.35 p.m. kick-off and put live on Sky, despite the fact that we have been on Sky twice already in the last week or so. For it is written in the FA scriptures that Hereford United Football Club shall always be on television, regardless of the attractiveness of the tie, out of respect for the famous Ronnie Radford goal and a thousand Parka-wearers' pitch invasion. It's the law.

It's a strange route via Chester, Wrexham and Shrewsbury, the rivers we drive over look to be top white-water rafting tackle, I half expect to see an episode of *Paddles Up* being filmed. We have our customary goalscorers' draw. Ninety raffle tickets are drawn out of a Morrison's carrier bag, each containing a minute, and if a goal is scored in that minute, you win a share of the pot. Despite chipping in £2 almost every time, I've only ever won it once, a measly £22.50 share as the game was a four-goal thriller. My lucky numbers today are 3 and 69, which obviously invites hilarious 'Only time you'll ever get one' comments from Carl H.

Our pub stop is The Wellington at Wellington, an unimaginative name for an unimaginative pub. The tour organiser, Arky, isn't here today, but has asked them to provide us with a 'toned down menu'. When he first enquired about the food, they were talking quail's eggs and stuffed pheasants, whereas 99 per cent of our travelling band would undoubtedly be scanning the menu for the steak pie and chips option. It is a Wiganer's duty to sample pies from as many corners of the country, or globe, as possible. The prices on this low-budget menu are scandalous: fish and chips can be purchased for around about £8, or if your budget won't stretch that far you can go for the cheapest option and have some stir-fried vegetables for £5.50. They are also pissing us off by coming around badgering for food orders, telling us the kitchen shuts in two minutes. It's a one-pub village and after one swift pint, a few of us plan our escape. We ring taxis with the intention of heading into Hereford.

Four taxis head for Hereford. I don't know who called the pub we were going to, I think the original idea was to head for a Wetherspoons: 'It hasn't been built yet' is the response from the yokel taxi driver. Nevertheless, we end up in an establishment called The Litton Tree on his recommendation in what could be described as a minor error of judgement. Stitched up good style! As we enter, there are a few uneasy stares from a mob of 20 or so locals, followed by a few mutterings and several phone calls: yep, we've walked straight into their main boozer. Twenty soon becomes forty and they're still getting on their phones, how many do they need?

It soon becomes clear that it's going to kick off in here, we've naively taken up a position at the rear end of the boozer as well. There's some handy lads amongst the 16 of us, but we make a collective decision to simply sup up and head next door. It's slightly humiliating but it's only three o'clock and we know full well that there's a battle bus on its way containing some of the lads for whom having a fight is, shall we say, more of a priority than in our little party.

A few hostilities exchanged from either side and half-hearted attempts to get at each other, and we enter The Commercial down the road. If it goes, it goes. It would be much better to have a chat about the beautiful game but they clearly don't like Division Two fancy Dans, coming in their pubs and taking the piss. We stay in The Commercial until around quarter to five. The police come in the pub at one stage and are told in no uncertain terms that we're stopping in here. If the Hereford lot want to come in, then let them, we've come for a drink and that's what we're having, if they want to try and move us then they can. We're not moving from pub to pub for their benefit. If they try and come in here, we're going straight at them as soon as they step in the doorway. That is the script. Why should we move on their account?

We are then paid a visit by what we are to assume is Hereford's 'top boy'. A short, bald, bespectacled, harmless looking 40-something recognisable from the previous pub enters, approaching one of us and is basically telling us when and where parties will 'get it on' so to speak. We just nod our heads and send the silly old fecker on his way: an arranged fight in a graveyard, ace! We also know that the 20 lads they are claiming to bring to this event is closer to 50. It's all a game, and I find it funny more than anything, and that's not intending to make light of the situation. We eventually find out where the bulk of the Wigan mob are drinking, and it appears that they are otherwise engaged. We move to a pub in the centre, which is down a long, thin alley, just in time to witness all hell break loose between two groups in what looks like a scene from a Western. I've not got a clue what went on beforehand but no sooner have we arrived than it's time to disperse as the police have turned up and are looking to nick folk. The Wigan mob have arrived and the Hereford mob, including the fat Don Estelle, have scarpered.

We make our way to the ground and have a quick pint in the JD's pub across the road from the ground, a bit more welcoming in here. The locals have turned out in numbers for us today, it seems, many with the sole intention of kicking a bit of northern arse. No more incidents, and we get on the ground for a very reasonable £8 and try to find a decent view to watch yet another live game.

I'm not a complete ground hopper, but the stand is quite quaint in its own way, in that it's twice as steep as it is wide. When you go in the seats, it's only about six rows deep and you feel like you are right on top of the seats when in this upper tier. Unfortunately, we have paid into the standing area of the lower tier, where the huge concrete pillars obscure our view and it's comparable to watching a match in a multi-storey car park. But what do you want for £8? The away following is a bit poor really, officially recorded at a mere 315. Once again the telly and the two games a week we've had for the last month are taking their toll.

The game is unbearably dull, it's one of our worst performances of the season by far. We've been on telly three times in the space of a fortnight, and with the exception of the pure grit shown against Man City, we've played terribly, yet won all three. Is it a deliberate ploy to make the nation think we are worse than we are? If so, it's working a treat!

Hereford are having a real go at us, reminiscent of their comedy-accented hoolies earlier on that day. Filan is again on top form, and when Hereford do get the ball in the net, midway through the first half, it is thankfully disallowed for offside. The cameras apparently show the Hereford fella to be onside. Cameras, shameras, not what the FA Cup is about, I'm afraid: you can't use them at Bridlington Town vs. North Ferriby in the first qualifying round, so you shouldn't be able to use them in the latter stages either. There's no denying, though, that Hereford deserve to be in front, and this is underlined when their winger hits the inside of the post with a fierce shot that bounces clear.

Half-time brings a break from the action and a health-conscious balti pie for my tea. The second half is dire. The vocal chords of the away end have long since died, and we now watch in silence, awaiting our last rites. Just as we concede the fact that we're going to have a replay to contend with next week, and people all around me are moaning about having to pay 'another £14 to watch more of this shit', we finally, with 89 or possibly 90 minutes on the clock, create a real chance.

An Ellington flick is controlled on the edge of the box by Green, he brings it down, and his touch is a quality Bergkamp-esque effort to drag the ball wide and turn away from the defender. He then thumps it in the net to give us a late and very undeserved winner. Are we bothered? Like hell we are! Are we going to celebrate? Damn right!

The previous 89-odd minutes of crap are forgotten as the players, on departing the field, are treated like heroes, Scott Green in particular is taking most of the plaudits and deservedly so. Then, there's nothing left to do but file out and once again the rival factions are at it. No sooner have I got on the coach than I watch a large mob of Wiganers charging at the police lines. Never had Hereford down as a trouble hotspot, but it's the lairiest place I've been to so far this season. The magic of the FA Cup, eh?

Our coach pays directly for the incidents going on throughout the day, as we are given what might be termed as an 'extensive' police escort home. We are taken south of Hereford, I know we are on the M50 for a while and head somewhere near Gloucester, which is well south of our route home, before eventually heading north on the M5. A big bloody detour by any stretch of the imagination, although I do recall coming this way at least once before.

We pull off at one point to try and stock up at the, ahem, services, only for the coach to get surrounded by bobby vans as soon as we hit the slip road. It's eight o'clock on a Saturday night so why is it, when there's all these moves towards 24-hour drinking and relaxing the licensing laws, that travelling a hell of a long way on a football coach and having a drink is tantamount to murdering a nun? All over the country, nightclub revellers will be getting coaches to towns and clubs in other cities on stag dos and birthday parties, and they will all be drinking Smirnoff bloody Ice by the bucketload. Not us though, not even a sparkling Perrier water.

The escort is still with us ten miles outside Birmingham, when we've been on the road for about an hour and a half. The usual arguments start up over whether we should stop or not. A compromise is reached, so we stop at Corley service station, only fair as the journey home is around three hours long and hardly anyone has anything to eat or drink on their person. We are greeted by the amusing sight of a few dozen green-and-yellow-bedecked flag-waving Runcorn fans, whose coach has broken down on return from Bristol Rovers. Poor old Linnets, their game finished four hours ago and they've not even made it past Brum. We arrive back in Wigan just before 11 p.m., I'm tired and weary and my head's banging as my Sunday morning hangover has already settled in. Just time for a couple of hours in the Orange House and Rik's, then I toddle off home.

Sunday arrives and the only hangover I am in possession of is a betting hangover. For some reason, I read about Team Bath, believed the hype and decided to stick a tenner on them at 9/2. After all, I already know from experience that Mansfield are crap, and the Bath team contains players who all have league experience under their belts. It's being televised, and these romantic ties which the press pick up on often turn into upsets. Not this time though, and I am slightly upset at being a tenner down on this speculative effort.

This is small change, though, compared to my 'little' rugby league bet. Saturday saw the second of three tests between the GB rugby league side and the touring New Zealanders. Now every time there is one of these test series the score after two tests is always 1–1 to set up an exciting finale. Whoever wins the first test has a tendency to lose the second, which makes for an exciting third one and boosts ticket sales. That's a fact, I wouldn't dream of suggesting that anything more sinister is going on, I'm just following the form as a betting man. After jibbing out on a safe £100, I go down to £50 on a straight GB win to even things up at odds of 2/1.

The woman in the bookies asks me when I put it on, 'Are you sure you want a straight win, it's 10/11 with GB on an eight-point start?' If only I'd listened!! The game finished as a 14–14 draw, a rarity in rugby league circles as I'm sure you will be aware. The cheeky gits who organise these events then come on the radio the next day and say that both parties have agreed that the final test will now be a one-off with the match winner winning the entire series and effectively voiding the first two. I have learnt a very valuable lesson in betting, and will understandably be knocking it on the head for a few weeks! Would this happen in the Ashes? Would the Aussies say, 'Yeah, we'll forget the previous four tests which we've stuffed you in and just have a straight knockout to make it more interesting.' Would they buggery! Another reason to hate rugby league.

One other Sunday event sees us draw Luton at home in the FA Cup second round. A tough draw but a home draw. It's got 1–1 and a Tuesday night replay in Luton written all over it! Wonder if shell-suit boy will make the trip up north?

I'VE ALWAYS LIKED THE WELSH

23 November 2002, Brentford (a). Won 1–0.

My alarm clock goes off at 6.10 a.m. for an early start and a trip to the capital to a ground which is one of everyone's favourites. Unfortunately, as they are still screwing around with the train lines, the old choo-choo is a strict no-go, unless we fancy landing back in Wigan at 1 a.m. This prevents us having the customary drink up around London and the obligatory trip to the legendary Flying Scotsman, but not to be deterred, we set about filling a coach up.

It's a real struggle getting names together: a Wigan travel company has been offering a coach down and overnight B&B for under 40 quid, this is a steal and quickly tots up around 150 or so names. Our coach, a 33-seater with no bog, comes very close to not going at all due to a poor take-up, but eventually we muster up 30 or so names for the trip. Full respect to the likes of Stey, Dean Martin and Arky himself for ringing around and generally pushing people into going. There's more casualties due to the 7 a.m. start. Canny was meant to be going, but after three attempts to ring him at 6.45 a.m., Mushy answers his phone and, in a poorly disguised accent, starts shouting at me in fluent Spanish. 'I take it he's not going then?' I've paid £17 for the bugger, although fair play to him, I do eventually get it back when he sobers up, sometime in January. The coach driver turns out to be a diamond geezer but he doesn't exactly inspire confidence when he asks the question, 'Do any of you lot know the way to the M6?'

Our destination today is the splendid Hayes Football Club in west London, and the driver's timing is impeccable, as we arrive soon after

11 a.m. I eye up the £250-jackpot bandit, the pool tables, the dart board and the big screen showing *Soccer AM*: great – a proper supporters' club. It looks like a normal boozer from the outside, although there is also a function room (The Ferdinand Suite, named after Les, not Rio) and inside the beer prices are very un-London like, at £4 for a lager and a Guinness. No sooner have we settled down than the staff are coming round taking orders for pie and chips. Well, it'd be rude not to. There's no roasted badgers testicles on the menu in here thank you very much. The manager of Hayes FC, Billy Wordsworth, comes to sit with us and have a chat about today's game, a very decent geezer who certainly knows his football. Although, he does express a wish that the rain keeps up so that we will stop here and watch his boys instead, as crowds have understandably dropped somewhat since they fell out of the Conference. At least we know we'll get to see some football today although I think we'd struggle to support a team who play in red and white stripes.

After myself and travelling associate Neil Goon demolish the best part of six pints apiece while watching a classic Man United vs. Newcastle 5–3 thriller, it's two o'clock and time to make a fond departure from Hayes Supporters' Club. I am forced to revise my previously ill-founded view of Cockneys as their hospitality has been superb throughout. The only exception to this is the handful of snides at the bar, almost wholly QPR fans who couldn't be arsed travelling to Luton, except one who is curiously chanting 'Come on you Spurs' as we file out. And talk about timing, our coach departs just as the two Bedford Town coaches arrive, the occupants giving us a slightly bemused 'Who the hell are they?' look. For us, it's back down the M4 and on our way to Griffin Park, with the odd wrong turning as we try to negotiate the flyover. As for our driver, well, Phileas Fogg he ain't, but he's not aided by listening to the myriad of bad directions coming from all quarters of the coach. We park up across the road from the ground at a quarter to three and at exactly twelve minutes to three chance a quick scoop in the New Inn on the corner of the ground, which is awash with the bulk of the travelling Wigan support.

The weather is still a bit changeable, but faced with a choice of standing on a terrace for £12 or paying £15 for a seat, there's only one outcome. Let's hope it doesn't rain! The game has, predictably, already kicked off by the time we get in there, and it's good to see a reasonable support of around 500 or so have made the trip. The game isn't exactly a classic. Brentford have some bloody big players in their side and play quite a direct style. I've always liked Brentford, it's quite a friendly club with decent fans, they always seem to survive and they always manage to raise a good, young team up. This summer, they have again lost a few of their better players to bigger clubs but they always bounce back and unearth some new young talent. However, I realise that now I'm starting to sound like one of those patronising buggers whom I hate so I will cease this line of conversation before I find myself calling them the 'Crewe of the South'.

There really isn't much to tell about the first 44 minutes, a desperately dull, dreary game, with very little in the way of opportunity or incident. That is, until the 45th minute, when Wigan's Welsh international centre-forward, fresh from his two-minute substitute appearance in Azerbaijan, takes the stage. A decent attack from Latics is foiled partly when Ellington chases down a ball which eventually runs into a defender. I think he might have blocked a shot from The Duke, it's hard to see, but whether it's a clearance or a deflection it falls out wide towards the edge of the box from where Neil Roberts slots home from an acute angle. 1–0 to Wigan and there's barely time to restart before the ref blows for half-time. We haven't played very well but due to the persistent diving, play-acting and trying-to-get-their-opponents-booked-type play that a few of the Brentford players have engaged in, I feel this is just deserts for them.

The second half sees us hanging on grimly, while Brentford are attacking grimly. Now it's our turn to waste time and dive about. Nathan Ellington gets a lot of shit for doing this, but I've seen far worse from other players. If he is pretending, then he's very convincing as half the away crowd wince every time he is felled by a challenge. The Duke probably has our two best chances of the second half. Chances should really be in inverted commas, though, as these two efforts are from 30 yards out, with no support and can be described as slightly wayward at best. De Vos also hits the post at one point, he seems to be doing that quite a lot – try aiming for that area in between the two posts, big fella!

Brentford do edge the second half, I'll give them that, but only in terms of possession – their failure to trouble John Filan between the sticks means that they were always going to struggle to score an equaliser. The game finishes at 1–0, a very professional if not spectacular performance, our away record is certainly doing us proud at the moment. It is not only a welcome away win but a necessary one, as the pressure up at the top is unrelenting. Brentford haven't been beaten at home before today since April, when the visitors were Wigan Athletic!

The journey home is a somewhat raucous one. After stocking up at Sainsbury's in Hayes, where that old teenage favourite of mine, Merrydown, is on offer at a mere £1.68 per litre, it's time to let the debates and singing start. We doubt whether we'll get back to Wigan before ten o'clock, but as long as we've got plentiful supplies and a driver willing to pull over for the occasional piss stop, then we're contented souls. A drunken Neil Goon is touting interest on the coach for our forthcoming European jaunt next season. 'Yeah, we'll beat Fulham, get a favourable draw in the quarters and then go into the semis along with United, Liverpool and Chelsea, who will all qualify for the Champions League, meaning we'll get the UEFA place: Malaga, here we come!' 'I fancy Rapid Vienna away, or maybe Paris St Germain, or what about somewhere in Italy, Parma – or maybe Milan, I could do with some new threads!' The more this topic is mooted, the more it becomes a realistic notion. The song for the way home goes as follows:

> We're on the march with Jewell's army,
> We're all off to gay Paree,
> And we'll really shake them up,
> When we win the UEFA Cup,
> 'Cos the Latics are the greatest football team!

Coupled with some of the older members on the trip, whom I'll not embarrass (Vaughanie) coming out with some of our classics of yesteryear: 'Like a knock-kneed chicken' . . . 'My old man said be a rugby fan', and 'We are the famous non-league hooligans', the journey home flies by. The mood is an excellent one, we've put in a mediocre performance today, but we nicked the points, and it's this sort of fortune which has us all convinced that our team is destined for greatness. Maybe even a UEFA Cup run! There's a great, wonderful feeling about the day, that this really is going to be our year and a coach full of cynics has been turned into a coach full of believers by the time we arrive back in Wigan at around ten o'clock. Time for a few in The Swan and Railway, or a sprint to the bogs in my case, as I have been bursting since we hit the Thelwall, and then savour a few more Saturday night beers around town in honour of the fabulous Latics. As the genial Ray Dorset once sang 'One day we'll be at Wembley, winning the FA Cup!'

PINTS AND POINTS

30 November 2002, Northampton Town (h). Won 1–0.

I could just do with a quiet run-of-the-mill home game to sort my head out this week. Unfortunately, today is the day of the *Cockney Latic* 2nd Annual Charity Pub Crawl, so I have resigned myself to ending up completely blotto, resistance is futile. We usually take a back seat for this event and certainly can't take much credit for the amazing sums of money raised by it. The likes of Arky, Parky, Penk, Brasso and the Dean Martin family are the real stars of the day and last year presented Wigan Hospice with a cheque for over £2,500 on the pitch at the JJB, a wonderful effort, and the prime intention today is to beat it. I'll still attend but as I'm hopeless at raising money for charity, I usually end up parting with a large portion of my personal fortune (i.e. about 20 quid) by way of compensation.

The script for the day is simple: a selection of Latics-friendly pubs, collecting on the streets and in the grounds and a few high jinks and fund-raising events en route. I've got a few jobs to do in the morning, so I join the crawl at the ridiculously late time of 11 a.m. Many of the others are already into the swing of it, due to Fever opening early with bacon butties at 9.30. It's now closed, however, as myself and John Heeley (his excuse: pissed out of his brains the previous night and overslept) find ourselves banging on the door in vain. A few phone calls and it's on to The Swan and Railway where we buy our official pub crawl T-shirts, well I'll buy one but I'm not bloody wearing it. A couple of bacon butties and let the drinking commence. A good turnout of 40 or so are in attendance, and the somewhat disturbing talk is of whose head is going to be shaved.

I've got to give credit to those out of the squad who go out into the streets of Wigan with buckets to collect in some of the most horrendous weather I've seen so far this year. Somewhat shamefully I have stayed in the pub to play catch-up with some of the others. Next stop is The Orwell; as we head in the direction of the ground, it's only a five-minute walk but we get drenched en route. A quick pint in here and our aim is to head for The Bowling Green at Newtown for one o'clock as Arky is rumoured to be getting his 'tache shaved off and Caddy his hair shaved off if the ransom of £50 each can be raised. Unfortunately, it's a quarter to two and it's absolutely pissing it down outside. Do we stay and have another pint or make a run for it? At £2.14 for a pint of Carlsberg, the decision is made.

After another severe soaking we compare unfavourably to drowned rats. Myself and a few of the other stragglers take refuge in The Seven Stars, not an official pub crawl venue, but a useful halfway house with our next port of call. This must be one of the few pubs in Wigan that I've never been in, as every other time I've tried to get in, it's been shut, but it's a proper boozer by all accounts, if a little bit in need of a refurb. From here we head to The Bowling Green at Newtown, negotiating the wonderfully named but badly designed Saddle Gyratory System and receiving another soaking for our troubles: why the hell didn't I bring a jacket out with me? We arrive at The Bowling Green drenched to the bone to find Arky minus a lip-slug and Caddy minus his hair. Beany has also had his head shaved, not particularly for charity but because it needed a trim anyway, and it was free. Mrs Dean Martin, despite being a hairdresser by trade, has carelessly left a big clump unshaven at the back of Caddy's head. Clumsy! Caddy is clearly the only one in the pub unaware of this.

We have also missed the masses of food that they have put on. Yet another drenching is suffered as we make our way from The Bowling Green to Champions Bar near to the JJB Stadium. Just how hard can it rain in one day? I am seriously contemplating jumping in a taxi and going home and getting changed, but it's not really pub crawl etiquette, so I settle for a quick warm under the hand dryer in the Robin Park complex and get back to the job in hand. I've probably had about eight or nine pints now and I'm looking noticeably 'on me way' to some of the other Latics fans in here. Oh well, just time for another scoop and then time to make my way on to the JJB.

My recollections of actual games aren't exactly accurate at the best of times but due to the level of alcohol consumed and the consensus that this was another extremely dull game, I make no apology for the lack of football in this report. As Paul Jewell said afterwards, 'It's 1–0 wins which are the making of a promotion-winning side.' Of course, it would be much more preferable to win 4–0 every week and do it in style, but when you've suffered as many near misses and heartache as Latics fans have done in recent years, then all I can do is echo his sentiments. For the first 35 minutes, nothing happens, I basically sit there and catch up with the gossip from my usual matchday crew of Moore, Ian, Liam and Naylor, who all find my state highly amusing. After 35 minutes, I start to get a bit peckish due to missing the food in The Bowling Green so venture down to the concourse for a pie and a Bovril. Just as I am purchasing said items, a roar goes up from the ground. 'Fuck!', I utter at the 14-year-old girl serving me. That's two goals missed for the season, both ours as well. As ever, better for them to score and for me to miss it, than for them not to score at all. Neil Roberts sweeps home his third goal of the season from close range to put us 1–0 up, so I am told, and there endeth the goals for the day.

Northampton have come into this game on a good run of form, but are quite possibly one of the worst teams I have seen all season. The two up front, Forrester and Gabbiadini, look a bit lively, but are so starved of service that they may as well be on hunger strike, the latter of the two definitely should be. Their frustration is evident in the second half when Gabbiadini receives a red card for a rash challenge leaving them with ten men. I am actually a little bit surprised to see old Flabby playing, although I have heard that he has banged a few goals in lately. I remember watching him a couple of years ago and thinking that he looked past it then.

We spurn a couple of other openings and enjoy a great deal of possession without ever looking too interested in trying to score more goals. John Filan earns his money for the day in the second half as a whole two crosses come his way. It's another day when we win 'ugly' and the performance isn't half as important as the result. Our small but perfectly formed 1–0 victory has put us back on top of the division, one point clear of Cardiff, who had destroyed an out of sorts QPR 4–0 the previous night.

Back to the arguably more serious business of our pub crawl, which continues in The Brickmaker's Arms, the unofficial base for the

Cockney Latic. Another head shaving takes place, with Sharpy being the victim. Another patch is mysteriously left at the back, although he is insistent that his 'tache must remain intact. I refrain from putting myself forward for a follical scalping on this occasion, and stick to the more familiar pastime of drinking lager and talking bollocks.

Next stop is The Pear Tree, who have kindly reduced their beer prices. I believe that numbers have increased, possibly upwards of 70 or 80, but then again, as this is another big Latics pub, half the people might just be in there post-match anyway. A hastily arranged charity game of Kings and Queens is next. A coin is tossed and depending on whether you make the right stance (hands on hips or hands on head), you either remain stood up in the game, or sit down if you get it wrong. The sight of folk agonising over whether to pose like a big, hard boxer or a mincing queen always goes down well, despite several allegations of cheating and match-rigging.

From there on in the night is something of a blur, from the John Bull, a pub I would never have dreamed of going in a few years ago as a house music fan. Nowadays I heartily agree that it has the best jukebox in Wigan. Then on to God knows where else. We inevitably end up where we started, in Rik's Bar/Fever. I have very little recollection of the evening, but managed to confirm my attendance later on in the evening as I appear on several of the photos, eyes and hair all over the place, trying desperately to get taken on by all the women. I also recall agreeing, for the umpteenth time, to arrange an interview with former Latics star, Neill Rimmer, who's a great geezer. He's retired from the game now, but we frequently see him around town and he always has time for Latics fans. No idea of how or what time I got home, and on checking my pockets the next day I am sure I've been mugged and can only hope that the extra spend that has disappeared has found its way into the charity buckets. The amount raised, even within a few days of the event, looks certain to raise much more than the £2,500 raised last year, for which I can only applaud all those who participated or contributed. Football fans generally get a bad press these days, and there is no better example than this to dispel the myth that we're all baby-eating yobs. (In early 2003 the final figure raised is announced as over £5,000!!)

DECEMBER

ANOTHER ONE BITES THE DUST

4 December 2002, Fulham (h). Worthington Cup Round 4. Won 2–1.

I'M RENOWNED FOR MY ABILITY TO PICK UP ALL KINDS OF AILMENTS WITH RELATIVE ease, which means that I am often tagged with a 'sickboy' moniker. I play football and go to the gym a few times a week so there's no reason why I shouldn't be in good health, but for some reason I just seem to pick up bugs like Rod Stewart picks up nubile glamour models. On no occasion does this ever merit any sympathy, more often than not I get ridiculed, but the previous Saturday's festivities have left me with a heavy bout of the flu coming on. I have shivered, sneezed and spluttered my way through work during the three consecutive days and despite colleagues saying to me 'you should get off home' (anxious more than anything that they do not catch my germs) my argument for staying put is, 'Well, I'm going to the football on Wednesday, so I'd be a bit hypocritical if I did go off sick.' On the day of the game, I am ill. I'm sicker than a paedophile ring and I really am regretting not taking a coat out with me on Saturday now. Still, despite all this, I get decked up like a *Crimewatch* suspect and take up residence in The Pagefield an hour before kick-off, drinking a singular bottle of Holsten Pils while codeined up to the eyeballs.

Time to renew acquaintance with our old foes from Fulham. Since the days when we beat them to the Third Division title, they have booted out Adams for Keegan (felt a bit sorry for Adams there, he slagged us a bit but he was only backing his own team) followed by Tigana, the Premier League, class international players, and European football. Meanwhile, we're still playing the likes of Colchester and Northampton in Division Two. They are a benchmark of where we could be, I suppose.

We just make kick-off, and our little spot is busier than usual but there's none of the City problems this time. The away support is appalling, no more than 150 have made the journey up. Still, Wigan or Hertha Berlin, I know which I'd choose. Their team is also very weak, the oddly-named Maik Taylor is in their nets, and apart from Inamoto I barely recognise any of them. I am told by the scoreboard that Clark and Collins are playing as well, but I fail to see evidence of any sort of midfield skill or endeavour from either of them throughout the game, so they could mean Petula and Joan for all I know.

My pre-match pessimism has determined that, as we have already taken two Premier League scalps, this time we will be put to the sword, reality will take over and we will be dumped out of this competition. Fifteen minutes gone and Fulham defender Ouaddou (sounds like what a Wiggin bird says when she's about to get married!) swings a flailing elbow at Neil Roberts, for which he receives a mere yellow card. It looks clear that this game is going to be even at best, there is absolutely no difference between the two sides and it will probably come down to who wants it more. The evidence of who that is comes in 20 minutes. Fulham are cut apart due to a steady build-up by Latics which results in Neil Roberts backheeling the ball into the box and Nathan Ellington slotting home. We're 1–0 up and the European dream is still alive!! Now, despite all I've said, both positive and negative, about this competition, the most important thing about this goal for me is that it's scored by Ellington, and he has broken a nine-game drought. Although results have been superb anyway in the games where he has failed to register, it's always good to see your number 9 scoring goals, and he tucked that one away brilliantly.

Eight minutes later and what can be best described as a 'mix-up' in the box occurs. Fulham fail to clear a ball, Ellington has a swipe at it, but misses the ball completely. He then goes up to head it, so does a

Fulham defender, but it's a ten-bob header. It drops again, and Ellington reacts first, he takes a touch, and tucks it coolly past Taylor to make it 2–0. This time, the ground really does go barmy, everyone is bouncing up and down, hugging one another, myself included, until my legs nearly buckle and I remember that I've got the flu. The chants of 'Duke, Duke, Duke' are ringing around the ground but, quiet fella that he is, he walks back to the halfway line and gets ready for more. He's got one hell of a record against Premiership clubs, and although he fails to add to his tally later in the game, he frightens the life out of them every time he goes near the ball. He has a hat-trick chance soon after, but chooses to square the ball across the box to Peter Kennedy, who hits a first-time drive over the bar.

Neil Roberts also has a chance to extend our lead, but only manages to find the 'keeper's gloves due to the close attention of Fulham's defenders. Once again, a Premier League side come to the JJB and find themselves all at sea. Whereas The Duke will undoubtedly get the plaudits, Roberts is putting himself about relentlessly, Tony Dinning is having an excellent game marshalling the midfield, and Jarrett is showboating against international footballers, flicking the ball over their heads and turning them inside out. Fulham, like many before them, are shell-shocked and are restricted to long-range efforts and a bit of oriental trickery from Inamoto, their Japanese World Cup (and my Fantasy League) star.

Half-time comes and goes and all the talk is of 'how many', which might sound arrogant but very realistic after the first half performance. Fulham respond by upping the stakes a bit, throwing on Sean Davis and Luis Boa Morte. I don't know much about Davis, except he is a good young prospect, but Boa Morte, despite struggling at Arsenal, has scored some great goals this season on the telly. He seems to have electric pace, and our back four aren't the quickest. Still, we've a two-goal headstart. It certainly gives the impression that Fulham are going to have a go this half, and they do. Their first real chance falls to Davis, who blazes gloriously over from a few yards out, and shortly after, some Inamoto dribbling sees him beat the last man and John Filan, who comes charging out way too early. He chips the ball deftly towards an empty net, but another Fulham player wants the glory, and taps it home. Bad move, as the flag is raised! In the words of Terry Gaskell, 'Tell him to read up!' Hilarity all round from the home fans, sometimes an easy opposition miss is as pleasurable as seeing your own team score, especially when their players and fans are celebrating, totally oblivious to the flag, and it doesn't get much funnier than this one!

Ellington gets more chances to add to his tally and claim another hat-trick: a shot is deflected and saved by the keeper, a header narrowly goes wide and he also hits a fierce volley which stings the keeper's hands. We still look quite comfortable, although Fulham are pressing more. Fulham eventually get a breakthrough with five minutes to go, a through ball from Petula Clark is latched onto by Boa Morte, who bustles past the Latics centre-halves and uses his electrifying pace to leave them in his wake before coolly finishing past Filan. This sets up a slightly nervous five minutes, but there are no more Fulham chances. We still press for a third, Mike Flynn races down the right touch-line with a chance to cut in for goal. He pauses and then chooses to run the ball down to the corner flag. I'm not so sure whether he could have gone for goal there, but never mind, it's a few more seconds wasted. The crowd sees the Latics home with all the usuals, 'You Are My Sunshine', 'Mudhuts' and the ever pertinent 'Let's Hang On', not that I join in because my Halls-Mentholyptus-lined throat was completely knackered an hour before the game even started, and is now in a considerably worse state. Just time for Jewell to carry out a vital 90th-minute substitution, and we are left to celebrate another famous victory. Somehow, there's not the same euphoria as when we beat City in the previous round, but both players and fans acknowledge each other. And although it would be unfair to single out individuals in what was a fantastic team performance, the sight of Neil Roberts trudging off the pitch, caked in mud from head to toe is a wonderful representation of the pure graft tonight is about.

We make our way out and back to our local when someone tells us that the draw for the next round is actually taking place now. When we arrive, we find that the cable is on the blink and we're not going to get the draw on; we're not too happy and discuss alternative drinking establishments. But our decision is made as, by the time the landlord has sorted out a radio, it's done and numerous phone calls confirm another home draw against Blackburn Rovers. Great!

In contrast to my usual habit, I bugger off from the pub early due to my physical state and am tucked up in bed watching the highlights on ITV. No surprise to see that we're bottom of the bill. I've just enough strength to shout a few words of defiance: bollocks to you TV producers, shove your 'Wigan is a rugby town' research up your arse, we're Wigan and we've stuck it up your Premier League boys again!! The Worthless (*sic*) Cup is rapidly turning into something of a talisman for us this season, we have already gone two rounds further than we have ever done before, and are now only two rounds away from the final. Whereas myself and Paul Jewell still share the same vision that the league is our first priority, it's certainly doing us no harm, with Blackburn at home shaping up to be another good pay day. Bring it on!

THE MAGIC OF THE CUP . . . YES ANOTHER ONE

7 December 2002, Luton Town (h). FA Cup Round 2. Won 3–0.

Completely and utterly bedridden with flu for the two days after the Fulham game, I still manage to surface for this home FA Cup tie, which is more than can be said for several thousand thrifty Wiganers. Had it been an away game I would have had no chance, as it is I can muster up a quick in-and-out mission, so venture off to The Brickmaker's to pick up some magazine articles for my sad Saturday night in with the Beechams. That's the powder, not the ex-*Dynasty* star, Stephanie, and her daughter, unfortunately. It's a quiet home game in our eyes, despite the recent rivalry we appear to have built up with those horrible plastic mockneys from Kenilworth Road. No beer for me today, just a bottle of Lucozade, and surveying the scene, there's not as many faces in here as usual, a surefire sign that there's going to be a poor crowd today.

It comes to something when the best part of the FA Cup is the actual draw, but that does actually seem to be the pinnacle of each round for 90 per cent of the clubs involved. I don't have any mind-blowing theories as to why the FA Cup doesn't seem to have the same appeal as it did a few years ago but I'd guess it's just filtering down from the big clubs who don't take it seriously. I can't imagine a

50,000-plus crowd at Goodison Park, including 20,000 Wiganers, for a fourth-round tie nowadays, as was the case in 1980. The top half of the Premier League are hankering after European and Champions League places, the bottom half are solely concerned with staying in the Premier League, and prices have risen to such an extent that many season ticket holders don't take up the option of the additional expense a cup run brings.

It now appears, judging by today's crowd, that Wigan Athletic fans don't take it too seriously either, unless we're playing a bigger club, who probably won't be taking us too seriously when that happens. Luton have brought a decent following, to be fair they have been mouthing it at our own support down there all week, so at least they're making an attempt to back up their name-calling.

It's trademark December weather now, i.e. it's bloody freezing and the pitch looks a lot worse for wear after the two previous games. Paul Jewell has sprung a bit of a surprise by giving second-year YTS-lad Leighton Baines another start at left-back. I always feel pretty pleased when we have a youngster playing for us, as we are often hit with the 'moneybag' jibes and the only way to conquer this is to nurture and develop our own talent. It's just a shame they always seem to be left-backs and not centre-forwards! Still, from what I've seen of young Leighton he looks a very fine prospect, even though his name sounds uncannily like a Bedfordshire village. The newly crowned Division Two Manager of the Month names an unchanged team, apart from young Bainesy, as I've heard him called. Footballers these days, no originality at all when it comes to nicknames, even The Duke is somewhat predictable, yet nevertheless a great monicker.

So to kick-off, and I watch the game with reasonable attentiveness, probably due to the lack of alcohol inside me. Three early Luton chances fail to produce a goal. This, coupled with some sterling keeping from the Super Aussie between the sticks, ensures we manage to keep the Hatters at bay. Reading the team news prior to the game, it appears that Luton have had an exodus of strikers to the treatment room and are relying on some kid and a right-back up front. It's probably just as well, because two of the chances in particular were easier to score than miss; as it stands the game remains goalless with half an hour on the clock.

With 37 minutes gone, the Latics find themselves creating their first real chance. A low ball is played into the edge of the box to Ellington's feet – he turns in that familiar unorthodox style, and takes a touch, he feints a shot and the Luton centre-half loses his footing. The Duke coolly tucks the ball into the far corner to make it 1–0, not the firmest of shots, but well enough placed to put us in front. Certainly a goal against the run of play, but that's why we paid £1.2m for The Duke – his ability to create something out of nothing has paid dividends again. With a full half to go, an inexperienced and jaded Luton outfit no longer seem to want to know. It also earns my good self a tidy £22.50 return on my £5 first goal bet, probably just as well as I've gone for a big fixed-odds bet today with a one from each section of the coupon, and my top section bet (Liverpool at Charlton) is looking like bolting.

Not long into the second half, Jewell makes three changes to the midfield, all of which work well. Mitchell comes on – always bringing the defensive midfielder on first when we're winning 1–0, eh Paul? – soon to be followed by winger Gary Teale, with both the wide midfielders, Green and Kennedy, making way. It proves to be a wise move, as within minutes, Teale supplies a great pass through to Ellington who is charging down the right wing. The Duke meticulously watches the ball rear up and over his right shoulder and, on its way down, launches an Exocet first-time half-volley past the despairing keeper and into the far corner. As Alan Partridge would have undoubtedly said, had he been providing commentary, 'SSSHHHHHHIIIIITTTTTTTT!' It is the strike of a forward who has quickly rediscovered his confidence. I remember in the alcoholic haze of Brentford away, just two weeks ago, when the Duke lashed a couple of similar attempts woefully high and wide, but he's back with a vengeance as Luton have just found out to their cost and, ultimately, their FA Cup exit.

There's no way back for the Bedfordshire lot, who have now taken to abusing the ref, like it's his fault? Wigan get a couple more chances which really should be put away. Tony Dinning uncharacteristically blazes a shot wide and Ellington puts Teale through one-on-one with the keeper, who eventually manages to save something. Ten minutes left, and Jewell brings Flynny on to play up front in place of Neil Roberts. Mike Flynn's first touch is a superb 50-yard pass from the left-hand side of the halfway line to Gary Teale near the right-hand corner flag. Three minutes later, with probably his second touch, he gets on the end of a Nicky Eaden free kick to loop a header over the Luton keeper, making the scoreline an emphatic 3–0! He did the same at Blackpool, talk about a 'Supersub', not that it's a tag he wants.

The Luton fans exit the JJB en masse. Have a safe journey home, why don't you! I wonder if they are genuinely dejected with their cup exit, as we have been in the past, when there's little else to play for, or whether, going back to the 'Has the FA Cup lost its magic?' argument, they couldn't care less. And we never got to renew acquaintances with the tosser in the shell suit either, although we do later hear one of them throws a pan out of a transit van at some Latics fans. That's about right for Luton. The crowd of 4,500 is slightly disappointing, but on inspecting the attendances in the Sunday papers the next day, it seems the malaise is affecting the FA Cup in general, as gates are down almost everywhere.

Straight home after the game, only leaving the house on Sunday afternoon to watch the Oxford vs. Swindon live game in the pub as I've heard all about the rivalry between these two. I'm still drinking pop, and I've only really gone out to watch the draw with a few like-minded football souls in the local. That's a bit sad really, isn't it, but as I've already said, often the unfinished business of who we are going to draw in the next round is much more exciting than the game itself. Will it be Arsenal? United? Spurs? Or even every Latics boy's dream tie – Bolton Scumderers?

For the record, this year's prestige third-round tie will be Stoke City, away. Not the best draw, but certainly not the worst. They are another club with whom we have a lot of recent history. Just like Preston North End, Burnley, Millwall, Man City and Reading before them, we have fought a dogged promotion play-off battle with them in recent years, and just like PNE, Burnley, Millwall, Man City, Gillingham and Reading before them, they won, while we failed miserably. A lot of people seem to think we've got a great chance of winning the Second Division title this year, and without being presumptuous – yes we have, along with a few other clubs. But if we finish second or go up in the play-offs, the consolation will surely come from settling a few scores with a few of those listed above next season. Last year we tonked Stoke City 6–1 on a fantastic night where everything we tried came off. While it was great fun to utterly humiliate them, they are now in Division One, albeit temporarily, so it's fair to say they had the last laugh.

However, I don't think many Wigan fans will dwell too long on our FA Cup draw, as we have more pressing matters to deal with. A trip to Ice Station Zebra in the frozen plains of Yorkshire to visit those arrogant tossers from Oldham in an almighty league clash. Let's have it!!

THAT MOBY'S NOT AS AMBIENT AS HE MAKES OUT

14 December 2002, Oldham Athletic (a). Won 2–0.

If points were given for mouthing off, the Oldham lot would have had this league wrapped up a long, long time ago. The Internet has offered a whole new angle to fan interaction; it has positive aspects in that it enables supporters to forge new friendships and camaraderie, but there's also that dark side, where abuse gets taken too far by people getting a sad kick out of their anonymity. The rivalry between Oldham and ourselves has already been well documented, and in the week leading up to this game there's all manner of crap flying about between the two factions. We are 'scousers' who are 'going to screw up any minute' because we're just a 'small-time club with no fans and no history'. Yawn. Beating them means so much to us for one reason only: we need the points to stay top.

Although the Oldham lot try and claim that we're not their rivals you can tell by the way they are foaming at their keyboards that this is their cup final. They are incessant in their hatred of us. I have developed a loathing of them simply because I am sick of them spouting crap about Wigan Athletic, a team they know nothing about. Apparently, because Oldham have played in the top flight and a Rumbelows Cup final, we are inferior and should, by rights, just give them the points. Bollocks! They've not had to endure 45 years of rejection by the establishment or battle their way through from the Cheshire League to finally obtain privileged membership of the hallowed 92, as little Wigan Athletic have done. They, therefore, have no right to patronise us by droning on about their history as our own unique history is every bit as proud and colourful as theirs. That's the beauty of football, every club has its own unique history to tell, if only the bitter little cretins bothered to read up they would realise that.

I think their real beef is that our future is looking considerably brighter. My theory of their irrational hatred is that they can't bear to see us do well because we share the same nickname as them, hence all this 'Plastic Latics' shite they come out with. If we carry on making progress as we have been doing and encounter success this season, we will be the Division One Latics and they will be the Division Two Latics, getting ever so slightly less press coverage. Before you know it, Wigan *are* 'The Latics' and Oldham are just 'lower-division Oldham'. Hopefully! No, seriously, I suppose we're pushing their nose out of joint in that respect, but if they're getting so riled up over a club nickname then that is just pathetic. Arrogant in the extreme, the bulk of their bitter, small-minded fans have been insisting that they would stuff us all week. 'Justice will be served,' quotes one particular East Lancs Confucius. Wrong again, Nearly Yorkshire Bastards! (One of our own little nicknames for them.)

Whoever deemed, back in 1932, that Wigan's newest football team should be given the suffix 'Athletic' has incurred the wrath of every Oldham fan. Whatever! I'm here in Oldham for the football and decide to sample a few scoops in The Bluebell. It's going to be a quiet day today, because I've still got the flu and a visit to the coldest place outside the Arctic Circle isn't going to help my condition.

The Bluebell is absolutely chock-a-block with Wiganers. There are a few Oldham fans in, and they look, well, reasonably human, anyway. They make no attempt to accuse me of having sex with Labradors or pimping out my sister, as is their wont while on the web. Blimey, I even manage to have a decent conversation with one of them. However, situation normal upon making our way outside, a slack-jawed yokel with a bad Henry Lloyd on is blabbing away in his mobile. 'These Wigan bastards are gonna get it today blah blah.' He's about six stone, incredibly ugly and walking like a Harlem Globetrotter. Whatever it is we're going to 'get', he's clearly already 'had' on many occasions.

No need for all this bitching though, the points are the priority and as we file on to the ground there is a pleasantly large away support on view, and to give them credit (for the first and last time today) the home fans have turned out in numbers as well. Wigan are missing McCulloch and Lidds, whereas Oldham have recently suffered injuries to Clint Hill and Clive 'The Jive' Wijnhard. (Sorry, I was a big *Hit Man and Her* fan.) The game starts off tight, neither side wanting to give ground early doors. Oldham are not impressive at all, but we're hardly rampant ourselves. We amuse ourselves by laughing at the muppets in the stand to our right. A few of them are doing egg-chucking movements insinuating that we are rugby fans. They look silly. There is one in particular who is tall and skinny with a bald head and looks like the American DJ Moby, and he is making a right prick of himself. It can't be their firm because no self-respecting football hooligan would behave so pathetically. The Wigan support is loud and vocal, ringing around the ground 'Small town in Yorkshire', a particular fave where Oldham are concerned.

The Oldham geeks are keeping us entertained but I'm going to be mightily pissed off if they score. There is no need to worry, as on 30 minutes a clever Roberts flick puts Ellington through on goal and The Duke lashes a volley past the hapless Oldham keeper. YYYYEEESSSSSSSSSS! Have some of that, you Oldham bastards! I can't help going crazy at this one, the banter between the fans, the top of the league stature of the game takes over as we all go charging down the stand and over to give it to the now strangely subdued Oldham tossers. The away crowd are enjoying a sense of euphoria, while the Oldham lot are restricted to sporadic gestures of anger at us when they occasionally pop their heads out of their coats. 'Moby, Moby, what's the score?' is the chant aimed at the turtle-necked one. Ha ha, brilliant.

The momentum from the goal carries both players and fans through until half-time, and the second half begins in a similar vein. Oldham's passes are starting to find touch and there's a spell of four minutes or so where they simply cannot get the ball off us as we do that infantile 'Ole' cheering-thing in unison. A Dinning long ranger just scorches wide and a Roberts header goes over the bar, we are totally dominant and I don't think Oldham get a shot on goal all day. Dinning is also winning his own personal battle with former Latics player Darren Sheridan. Dinning has been known to lose his rag and

Sheridan is constantly niggling him to try and get him sent off. If that's the best Oldham can do in their efforts to get back in the game then it's a very sorry show.

A corner to Wigan on the hour mark is swung in by Scott Green and, bugger me, if that isn't Jason De Vos meeting it and slamming home another brilliant header. 2–0 and absolutely no surprise at all, as this game is completely one-sided. I look over to check Moby's reaction and can only presume he is doing a set at the Ministry of Sound later on as he has disappeared without trace. We've silenced their fans, we've silenced their team and we've totally outplayed them, somehow I don't think the Oldham fans will be visiting cockneylatic.co.uk for a few days to tell us how good they are. Sheridan is already on a yellow, and once again kicks out, this time at Neil Roberts. He is sent for an early bath for his troubles, just to further cement the result. If this game was a street, it would be Pottery Road, Wigan. That's a one-way street, for those of you not familiar with God's own country. The home support are leaving in their droves, shaking their heads as they really don't have any excuses this time.

Five consecutive wins with no goals conceded, and our closest rivals sent packing with their tails between their legs, a great, great day to be a Latics fan. We arrive back in Wigan and watch our two nearest rivals, Cardiff and Bristol City, fight it out at Ninian Park. As with Oldham, similarly unimpressed with the pair of them.

As a footnote and in the interests of fair play, I contacted several Oldham fans prior to the game with a view to them giving me 'their side of the story'. I'm still waiting.

EUROPE BECKONS . . . BUT NOT FOR US

17 December 2002, Blackburn Rovers (h). Worthington Cup Quarter-Final. Lost 0–2.

Talk about excited. 4.30 p.m. and a grown man (plenty would dispute this) is driving up the M6, rocking backwards and forwards, banging the steering wheel, singing 'We're on the march with Jewell's army' and grinning like a loon. More of the same occurs as I arrive home at five o'clock, bouncing from room to room, singing and jumping about, without even a drip tray's worth of ale inside of me as of yet. The Worthington Cup has won a reprieve this season, from myself and many, many others. I'm not just talking Wiganers here, even the likes of United and Liverpool seem to be taking it seriously this year. I never contemplated on that night in Northampton in the autumn that we would get this far, but nevertheless, here we are, in the quarter-final, only three games from Cardiff and facing another Premier League outfit. Big deal! We've knocked three out already!

The FA Cup run of 1986–87 must rank as one of Latics' greatest achievements as a league club. Could tonight eclipse that? I think there is an inevitable resignation in the air about tonight, the old 'we've had a good innings, let's just go out there and enjoy ourselves' cliché coming out. It's usually the case that results correlate closer to league position the further you progress in a tournament, lightning never strikes twice. Or four times, in our case. Still, win, lose or draw, it has been an unbelievable achievement to actually get this far, so the notoriously fickle sporting Wigan public turn out in their droves.

Blackburn scare me: Yorke, Cole, Jansen, Ostenstad, Dunn, Duff. Jason De Vos can keep all that lot quiet, but who's going to keep an eye on David Thompson? Still, Blackburn are playing against a club on the crest of a wave, unbeaten in the league since August, with our only cup defeat coming against Donny in the LDV when half the team looked like they'd rather be in the boozer. So let's give it to 'em!

A couple in The Pagefield pre-match where I am armed with the local papers, digesting the Latics news, and to give them credit they have given excellent coverage and build-up to the game. We're playing the usual game of 'guess the crowd' and agree that anything over 15k is a decent turnout. Martin, a Blackburn lad, is telling us that he expects Rovers to bring around 2,000. The town has been buzzing about the tie since the draw was made and all the usual connections and stories about Dave Whelan breaking his leg in the FA Cup final are ensuring we receive coverage on the local and national TV programmes. It's certainly captured the town's imagination, as when we make our way across to the JJB I've never seen such a mass of people making their way over from Springfield. We go straight up into the South Stand and take up seats quite close to where we usually go, but the stand is pretty full already. The opera singer is on the pitch, and while I may have taken the piss previously, I must admit that this time there is nearly a tear in my eye, or maybe I'm choking on a pie, as he hits the final strains of 'Nessun Dorma'.

At kick-off time, the noise levels are wonderful, the South and West stands are all but full and Blackburn, to their credit, have brought an excellent following, probably in the region of 4,000 to 5,000. There's a constant cross-fire of 'Small Town in Burnley' (us to them) and 'Small Town in Bolton' (them to us) being jettisoned across the ground. The only surprise and disappointment is that the North Stand is only half full. It should be packed to the rafters with kids watching a team of Premier League stars play against their local heroes, and I find this a little hard to explain, but never mind, we're ready for kick-off.

Latics start with the same side that defeated Oldham, and Blackburn are fielding more or less their strongest team. Right from the off, Blackburn bloody murder us, real men-against-boys stuff, and they should be 5–0 up after 15 minutes. We try to get behind them vocally, but we are shell-shocked. Whether it's nerves, or showing their Premier League counterparts too much respect, I don't know, but when we do manage to get the ball off them, it is given away cheaply or sliced into touch. We're going to get walloped if this carries on. Having said that, we actually manage to create a couple of reasonable chances of our own during the early stages, a De Vos header and a Dinning volley, but nothing like the calibre of chances Rovers are creating. David Thompson shoots wide when more or less clean through and Lucas Neill hits a tame shot straight at Filan after a strong forward run. Another Thompson effort, Flitcroft is thwarted and then Andy Cole hits the post following a wonderful passing move. The two lads up front, Cole and Yorke, are making our colossal centre-halves look like mannequins, latching on to superb through balls from the flawless Tugay, who is cutting us apart like he is slicing up kebab meat.

And then, 16 minutes in, the inevitable occurs as Andrew Cole latches on to a Tugay pass to smash the ball past Filan. Suspicion of offside? Maybe, but that's Cole's game, throughout the night he sits right on the shoulders of our back line, playing the percentage game and using this tactic to cause mayhem. Dwight Yorke is also lively. He is gifted a ball by Jason Jarrett and he races in on goal and really should put the game to bed, but he doesn't. Following this incident we regain a bit of composure and make a game of it. The most encouraging moment sees Ellington break clear of the Rovers defence, only for the linesman's flag to spoil our excitement. With only one goal in it there's always the hope we can claw it back. Half-time and a tame Ellington header and a tasty Dinning volley, both from distance, are the best we can muster.

There's bugger all chance of a pie or a pint, indeed it takes 15 minutes to get through the crowds to the bogs and back in order to relieve myself of the several pints of premium lager I have been painfully holding onto for the latter part of the first half. There is an amusing moment as I'm 'in the stalls' so to speak. I can hear the Tannoy as the WISH FM DJ is obviously going along a row of kids in the Glitter Stand with the microphone, asking the innocent little cherubs to shout their names out: 'Tom . . . Chris . . . Dave . . . John', then 'DICKHEAD!' shouts one – raucous laughter all round in the piss stones! Clearly a future star in the making, the kid will go far! Shades of Matt Bianco on *Swap Shop* all those years ago!

The second half begins with the Latics kicking towards the South Stand, and there is a renewed effort to get behind the lads. We force a succession of corners, each one is accompanied by the sound of 'Come on Wigan' roaring around the ground so loud that folk in Warrington can hear it. Alas, Rovers' Brad Friedel picks each one of them out of the air with cherry-picking ease. However, one of our corners clearly isn't one, the ref undoubtedly listening to the crowd's appeal (wow, we've got a crowd and they're actually influencing things). The usual routine here is for the home crowd and players to look a bit sheepish and get on with it, but in this instance, it's also a signal for Graeme Souness to perform his own party piece. He flips completely two minutes later when we are awarded another corner (this time the ball *was* out, I'm afraid Graeme!) and gets sent off for arguing with the linesman. I can see the physical mass of people baiting him in the West Stand as he heads up the tunnel.

Blackburn are still dominating the midfield, I'm very impressed with Tugay's supreme passing, possibly one of the best in the Premier League, and Flitcroft is doing his spadework and certainly not getting on the receiving end of any abuse! Ellington is working hard up front and troubles the Blackburn defence with a great cross which Neil Roberts manages to get on the end of, but it lands safely in Brad Friedel's midriff. The next great chance falls to Gary Teale, who has just come on for Kennedy. His first touch sees him running at two men, and he just skips through them with electrifying pace to get a sight on goal. The crowd are up off their feet again as he hits a fierce near-post shot. An inferior keeper would have let that in, however Friedel manages to scramble it away for a corner. Teale is absolutely white hot on his day and easily leaves Premier League defenders in his wake, he must be pushing for a recall to the starting line-up on recent performances.

Blackburn are still causing problems, as Andy Cole races clean through from a Thompson pass, John Filan comes out and makes a fantastic save with his legs just as the forward is preparing to pick his spot. However, that same combination kills the game off after 80 minutes as Cole scores with a similar finish to his first. Bugger! Again, suspiciously offside, but I don't want to introduce any sour grapes, maybe he's just too quick for us. Following this, we immediately create possibly our best opportunity of the game as an Eaden free kick isn't cleared by the Rovers defenders, allowing Jackson time to control and shoot. The central defender, reliable as he is at the back, doesn't quite possess the same cool head in front of goal, and blasts wide to deny us a consolation. The Wigan crowd back their boys to the end and nearly all make a point of stopping to the end to applaud them off.

On tonight's display, it's easy to see why Blackburn are the holders of this trophy. Just like that Man United game of a few years ago, I marvel at seeing such talent on display at the JJB and with a bit of luck, it will give the players and fans the appetite for more. I was a little disappointed not to see Dunn or Duff but very pleased to see some great skills by Tugay and Thompson. It's certainly better than watching Scott McLeish of Colchester or Darren Sheridan of Oldham strutting their stuff in the centre of the park, and I take consolation from the fact that the crowd have all got good value for money, if not the right result.

If the team have made a mistake tonight it is possibly that we have given Blackburn a little bit too much respect. The players were a little in awe of them, we simply gave them time on the ball, which they used to hurt us. A bit of blood and thunder and we could possibly have stifled them, but with their keeper and centre-halves all so solid, we were always up against it. For our sins, we tried to play football against them and got our fingers burnt.

By the time we've negotiated the huge bottleneck at the canal bridge, and are safely camped out in the pub, all our thoughts move back to our league campaign. The main concern is that the players don't get downbeat and let tonight's defeat affect our league form. The atmosphere is obviously deflated, though, and I get home just in time to see Souness slagging off our pitch and giving us very little credit whatsoever, although Frank Stapleton's comments are spot on. So, it's two cups down, one to go, but we can return to the more pressing matter of the league for a while now. The only interest now is obviously to hope Blackburn go on to win it so that we can say 'we lost to the eventual winners' like that's meant to be some sort of consolation, and to take a sideways glance at who they get in the semi-final. Manchester United, of course!

AFTER THE LORD MAYOR'S SHOW

21 December 2002, Huddersfield Town (h). Won 1–0.

The Wigan public are as fairweather as Carlton, the former Wimbledon winger, and really piss me off at times. Exactly how many of the 17,000 (less a few thousand travelling support) return after the Blackburn game on Tuesday? Six thousand and thirteen to be precise, including an away contingent of several hundred singing their strange 'Udders, Udders' chants throughout the game. Defeat to Blackburn is hardly a shock, but I still think that the majority of the crowd are deflated due to the ground looking so empty today compared with the atmosphere on Tuesday night. It's not their fault though, it's those bastards who are trying on kecks in Burtons at 3 p.m. on a Saturday afternoon when they should be watching the best team that Wigan has ever produced secure another vital three points in their quest to make it to Division One.

Fanzine day and I nip into The Red Robin about two-ish, undeterred by my previous very scary experience with Crewe's finest,

Nathan 'Duke' Ellington celebrates his hat trick against West Brom in the Worthington Cup. (© Paul Simpson)

HMS Destroyers – Teale and Dinning re-group after putting Plymouth to the sword. (© Paul Simpson)

Ellington scores a spectacular equaliser against Stockport. (© Paul Simpson)

LET'S HANG ON

Latics vs. Man City (Worthington Cup). 'Who put the ball in the City net? Super Neil Roberts!' (© Paul Simpson)

A great away following at Blackpool heralds a fortuitous 2–0 win. (© Paul Simpson)

LET'S HANG ON

Another Premier League scalp is claimed as Ellington slots home against Fulham. (© Paul Simpson)

ABOVE: De Vos powers home the second against Oldham in December. (© Paul Simpson)

LEFT: 'Can we have it back please?' Nearly half the Oldham team still can't get the ball off Leighton Baines. (© Paul Simpson)

BELOW: A motley crew gets ready to hit Port Vale on Boxing Day. (© John Heeley)

Tired and emotional on the way back from Peterboro'. (© John Heeley)

ABOVE RIGHT: Captain De Vos celebrates a vital win at QPR. (© Paul Simpson)

MIDDLE RIGHT: Chairman Dave Whelan salutes the travelling support at QPR. (© Paul Simpson)

BOTTOM RIGHT: Neil 'Bomber' Roberts wins the aerial battle to equalise against Oldham at the JJB. (© Paul Simpson)

LET'S HANG ON

Tony Dinning celebrates the strike that secured 100 points against Barnsley with Jimmy Bullard. (© Paul Simpson)

Lifting the trophy at the JJB. (© Paul Simpson)

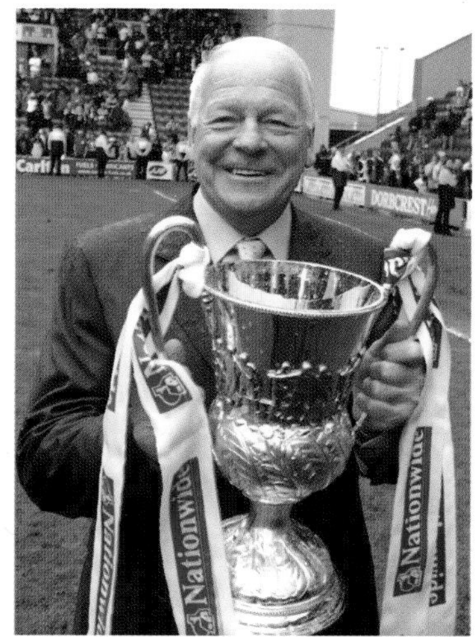

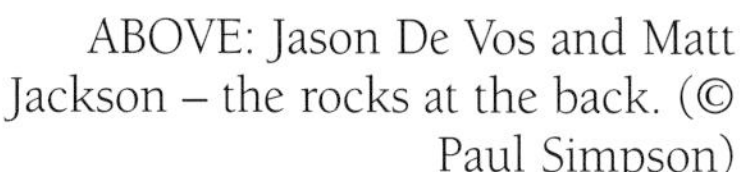

ABOVE: Jason De Vos and Matt Jackson – the rocks at the back. (© Paul Simpson)

ABOVE RIGHT: Dave Whelan brings home the silverware. (© Paul Simpson)

RIGHT: A fan gives Division One the thumbs up. (© Paul Simpson)

BELOW RIGHT: 'And now you're gonna believe us . . . the Blues are going up!' (© John Heeley)

BELOW LEFT: The author getting ready to play football, badly. (© Carl H)

A taste of champagne for manager Paul Jewell! (© Paul Simpson)

'Relax, boys, we made it!' From left to right: Flynn jnr, Studs McMillan, Flynny, The Duke, JDV, Lee McCulloch and John Filan. (© Paul Simpson)

LET'S HANG ON

and sell a sum total of two copies in there. So that's one to scrub off the list then. For some reason, and I think that the reason may well be the opening of the new supporters' club underneath the South Stand, very few Latics fans go in here now and it's more or less been designated as an away fans' pub. They are welcome to it – I always have to wait at the door for five minutes while the bouncers clear it with the manager to go round, and when I do have a drink in there it's served in a plastic pot. And rightly so, what with such scary Crewe thugs frequenting the place.

On to the ground, and it's looking very, very sparse. We're top of the league, unbeaten in the league for months, we haven't even conceded a goal in the league since October, and there's a dead atmosphere. Desperately disappointing, and I can hear fans of other clubs laughing as I write this, but I cannot lie and say it's like the Maracana. We saw the ups of a brilliant Latics crowd on Tuesday, now we suffer the downs of fickleness in the extreme, with a very poor and lethargic crowd today. Of course, the ones that are here are worth ten of the ones that aren't, but it's just bloody frustrating for us, and I think this is why the crowd is so quiet. It's us, the loyal fans, who take all the flak when the crowd is poor, not the people who just turn up for the big games. I'd call them something nasty, but if we're perfectly honest we need them if we're to continue growing as a club, and everyone at the club knows it.

Anyway, enough about that. Huddersfield are a club in a bit of a mess. Three years ago, they were battling for a play-off place to get into the Premier League, now they are in the bottom four of Division Two, staring the basement division in the face. In a moment of desperation, they've even taken Lee Ashcroft on loan, who is currently our sixth-choice centre-forward, just behind Jimmy Krankie and Osama Bin Laden. We have, naturally, refused them the opportunity of playing him against us, in the improbable event of him banging the winner in for them. I'm sure he is grateful, as it will give him more time to concentrate on some of the pursuits with which he has been much more familiar during his time at Wigan, none of which involve playing football. We can't take them for granted though, as they still have a decent side on paper, and it's basically the same team that was top six for most of last season, and of course a team at the bottom is always fighting for points. Is that enough clichés for now?

Teale is restored to the starting line-up at the expense of Green, with McMillan coming in for Leighton Baines. Shame for Baines, and Flynn for that matter, who now find themselves completely omitted from the 16, but they're young lads and I'm sure will bounce back. We also see the welcome return of Lee McCulloch and Andy Liddell to the bench after a couple of months apiece out with injury. We're really getting back up to full strength now, although the game doesn't really back this up as there are very few chances. With half an hour gone, the first real chance of the game falls to Huddersfield. A brilliant point-blank save from John Filan is only partially cleared and the same player who has the first effort, Danny Schofield, gets his head to the rebound which looks a goal all the way but for De Vos producing a great clearance off the line.

This sparks the home crowd and players into life as a Tony Dinning strike from 25 yards is tipped over spectacularly by the Huddersfield keeper. The scoreline remains goalless until first-half injury time when De Vos nods home a Kennedy corner to give us a 1–0 lead. Jubilation for Faz and Co who sit near me and have lumped on the value bet, De Vos first goal at 18/1. Much better value than the measly 7/2 offered on The Duke.

Town look quite lively in parts, and certainly don't look like a team destined for the drop, but nevertheless they fail to seriously trouble our lead. As for the Latics, well, The Duke has a couple of close-range efforts parried, whereas sub, Paul Mitchell, produces a fantastic run which ends with him shooting just wide. The crowd resort to hurling abuse at Town's massive centre-half who is doing his all to rip Roberts's shirt off his back throughout the second half.

Latics eventually put the ball in the net with a few minutes to go, following a great run and ball across the face of goal by Gary Teale. It eludes both the Wigan attack and the Huddersfield defence, only for Tony Dinning to run in at the back post and smash it home. A quality finish to wrap up events! The ref, however, has other ideas, and decides to disallow it for a shove which only he appears to have seen. It all turns out to be academic in the end, as the 1–0 result stands. Other results are irrelevant as we're top and we're staying there: Cardiff are four points and Bristol five points behind us.

I'm not a huge fan of statistics but reviewing our season at this stage makes fantastic reading and, while pleasing, makes it all the more mystifying why our crowds are not improving. Fifty points after twenty-two games, no goals conceded in six games, no league defeats home or away since August and four points clear at the top of the league. The one worrying statistic is that our record shows that in previous (failed) promotion campaigns we have traditionally done badly in the second half of the season. We hope that the momentum that has carried us this far will continue into next year and this post-Christmas blues effect doesn't come into play. Roll on Boxing Day.

OH I WISH IT COULD BE CHRISTMAS EVERY DAY

26 December 2002, Port Vale (a). Won 1–0.

Ill in bed over Christmas, apart from Christmas Day when I nipped to The Pagey for a game of dominoes. I still managed to dish out a tonking at 'fives and threes' – I am acknowledged as a master of this sport, if you can call it a sport. If only it paid 40 grand a week. In another year it may well have been different, but this year I was well prepared to stop in on Christmas Eve in order to be in good shape for Boxing Day. So I start Boxing Day in good shape, but certainly don't finish it that way!

Half ten is the coach departure time, and as I turn the corner of the Old Gas Showrooms or OGS (it hasn't been a British Gas building for 15 years but no one calls it 'The New Council Offices') I'm greeted by several amusing sights. Boxing Day in Wigan equals fancy dress. I must admit, I've refrained this year, I just couldn't get organised. If I could have come up with something original, practical, cheap and easy then I would have done, but old lazyarse here couldn't be bothered. I remember a couple of years ago when I was charging across the terraces at Oldham, dressed as Superman, whistling the theme tune. It was bloody freezing and I should have added some padding! Superheroes don't fall asleep on their front lawn, though, in fact I don't even have a front lawn, I live in a terraced house and actually fell asleep in the snow at the front of our house. And I wonder why I'm always ill?

It was only when I travelled a bit that I realised that other towns and other countries just don't do this 'go out in fancy dress on Boxing Day' lark. The split is about 80/20 in favour of those who have dressed up and I'm one of the 20. There's some classic sights: Rob, dressed in full cricketer attire, 'They'll not let you in the ground with that!' pointing to his bat. There's numerous '70s types ('Thought you were coming in fancy dress?' 'Nay, I've been round and robbed your wardrobe', etc. etc.), Marked Man has come as a referee and Keith Lard, complete with dog, is instructing everyone to be careful because 'fire doesn't kill, ignorance does'. Great! My mate, Ian, who is more familiar to Suddy's more liberal transportation, turns up in a Hackett jacket with a very indiscreet eight cans of Murphy's for the hour-long journey. 'We're going to Port Vale, not Portsmouth.' He gets them all confiscated upon entrance by a mean-looking clown. That would be Arky, the tour organiser.

Off down the motorway, we pass several Everton coaches on their way to Brum, containing some of the scariest looking bastards you've ever seen. Usually we'd engage in a bit of cross-lane shithousing, but let's face it, it wouldn't be much of a contest, after all, no one messes with Elvis or Spiderman. A bit of traffic here and there and we head past the Vale turn-off to try a few pre-arranged scoops in The Staffordshire Knot, deep in Stoke country. The numbers are bolstered by several cars and, inevitably, the Wigan coppers turn up an hour in, to be met with cries of, 'Bloody hell lads, you come as that every bloody year!' Fair play as PC Dawber and Co. pose for photos, there's plenty who would deny it, but there has been a rapport built up over the past few years between the Wigan bobbies and ourselves. They're just doing their job, and could make it a hell of a lot more uncomfortable for us if they wanted. Because we don't misbehave, they usually leave us to it. Even though the potential has been there at many games, there's not really been an incident. It doesn't stop a couple of Stokie scrotes bobbing their ugly mugs into the pub though, before walking out, and engaging in a spot of frantic, and probably fake, mobile phone activity.

At a quarter past two we head for the ground. The queues for the away end are hideous, and they eventually see sense and open a few more turnstiles. The weather is not too bad for this time of year, but I pity the 'Zulu Latic' who is dressed, as his name would imply, in nothing but a loincloth and facepaint. Seventeen pounds to get in is a bit of scandal for seats bolted onto terraces, but Vale are in administration so I'll begrudgingly part with it, like I've got a choice. I also donate a quid to the 'Save The Vale' appeal, and rightly so – I've no axe to grind with Port Vale or their fans, but even if I did, I'd still give cash because we all know what our local football club means to us, don't we?

The half of the terrace that is open is jammed so we find ourselves a seat in a 'closed' bit on the other side of the mesh netting right at the front. The view is terrible and the seats are piss wet through. The stewards come and move us and we are forced to find seats elsewhere. Right next to the players actually! Bainesy and Flynny are both sound, whereas Greeny and Brannan would clearly rather be elsewhere. Well, they'd all rather be elsewhere, i.e. on the pitch, but that's a sign of our season. It would be remiss of me not to mention that the former two were engrossed deeply in their read for most of the game – the *Cockney Latic* of course. 'Don't know why you read, that, mate, it's shite!' says I. Not sure what they make of being sat in the middle of a load of pissed-up loons who are calling Port Vale's Steve McPhee a 'kiddy fiddler' every time he touches the ball, but they stay put, so I can only assume that they enjoyed our company. McPhee had the plug pulled on a move to Wigan earlier on this season because someone tried to demand too much money. On this performance, I wouldn't pay him in washers.

We know by now, due to early kick-offs, that Cardiff have lost and Bristol have drawn, so a win today means we will go seven points clear. I've always got the doubting Thomas about me, and I know I'm not the only one who goes into every game thinking we're going to screw up. Those of us who've watched Wigan for any length of time have it implanted into us because we've seen it all before. Thankfully, the players seem to know the score, and have only let us down three times so far this season, for which I have quite rightly slated them. Harsh at the time I know, especially as we're having a good season, but that depressing drive to Colchester and back to watch an inept performance will live with me for as long as any of the many 'up' occasions we've had this year.

I'm afraid I can't remember much of the first half at all. I've got six pints of Stella inside of me, but even so, there ain't much happening. We keep it tight, build slowly, snuff them out, quieten the home support and go in at the break scoreless. Some hours and many pints later, I was pontificating on just how much we must piss the other team off. We've conceded a mere four goals on our travels in twelve league games. How much must that do your head in as a home fan, when you go to watch your team knowing that there's only at best a one in three chance that you're going to see your favourites score a goal? People watch football to see goals, and we just aren't conceding any! For many teams, including Wigan both in the past and possibly today, going away from home, scoring nil and getting a draw is acceptable, but at home, the least you expect is to see your team put the ball in the net at least once. You've got a right to expect at least that. Unless you're a Bolton fan, of course! It's great for us but shit for them, but over the years I've seen us concede more sloppy goals than most, so I feel no need to apologise. I don't want to see Vale go bust and hope that my team has not unwittingly contributed to their fate by refusing to concede, but I simply don't want them to score. There's sentiment and then there's football. The day hasn't passed by without comments about Robbie Williams not putting his hand into his arse pocket for his so-called favourite club either.

Half-time and I've been incessantly badgering Ian that it's his round. A full 35 seconds after the 4 minutes of added time are up he eventually goes and finds himself at the end of a very long queue. When he eventually gets served (the last one before the bar shuts – born lucky that lad!) he has a moan about the £2.40 per can of Carling that he has been charged, and bloody rightly so. If Vale are planning on getting out of administration then they are going the right way about it. Sorry, that's a bit harsh maybe as it's standard fayre for the way football fans are treated and Port Vale is no different to anywhere else. The sights knocking about include a chicken, a bunch of gay Cavaliers and numerous *Phoenix Nights* characters – Ray Von and Brian Potter, complete with wheelchair, to name but two. I would have at least tried to get in for nowt!!

We miss ten minutes of the second period while we sup up, not surprising really as the half had probably started when we bought them. On return to our seats I'm in overdrive on football-manager speak, just showing off really because I'm in the company of players. 'We've got this one sewn up . . . They're here for the taking these lot . . . We'll keep it tight and hit them on the break.' And believe it or not, and without even a smidgen of smugness, that is exactly how it happens. As the second half begins (in the fifty-fifth minute in our case) Vale seem to be attacking a bit more and the match is very evenly poised. Wigan have thrown Lee McCulloch on to add a bit more attacking threat and still have Andy Liddell warming up on the touch-line, waving to the crowd who sing his name.

The decisive moment of the game comes after 69 minutes. The Vale keeper lets a tame, wide shot slip out for a corner, and Jason De Vos powers home from the resulting set piece. De Vos is one huge, scary man at corners – no defence is safe, and what a great captain he is turning out to be. Our player of the year, and arguably our greatest ever player, Arjan De Zeeuw fled to Portsmouth in the summer and we all wondered how the hell we were going to replace the man. He barely warrants a mention these days. No offence Arry, I'm sure he's as pleased as anyone with our season so far. Six foot four of Canadian brawn has seen us home on more than one occasion, the man is turning into a legend every bit as much as De Zeeuw before him. If we lift some silverware this season no one could begrudge him.

'We'll never play you again' is the cruel but apt taunt from the Wiganers. None of that 'Is that all you take away?' rubbish from the home support today, we barely notice them. Once again, and in stark contrast to last season, when we take the lead, we hold it, and hold it well. Stroking the ball about, as the crowd sing 'It's just like watching Beech Hill' and a fancy dress conga is instigated around the away end by Elvis. It is also worth mentioning that we are down one '70s man complete with curly Afro, who ran on the pitch when we scored, but tripped over his flares. I hope they don't rough him up too much, he's just a peace-lovin' hippy cat!

We create a couple more opportunities, but nothing of significance. Full respect to all the players for this result, including those who are meekly sitting with us, they've all played a part in building this spirit and winning attitude and deservedly take the applause of the crowd. The fourth official signals for four minutes of injury time, but it could be forty for all it matters, the game is over. A mad crush to get out, followed by a few cheeky words either side of the police lines, and we're back on the coach.

Seven points clear at the top of the league, we should be as upbeat as an Oakenfold remix, but we aren't. There's an attempt to get the karaoke started but no one's playing ball. Completely deflated! Not too much is said in the hour or so journey home, and when we pile off into Wigan we decide on The Orange House rather than The Swan and Railway because according to Ian 'it'll be full of fit birds in little skirts'. And it is! And we stop there for a few hours throwing Stella back, not least because the queues outside to get in elsewhere are hideous. It's just a mental night, Boxing Night, and whereas you have to admire the masses of nurses, cheerleaders and schoolgirls, it's just too bloody hectic. Careful though, as lads dressed as birds are always aplenty. Lads dressed in pilots' uniforms just look like posing tossers, tonight's the night when the rule book goes out of the window. It must look crazy to an outsider, but any Wiganer will tell you that our town is unlike any other.

We eventually make it to our spiritual home (Fever aka Rik's) which is full of the usual drunken Latics contingent. Needless to say, I chat loads and loads of birds up, and needless to say most of them are actually blokes in drag and look like Jo Brand. I recall having a decent conversation with a dragged-up McCann but forgot to ask whether he'd been home to get changed after the match or whether the Port Vale press box had a transvestite jumping up and down in it when De Vos thumped his header home. The memory is very sketchy. Suffice to say, I recall being woken by a lad saying, 'Are you alreet mate?' as I had fallen asleep in the gardens of the Deanery High School. Nick Hornby I am not. Still don't know who you are to this day mate, but thanks, as I was so plastered I'd still be there now.

It's evident that I've fallen over as well, as my ankle feels like it's broken. I don't make any attempt to disguise my state when turning in for work at 10 a.m. the next day. Although people know I play football, they've not got a clue at what level, so I could easily have come out with the old 'did it making a last-ditch tackle in yesterday's Unibond League clash between Droylsden and Burscough' to get a bit of sympathy. I even consider writing a letter suing the council and blaming it on a wobbly paving stone. It's all very in vogue but I'm not a great blagger, if you can't do the time and all that. It's just another UDI (Unidentified Drinking Injury) to live with. I don't think it's broken but it's bloody sore and has swelled up to the size of Sam Allardyce's head.

The pain in my ankle will be a constant reminder of Boxing Day, but it came as a consequence of a pleasurable day where we saw our team go seven points clear at the top of the table. We can actually afford to lose two games now, and still win the league. This is turning into a truly great season for a Latics mon but as the main man PJ says, 'We've won nothing yet!'

TWELVE-NIL TO THE WIGANERS

28 December 2002, Swindon Town (h). Won 2–0.

Never let it be said that us Wiganers don't like making things hard for ourselves. In a game in which the Latics are so absolutely dominant the Swindon team might as well have not turned up, they would have come away with a point had it not been for a late off-the-line clearance by Matt Jackson.

The BBC website, which is often a godsend to those with poor memories like myself, reports 20 chances on goal for Latics, whereas Swindon manage just the aforementioned one. The crowd seems a lot bigger than the Huddersfield game, but is given out as just over 6,000, the reason for this probably being that Swindon's away following is non-existent. No bloody wonder, if their team plays like that every week. There are one or two faces missing from my usual crew, no doubt due to the ravages of Christmas excess, but those that are here settle down to watch probably the most one-sided game we have seen all season. Nathan Ellington should have claimed the match ball before half-time, he misses at least one clear sitter, blazing over from a few yards much to the amusement of the few dozen travelling Swindon fans. He's just having one of those days, but to his credit, from the first minute to the last, he hassles, chases and runs at the Swindon back line, refusing to let his head go down, and eventually gets his reward.

The whole team are up for it today. Paul Mitchell and Lee McCulloch are two additions to the starting line-up, and both of them are straight into their familiar styles – McCulloch with clever running and Mitchell with tigerish tackling. Another player worth a mention is Nicky Eaden, who is having an exceptional game at right-back.

Well, I say at right-back but due to Swindon's inability or unwillingness to attack us, he is more or less operating as an additional right winger. Our more orthodox right-winger, Gary Teale, is also on fire at present. After a month-long spell of benchwarming, he is another who has taken his chance brilliantly, terrorising Swindon's left-hand side.

Teale it is who draws first blood for Latics. With Nicky Eaden overlapping and Tony Dinning also covering a lot of ground, a slick passing move down the left ends up with a cut-back for Teale, who smashes it home with his left foot. A cracking goal and a good half an hour overdue. Our passing has been superb throughout the half, and this is just reward for our dominance. With 42 minutes gone, I join the exodus downstairs to the bar for a half-time scoop.

The second half sees more of the same from Wigan. No matter how hard we try, we can't seem to get that second to kill the game off. Even at 1–0 though, I feel that certain players seem to be showboating and enjoying our dominance. Neil Roberts attempts a couple of flash overhead kicks, ever so eager to please – spectacular to watch when you connect, but he doesn't with either, unless one is an attempt to send the ball back across goal. On other occasions, the Latics' attacks find the Swindon keeper, Homer's lad Bart (Griemink), in great form and midway through the second half sees an almighty goalmouth scramble of epic proportions which Swindon eventually manage to clear.

As the game enters its latter stages and we fail to add to our tally, Swindon grow in confidence and start to push forward in numbers, setting up yet another nervy finish for a team who should be about 12–0 up by now. We weather the storm quite comfortably until a dangerous ball into the box isn't cleared at all, there are a couple of goalmouth attempts (at last) from Swindon, one of which Matt Jackson has to heroically block with his face. We haven't conceded a goal in the league since October, but I reckon that each game there's always been at least one chance like this for our opponents. A post or crossbar hit here or there, a missed sitter or a goal-line clearance – the last of these three is sheer persistence but the first two, it's got to be said, are more than a touch fortunate. Or crap finishing, you could argue.

Once again, fortune smiles on us. As Swindon push everyone forward for an injury-time equaliser, Andy Liddell collects the ball inside his own half and runs at what's left of the battle-ravaged Swindon defence. He reaches the edge of the box with all but one man beaten and has every right to shoot. He unselfishly squares it to the oncoming Ellington, who slots it into the far corner. At 2–0 the game is safe and The Duke gets the goal his efforts have merited. Relief for him and relief for us as the restart sees the final whistle go almost immediately. Another team buried and another valuable three points for us.

Emphatic wins for Bristol City and Cardiff the same weekend mean that they are still keeping the pressure on, and Crewe and Oldham still aren't too far behind. The final scores reveal that those useless bastards Leeds, with their Cockney blagger manager, have won their first game at home since September, beating in-form Chelsea in the process and costing me a good £140 on the coupon. After successful negotiation of a couple of other aways in a treble, Leicester at Watford and Luton at Wycombe, I deserve better (or worse) than that El Tel! Latics' winning run seems to be coinciding with my own gambling losing run but I'll put up with it, I suppose.

Paul Jewell has been insistent all season that two points per game will get us promoted. He must be beginning to doubt that, as we'd be lying in fourth at the moment if that ratio were applied. As we move into a new year, he has won over the crowd, he has got us playing superb football, and he has built a team full of winners who, at the time of writing, have set us up for the best chance we will ever have of winning promotion to Division One for the first time in our short history. Where's his OBE, Ma'am?

JANUARY

AND THE BEAT GOES ON

1 January 2003, Notts County (h). Won 3–1.

ANOTHER YEAR, BUT THE SAME OLD TUNE BEING PLAYED BY THE LATICS. MY PRE-MATCH boozing is almost solitary for this one, having seen in the New Year uptown, getting bored and then being safely tucked up at one. There's something oh so false about all this back-slapping, hand-shaking lark when you consider I spent most of the previous night queuing for the bar surrounded by moody little tossers pushing and shoving and looking to pick fights with all and sundry. That's just a personal gripe, of course, and won't stop me wishing all the best to all the people that matter.

Today it's Notts County's turn to come to the JJB and defend like troopers for 90 minutes in the hope of sneaking a point. With Stallard and Allsopp up front, they present a decent attacking threat, but we are unpassable at home at present. The major change of the day sees Andy Liddell restored to the starting line-up for the first time since October, at the expense of Neil Roberts.

Just as with the Swindon game, right from the off we absolutely batter them, without exaggeration. Within the first forty minutes or so, we create about ten decent chances, none of which are put away. The best of these falls to Nathan Ellington; he makes the difficult part look easy, controlling an aerial ball brilliantly, bringing it down with an outstretched toe, almost ballerina-style. However, he snatches at his resulting shot, putting it well wide from about a dozen yards out. The best of the rest occurs when Lidds races through, but only succeeds in finding the keeper's legs.

The Duke does have a major hand in the first goal on the stroke of half-time. Another concentrated spell of Wigan pressure sees Ellington's shot bounce off the foot of the post, only for Tony Dinning to blast the follow-up home to give us a well overdue lead. I say well overdue, but Notts County have been resolute in their defending, putting their bodies in the way of absolutely everything, and it was beginning to look like a '1–0 Notts County' day.

The news from our rivals is good as Cardiff and Bristol are both 0–0, although the 'next best', Crewe and Oldham, are both winning. After the change of ends, Latics play some of the best football I've ever seen in recent years to press home their superiority. In the first half, De Vos has had a couple of goalbound headers cleared off the line, and I can only presume that this is a deliberate ploy to halt our towering centre-half. County have clearly decided that if they can't stop him winning the header, then they stop him scoring by putting several men on the line. It only works for so long, though, as De Vos scores another thumping header early in the second half to put us 2–0 up.

The third goal arrives soon after, and is undoubtedly the best of the lot. After much twisting and turning in the box, Ellington releases the ball to McCulloch, who is crowded out by the Magpies' defence. He manages to lay it off to Andy Liddell, who smacks a fierce shot right into the far corner from outside the box. 3–0 and welcome back Sir Andrew! With 90 minutes on the clock, and with us 3 goals to the good, the fourth official signals a whopping 5 minutes of added time to be played. Great, we'll get another – the players still look hungry for it. However, County don't read the script, as a freakish, extraordinary event occurs.

For the whole of November and December, in league football at least, our onion bag remained unchartered territory, and it speaks volumes for the progress that the club has made that the players are livid with themselves after conceding a late consolation. The goal itself is excellent, and as good as anything I've seen from any team all season: two neat passes play Mark Stallard in, who hits a delightful first time chip over the advancing John Filan from 25 yards. The

County fans are slightly more optimistic, singing their 'We're gonna win 4–3 chant' as per the LDV game between us. The story goes that after the game, in the dressing-room, the players were depressed and dejected at committing the heinous crime of leaking a goal, and had a minor falling out. Filan's reaction as the ball went in is one of infuriation as our defence has simply refused to leak goals with a back four as tight as a submarine door.

Results elsewhere mean that Wigan Athletic are now nine points clear at the top of Division Two, a feat not managed elsewhere in any division of any professional league in England or Scotland. Even though a very tough trip to Bristol looms, surely even we can't cock this one up?

THE SJOKE'S ON US

4 January 2003, Stoke City (a). FA Cup Round 3. Lost 0–3.

I've had recent taunts levelled in my direction, by a certain 48-year-old coach-trip organiser, of all people, that I am 'a bit of a lightweight' in the drinking stakes. Ever willing to pick up a thrown-down gauntlet, I find myself tucking into a full English breakfast accompanied by a pint of lager at 9.25 a.m. in an anonymous town-centre public house. On making my way to the coach, I bump into Mr Joe Hawkins; Orrell RUFC's game postponed then? Following a brief conversation, I decide to hand over the responsibility of reporting on matches and ask him to provide his own outlook on today's events. This was nothing at all to do with me wanting to get as blitzed as possible in the shortest necessary time. Anyway, here is 'Joe's View':

'When Jarvis Cocker sang(?) "Do you remember the first time?" I doubt he was referring to Wigan Athletic against Tranmere Rovers on a freezing cold November night in 1966, but that was my first time and I still remember it, not maybe, but definitely. My *other* first time was some eight years later behind a couch in a friend's house in Rainford, but, hey, the football game was much more romantic. It also, most certainly, lasted longer.

'Since those two momentous occasions, I reckon the female of the species and football have given me equal amounts of pain and pleasure. And some 36 years later I'm still eagerly pursuing each pastime. That first match I witnessed at Springfield Park is as vivid in my mind as any I have seen since, and here I am now on a Friday in January 2003 eagerly awaiting this year's adventure in the wonderful FA Cup. Well, I was until a couple of moments ago when my mate Cainy called and said, "I don't know why we're bothering, I'm in The Brick and everyone's saying they're playing half a team." Here we go again.

'A couple of seasons ago Bruce Rioch sent a reserve/youth team out for an FA Cup replay at Notts County. Needless to say we (just) lost, but what was the point. Little Wigan taking the piss out of "the greatest cup competition in the world" (copyright: ITV/BBC/Sky – delete where necessary) again. We'll see!

'This season we have been blessed by a marvellous run in the Worthington Cup, a run that saw us beat Manchester City and destroy Fulham and West Bromwich Albion. Splendid stuff that we all enjoyed with equal measures of euphoria and downright cockiness. It has also made us all a bit blasé about the great competition that is the FA Cup. Since that first game against Tranmere, when I was seven years old and the World Cup victory was only five months in the past, I've enjoyed so many ups and downs watching Wigan Athletic in this competition. I've been one of 17,000 Wiganers that went to Manchester City in 1971 and 20,000 Wiganers that went to Everton in 1980. I've been chased halfway around Northwich, bunked off school to go to Burscough, had my life threatened in Grimsby by a monster wearing a butcher's coat and cheered improbable results against Peterborough United, Shrewsbury and Chelsea, to name a few. I've also (in recent years) witnessed horrible games and losses against Altrincham and Canvey Island. The boot's on the other foot now and good luck to all non-league teams. We were there once and we must never forget this.

'That's what makes the news that we might be playing half a team even more galling. Anyhow, the news that Cainy's just given me (i.e. that Filan, De Vos, Dinning and Ellington aren't playing) is probably the usual pub bollocks. And what is with all these rumours that fly about nowadays? I remember, and not long ago at that, when you used to go to the match on a Saturday, you'd read the reports on a

Sunday and Monday and that would be it until next Saturday. Now there's a different rumour each day. If you believed them all we'd be preparing to watch Ronaldo lining up for the mighty Latics tomorrow. Alas no, and I blame the Internet and all those keyboard bores for it all. In fact, I blame them for every ill in the world at the moment. Anyhow, I digress and tomorrow we're on our way to Wembley. Oops, it's Cardiff for the foreseeable future isn't it, and a slight amendment to that old song is necessary. So it's off to bed with the strains of "Tell my ma, my ma to roll us a big fat spliff, we're going to Cardiff" ringing in my head.

'It would be nice to report that I awake on the morn of the game fresh from a dream of Jason De Vos lifting that famous old trophy aloft after a 4–1 drubbing of Manchester United, but unfortunately not on this occasion. My back-up dream of Destiny's Child popping around also fails to materialise. Get up, you silly old fool there's a match to go to – away at Stoke City! Yes, to confound the general apathy surrounding this year's FA Cup tie we've drawn that massive club down the road. When the draw came out a couple of weeks ago there was a groan from the Latics faithful that could have been heard in the Potteries. All we ask for is Man United, Liverpool, Newcastle or Everton, but, no, out comes Stoke City away.

'Stoke are now known as Sjoke around here and over the last few years a very unhealthy rivalry has grown between the two clubs. This stemmed from the 1999–2000 season when both sides were going for promotion from Division Two. Two teams up there, going for promotion will always lead to a bit of spice between the respective supporters, but this season the rivalry was stoked up (sorry) by Wigan taking a hooligan firm to Hanley (Stoke's manor). Now at this point it has to be remembered that when Stoke were in Division Two they looked down on every other club as if they were "not worthy". See, Stoke are a massive club that should be in the Premiership, that won the league on 29 occasions, the European Cup 8 times, Sir Stanley Matthews blah blah blah. Along with this attitude (that to a man all Stoke fans adhere to) they also have a huge proportion of supporters that still think it's 1985! Well, on this occasion Wigan's little mob turned these Neanderthals around and off they fled.

'This was sacrilege to these Herberts and they spent the rest of the season "getting their act together" for the return leg. And get their act together they did. Police reports reckoned they had about 800 "lads" in Manchester at noon on the day of the match. If they needed any excuse other than the game being a top-of-the-table clash and the incident at the first fixture, their hero Sir Stanley passed away in the week leading up to the game. Thousands of them came, and there were scuffles all over the place prior to the game. There was then a huge outbreak of disorder inside the ground. It was well documented at the time and most that was written was complete bollocks. Stoke fans claim the trouble started because Wigan fans disrespected the minute's silence held in Matthews' memory. This is rubbish. The silence was perfectly observed inside the ground with the only noise being outside the ground, and that noise could have come from Wigan or Stoke fans that were unaware a minute's silence was taking place.

'What happened was simple. In the row in front of us in the West Stand were six or seven Stoke fans, including a young girl and a granddad. As soon as the game kicked off they were up cheering and shouting. The Wigan stewards quickly spotted this and moved them from their seats to the Stoke end. They went without any trouble and that should have been it. But for some obscure reason the stewards decided to take them along the front of the stand. As they neared the away end their bravado kicked in and they started singing. Unfortunately this was in front of some of Wigan's more lively fans, punches were thrown and, seeing this as their opportunity to really kick it off, Stoke fans came flooding across the pitch and into the Wigan seats. All hell broke loose, the referee took the players off the pitch and the game was stopped for several minutes. The players came back onto the pitch to play out a 1–1 draw. The rivalry was now in full swing. Last season the Sjokers were promoted, but not before we "whupped 'em" 6–1 at our place.

'Ironically, we've drawn the prats again and we're all outside The Old Gas Showrooms waiting for two of Arky's coaches to turn up. And what a rum set of buggers are waiting there. There are old faces, young whippersnappers in checked caps along with the never-miss-a-match mob. The watering hole is the usual one near Congleton. It's in the middle of nowhere and in all honesty is ideal for this type of trip. No one is going to bother you and the young urchins amongst us aren't tempted to wander off. The pub divides off into various factions. The

Scholes mob appear to be eating the pub out of food, my mob (roughly The Brickmaker's Mob) reminisce about the olden days and trips on Robbie's Battle Bus and later Robbie's Blue Minibus, while the youngsters take up residence in the pool room and the gents' toilets, for some reason. Safe to say the place is buzzing and before too long we are back on the coaches and heading to the dreadful, dreadful Britannia Stadium. Stoke was recently voted the worst place in Britain in which to live and quite rightly so. What this survey failed to mention is that the football ground is the worst football ground in the country (just in front of that other shithole Vale Park). It's a breezeblock, it's on the top of the hill, there's one pub, no shops, no car parking spaces and is always freezing. Today, it's beyond freezing and the 2,000-plus Wiganers that have made the journey and paid the extortionate sum of £17.00 to get in have again been cheated.

'We've definitely been cheated when Cainy's "breaking news" of yesterday is more or less confirmed with De Vos, Dinning, Ellington and McCulloch all rested. We could beat this lot with a full team, but with one eye on next Friday's fixture with Bristol City it looks like Paul Jewell has conceded defeat by removing the core of the team plus our most-improved player this season, Lee McCulloch. We get behind the team, 2,000 of us taunting the Stoke fan(s). Where are they all? It appears apathy has hit Stoke as it's a pitiful turnout from their fans. They try and make some noise but for the first 12 minutes their side don't touch the ball. We are all over them, but we've no cutting edge. Our best chance comes when their goalkeeper deserts his area and handles the ball. He should be off, the rules state he must go, but not with this referee in charge. He doesn't even speak to him, and that's it.

'We're done, and after 20 minutes they break away and it's 1–0. It looks offside to me and then after 30 minutes they slot a corking volley to make it 2–0. Pity the referee misses a blatant foul on Jackson in the box, but what do you expect? Jewell brings on Ellington and McCulloch after half-time and we have a good 10 minutes, but it's too little too late and Stoke get a third on 67 minutes. The Wigan fans try their best to get behind the team while I argue with a fellow Latics mon who actually said, "I'm pleased we're losing, we can now concentrate on the league." Apart from being one of the most used clichés in football, it's a numbskull comment. He, along with many others, has spent £8.00 to get there, £17.00 to get in and £15.00 to get the beers and food in and he's pleased we're losing. Before it gets too heated I back off and join the others in taunting the Stoke fans with (to the tune of "Yellow Submarine") "Wigan's going up while the Stoke are coming down" and "You'll always be 6–1."

'We lose 3–0 and are back in the pub in Wigan before 5.30 p.m., cold, starving and slightly pissed off. I say slightly rather than totally because although we've lost to one of our despised rivals it doesn't feel that bad, and maybe we *can* now concentrate on the league. Then again, if we lose at Bristol City on Friday it'll make Paul Jewell's decision to rest his major players a bit bloody stupid. However, there's always next season!'

Thanks, Joe.

RAT-ARSED AGAIN

10 January 2003, Bristol City (a). Won 1–0.

I've been flapping all week due to my agreement to help run a coach, for which we managed to get an amazing 20 names. I, along with Brasso, have spent many hours of time ringing around coach firms, eventually settling on one from Skelmersdale. I have little choice, as most of the Wigan firms are still on their Christmas break. Dispels the myth that Scousers are workshy, anyway. We do plenty of mithering to drum up support, but apart from the faithful 20 or so, and the usual suspects who travel by other means, no one is interested, preferring the company of their local alehouse and Friday night Sky TV.

I have two main concerns leading up to the game. Firstly, to ensure that I can provide adequate transport to the game to the 20 good people who have come forth with money at the Stoke game, and secondly, with ground frost thicker than a miner's butty, to spend the rest of the week praying that the game is still on. Bitterly cold all week leading up to the game, many games on the Saturday fall foul of the weather, but the noises coming from Bristol are quite positive. The groundsman, God bless his soul, has put the ground covers over the turf and the club have employed hot-air blowers (their chief executive, perchance?) to thaw out the ground frost.

Concern about my own welfare is overcome following a chance conversation with fashion guru, Naylor, earlier in the week. He, like me, is, of course, a stylish chap but, like me also, a bit of a tart when it comes to braving the winter months. What a shame I am about to shatter the illusion for both of us, by revealing that the conversation concerned where one can purchase long johns. OK, so we now know who ISN'T the *Cockney Latic*'s fashion correspondent, but I have really been feeling the cold this week, so set off to Wigan Market to get my bargain on Friday morning, two pairs for a fiver. Blue ones, mind.

The coach has been booked, the money changing hands between myself and the proprietor in a lay-by off the M58, and now my main concern is praying that the game is on after hearing that there is a 2 p.m. pitch inspection. I contact Stuart Hayton at the club for an update, and he confirms that the Bristol lot are confident it will be on. You never know with these madcap refs though. Just time to buy a couple of papers and four cans of Guinness to soak up the journey and it's down to the Gas Showrooms at high noon. I am still slightly nervous about whether this coach is going to turn up or not, not that they are an unreliable firm, but because I am born unlucky and will have 19 Latics men after lynching me if it doesn't. As it turns out, we get a bit of a result in that their 20-seater mini-coach has developed a fault so they have sent us a 35-seater instead. Excellent, a bit of room to stretch out on the way down!

The coach turns up in good time, and we impressively make it as far as Hilton Park before the first piss stop is called. 'Ten minutes and back on.' Everyone obeys this request, except the driver, who we find 20 minutes later tucking into a baguette. It's at this moment that I get a text through from Stu at the club telling me that the game is definitely on – result! I'm sure that I'm not the only one present who has butterflies in their tummy about tonight, I'm still telling all and sundry that I will 'settle for a point' but whatever, this is a big, big game which I couldn't contemplate missing. I know the others present feel the same. If we should pull off a victory tonight it will arguably put us, maybe not a foot, but perhaps a little toe, closer to Division One. Tonight could see a little part of history made, and I want to be there.

The stop-off is our usual port of call, the splendid South Gloucestershire town of Thornbury. It's a great stop, we've been making The Wheatsheaf our pre-match HQ for years now. A cracking little town, both for a group of football fans or for individuals who like to potter about the various other pubs, cafés, bookies, etc. Funny reading on Bristol's hoolie sites after the game, how we 'shit one' by stopping in Thornbury, when we always do. History has shown us that if you start walking about in the area near to Ashton Gate on your tod, the shady bastards pick you off and cause a few headaches. Thornbury's a great little town, where we never cause any trouble, but fill the tills of the local hostelries full of cash, that's all there is to it, really. One other characteristic for which Thornbury has become famed is a phial of liquid which has the sinister title of 'Black Rat'.

We arrive at The Wheatsheaf at around half past three, at least three hours' drinking time is envisaged, due to the expected Friday afternoon sprawl through Birmingham never materialising. When we arrive, I notice that the place has had a facelift since our last visit, and tragically, the stunning barmaid isn't behind the bar. 'Oh THAT one?' says the landlord. 'Married with kids now, piled weight on.' We are the only ones in the place, but quickly make ourselves at home. Shortly after, a couple of locals turn up and one asks the landlord, 'Who's all this lot then?' 'Oh, it's Wigan Athletic,' replies the landlord, adding soon afterwards, 'not the team, obviously,' just in case there was any confusion!

Pretty soon, our numbers get up to around 40 as a van and a couple of cars turn up, the Stella is flowing and, in addition, a pretty toxic-looking substance is being passed around in a half-pint glass. Yes, it's Black Rat time. Strangely, there are few takers for even a half pint of this devilish concoction, whereas the burgeoning number of locals enjoying a Friday post-work drink are polishing it off with aplomb. I've had it before, I can handle it, so I down it. I've spotted that there's now a label on the pump, stating that it is '6.0 per cent proof'. I well recall asking the last landlord, on a previous visit, what percentage it was, just for him to shrug his shoulders and say, 'No one knows. Somewhere between five and ten, I reckon,' which usually means nearer to ten, but I suppose their inaccurate labelling is their form of revenge on the EU bureaucrats who have probably made them do it in the first place. The locals look, well, reasonably normal, so I head barwards and demand a pint of the cloudy cider stuff.

I've never seen it on sale anywhere else in the world, but I suppose it could be quite a widespread tipple in the West Country. It smells a bit funny, but goes down great. Sensing my bravado, a few others try a scoop for good measure. This teases me into buying another one, which also goes down great, and before we know it, it's time to hit the road. The locals are shaking their heads. The journey to the ground is very much a blur, and I may well have been hallucinating at some point. Before I get accused of being a lightweight, I'd like to recall the tale the landlord told me of the rugby union team from up north somewhere who turned up at The Wheatsheaf, and claimed to be 'big drinkers'. Five pints of Black Rat later, they were rolling around the car park like dying bluebottles! I think we get slightly lost en route, but can't be sure, I also recall that several of us, myself included, had to relieve ourselves at the back of the coach in a bottle. Whoops. I had every intention of ringing up the coach firm on the Monday after this game to thank them, but decided against it, just in case he mentioned 'the funny smell coming from the back seats'. But, hey, they usually take Everton fans, so must be used to it by now. As Clandon, our token Evertonian on board, commented as we boarded earlier, 'You've not prepared very well, where's the funnel and bucket?'

I enter the ground very much the worse for wear. Off to the food hatch for a pasty and a Bovril and then onto the seats bolted onto terrace. The game kicks off at a crescendo with the full force of both sets of fans behind their teams. Within five minutes, The Duke is put through following a great flick-on by Liddell but his effort is well saved by the Bristol keeper. There's one player who wouldn't mind bagging one tonight, as a former Bristol Rovers player he is mercilessly booed and baited from start to finish by the City faithful with their slightly original chants of 'He's only a poor little Gashead'. Ellington has never scored against City, could there ever be a better occasion to break his duck?

The pitch is in excellent nick, both teams knock it about, although City seem to have an over-reliance on hitting long balls down the right to their talisman, boggle-eyed free-scoring winger Scott Murray. The away support belies its numbers by outsinging the Bristolians throughout. There's all our lot at the front jumping up and down pissed, trying to get on the telly, along with a group of lads whom I've never seen before, but they're leading the singing – students obviously – after all, what working fans can afford £200 Evisu jeans? Not having a go, I used to do exactly the same when the loan cheque used to come through at the start of each term! Mike Flynn's mates from Newport are all there, thankfully no one tries to lamp them on this occasion, and there's a handful of Bristol Rovers fans, here to watch The Duke. Absolutely no one is sat down, and speaking personally, the fact that these seats have no backs on them means that I'd end up with yet more UDIs if I even tried to sit down. I'm swaying about in the sixth row back, and have taken up a position next to some bird. Unfortunately, the Black Rat has made me incoherent, so little conversation develops.

Back to the game, and the few hundred Wiganers are taunting the 13,000-plus Bristolians with the ubiquitous 'Shall we sing a song for you?' not very original but sums up the mood thus far. The Duke is well up for it, flying into them, and Bristol create their first chance of note, a tame header which Filan gathers up. The resolution which was sadly lacking the previous week at Stoke has now returned to the team, and Bristol City, if they didn't know it already, are going to have to play very well to take us to the cleaners tonight. Liddell finds himself with a great chance with 15 minutes gone and a Bristol defender has to handball it out for a corner. City break soon after, when Martian-faced whippet Murray gets clean through on goal by rounding Filan, only for a wonderful saving tackle from De Vos to clear the danger. De Vos, you are De Best. Midway through the first half, and it's situation normal: the Wigan defence have marked out their turf, the tenacious tackling of Mitchell and Dinning in the middle is snuffing out the City threat and the previously heard home chants of 'Is that all you take away?' have been replaced with our own retorts of 'You're supposed to be at home'.

The Wigan dominance is further emphasised when a great run from Tony Dinning puts Nathan Ellington in the clear, surely this time he must score. Alas, his shot bounces back off the foot of the post. Bristol City, the home team, top goalscorers in the division with great attacking home form, are stuck in their own half and are being forced back by the sheer persistence of the Wigan 11. There is one disgraceful incident, which I, and probably the rest of the travelling

Wiganers, were unaware of until the day after, a sickening stamp by Tony Butler on Wigan captain Jason De Vos. The scumbag must have a deathwish taking on big Jason, not a man to be messed with. Thankfully the cameras picked up on it, and I expect suitable punishment to follow for this pathetic display of petulance.

Peter Kennedy, eh? The enigma that is Peter Kennedy. A player who has been very low in confidence over the last few months. He came to Wigan with a first-class pedigree, having played in the Premier League with Watford. He has suffered a few bad injuries, so I suppose Jewell knew he had taken a risk, but the Latics fans have thus far seen very little of the much vaunted 'sweet left peg'. He doesn't look bad at left-back, but looks terrified on the left wing. The consensus on the way down for most of the 20 on board was that if we were picking the side, Peter Kennedy would be lucky to get an arse-splinter in his tracksuit bottoms, but we all knew full well that Jewell would play him. 'Maybe he'll get a hat-trick,' said I. Ho ho ho's all round. For so it is written in the scriptures that Wigan Athletic shall have a whipping boy, and lo, he shall more often than not be found on the left wing, hitting crosses into Matalan car park. I give you Peter Kennedy, the crowd's whipping boy. Not tonight, though!

Two minutes into the second half a Bristol attack breaks down and the ball falls to the feet of Ellington. The Duke purposefully runs out of his own half towards the Bristol goal, where he is crudely shoved out of the way by a City defender, five yards short of the penalty area. Up steps Peter Kennedy. I've seen him in this position many times before, and he's never really come up with the goods. As a fellow left footer I know that this is an ideal position, halfway between the centre and corner edge of the box. There's no great expectations, I turn around and while I am telling someone that 'you can't say he's not due one', the ball is up, over the wall and into the near corner. GOAL! There's pandemonium breaking out in the away end as the have-a-go hero stewards set about making our away following even smaller than it is already perceived to be.

After it calms down I go over to a steward who I saw manhandling a teenage lad, introducing myself as a 'fan's representative', telling him that that is assault and to turn around while I make a note of his number. He walks backwards into the other stewards and points me out as lead troublemaker. They say the power of the pen is mightier than the sword. Well, let me state here and now, that you, my friend (*sic*), are a cowardly fascist pig of the highest order, picking on kids and I hope your genitalia turns green and shrinks to the size of a gnat's dinner if it isn't already. I withdraw my complaint, safe in the knowledge that this cowardly nobhead is not worth the effort.

So we're 1–0 up, Peter Kennedy's first goal for the club and what a crucial and superb effort it was, which I did eventually get to see. It would be harsh of us Wiganers to rub it in, and much as I hate being presumptuous, I am compelled to join in with the '1–0 to the champions' and 'We'll never play you again' chants which are increasingly creeping into our away-match repertoire. If ever a side played and looked like champions, then it's the Wigan Athletic class of 2002–03, but I'd still rather wait until we've won the championship before we truly celebrate it.

There is a hell of a long way to go yet though, we know that from many painful games in the past. We are singing silly songs about 'ooh aah Ambrosia'. My God, we're even singing Peter Kennedy's name to the tune of 'Kum By Yah'. The verse of 'Are you Rovers in disguise?' doesn't go down with the Rovers contingent any better than the 'Sheep, Sheep, Sheepshaggers' does with the Newport lot, but, hey, they know we don't mean it. Their manager, Danny Wilson, throws on Brian Tinnion in an attempt to force the issue back Bristol's way. Brian Tinnion has very smelly feet. I read this in a football magazine a long time ago. I think about offering this topical nugget to the female Duke fan from Bristol stood near me, but refrain. I've come out with worse chat-up lines in my time. A dangerous Bristol cross floats towards the six-yard box and who is there to head it clear? Peter Kennedy. He is doing an exemplary job of keeping City's star man, turkey-necked flying midfielder Scotty Murray, quiet, and when Murray does find time to get a shot in, Filan produces a reflex save.

Both sides have opportunities to alter the scoreline, Bristol's attempts get more and more desperate, whereas on 72 minutes, Andy Liddell finds himself clean through with a great chance to score, but the City keeper, Phillips, pulls off another fine save to deny him. City are running out of ideas fast and just cannot find a way through us. Wigan remain composed and stroke it or hoof it, depending on what the situation merits. 'It's just like watching Beech Hill' is the cry, a little pun preferred by the fans in honour of a certain region of the town. Thirteen thousand Bristolians are now as short on voice as their team is of attacking nous, 300 Wiganers respond to the silence by helpfully singing 'It's just like being in church'. The ref signals for four minutes of added time. FOUR MINUTES! Well, we've managed to 'hang on' for this long, what difference will four more minutes make? None at all, and the elation of the final whistle can't be matched – the joy of victory certainly doesn't decrease the more often it happens. The players look as pleased as we are. What a team, what a spirit Jewell has built. There's a bit of mutual appreciation, then both parties go their separate ways. Full respect to the travelling support, and also to the 19 who joined us on the inaugural 'Jimmy and Brasso tour'. The man of the match, beyond any reasonable doubt, is Peter Kennedy – a few including myself would be ordering a bit of humble pie had they not shut the food kiosk.

I make my way outside still disorientated and end up going walkabout. Two of us head to the industrial estate, over the level crossing where the coaches are usually parked up. No sooner are we around the corner, than it seems like half of Bristol are after filling us in, 'Come on, you Wigan twats, fecking northern monkees!' We spend a few minutes watching our backs before running the gauntlet back to our own coach, where the rest are waiting and cursing us. Bristol fans are a sound, knowledgeable football bunch, but they've always had this element that likes to pick off lone away fans. Seems it's fair game to them to do this, whereas others would say it breaks the code. Whatever, boys, it won't take the three points away from us!

The coach gets lost on the way home and we stop to turn around at a pub, of all places. Had I been at my instinctive best, I would have talked the driver into pulling over for five while we got some carry-outs but everyone seems too worn out to bother. The journey home is a cold, arduous one – this coach must be just about the coldest place in the country on a Friday night, the heating is non-existent. We are tired, but happy, we're now 12 points clear at the top of the league, a phenomenal achievement! A generous whip-round for our jovial driver as we head over the Thelwall, and I'm dreaming of my warm bed at this stage, bollocks to last orders in Rik's. We arrive back in Wigan at 2 a.m., by which time we have all sobered up and can only laugh at the half-naked birds and pissed-up lads stumbling about King Street. One last thing before I hit the sack: Teletext – 'Super Wigan Go Twelve Points Clear.' Back of the net!

Saturday, just after midday. I wake up and my throat feels like I have been chomping on razor blades. I ring up Ashton Town, as I had been intending to go watch them on the first free Saturday I had. Game is off. Leigh RMI – same script. Late result: Back to bed 1; Football 0.

THE FEAR FACTOR

18 January 2003, Colchester (h). Won 2–1.

I have developed a morbid affliction when following my team. Because we are winning every game, I always expect us to lose. I can't think rationally – we are far superior to Colchester in every department and really should put six past them, but because of this long unbeaten run I can't help but think that we are going to get turned over. The fear factor is evidently with me, thankfully the players and manager do not operate under this principle. I find myself listening to the contrary evidence, 'Last team to beat us at home apart from Port Vale . . . only side capable of doing the double over us this season.' I get an idea in my head to stick a tenner on a Colchester win, I mean, Tote's are offering 10/1, we're not that good, and it will soothe the pain of the impending defeat. I never go through with it, of course, it's sacrilege, betting against your own team. And so, in my eyes, is backing your own team. I believe that if I back Latics to win, then they will lose. Plus, at 1/9 it's hardly worth it.

There has been a little bit of a drive in the media and on the websites to encourage people to come down and watch this Saturday. It fails miserably. The argument for this is that people want to see us play Forest, Wolves, Preston and Bolton, they don't want to see dirty, niggly Colchester with their 50 travelling fans. This is true, but I still dispute the logic of people who 'don't go because we're playing Colchester'. How can you turn it on and turn it off like this? And what does it matter who the opposition is when we're playing so well? You don't pay £12 or £14 to watch the opposition play. You pay to watch The Duke and Andy Liddell score beautiful goals, the exciting wing play of Gary Teale, the majestic aerial presence of De Vos and the superb keeping of undoubtedly, absolutely no arguments, the best keeper outside the Premier League. They are all playing, whether we're playing Southampton, Southend or South Liverpool (RIP sadly). I have tried and tried throughout the book to understand and explain what makes the notoriously fickle Wigan public tick, but I have to concede that for all that there are some right lazy gobshites in the town, and it may take 20 or 30 years until the next generation comes through who genuinely appreciate the fine footballing outfit on their doorstep.

Of course, by then we will be shite again, so I console myself with the fact that the 25,000 crowds we will be getting for our North West Trains games in season 2033–34 will be moaning that the present team aren't a patch on the Second Division title-winning side of 2002–03. Of course, all 25,000 will claim to have been inside the JJB Stadium on 18 January 2003, but those in the know, will know, if you catch my drift. We are getting a lot of shit off other fans about our crowd sizes at present, but let's face it, it is the *only* thing they can criticise us for. There is a hardcore support that follows Wigan Athletic all over the country and the club knows and recognises us as being amongst the best fans in the country. Does the fact that there's not many of us make us 'poor'? No it doesn't.

A quick pint in The Pagefield and nip to the bookies across the road. Skipping on my much-considered bet, I do a correct-score Lucky 15. Fifty pence a line and I take the four tightest games on the coupon at 1–0. With a 100 per cent bonus for only one correct, I only need one to come in to break even. All four and it's a couple of grand. Later on that day, the games finish 2–1, 2–1, 1–1 and 3–2. No free turnout for me tonight.

The Latics start the game brightly, putting some great crosses over, yet not really troubling the goal. Possession is nine-tenths of the law, and the law of averages at least dictates that we're going to score very soon and score quite a few. With nearly half an hour of the game gone, it's still 0–0 and my doubts are starting to creep in again. They're frustrating us, maybe today's the day that we can't score and Colchester go down the other end and sneak a sly one. Colchester have their first chance of the game, a fierce volley from distance which Filan manages to get his body behind. The Colchester lot are going down like Shifnall Street Suzy, every tackle sees them writhe about on the floor in agony for five minutes. They are timewasting and there's not even half an hour gone! Paul Jewell has also been saying in the week that the crowd need to get behind the team more, and although neither the atmosphere nor the crowd is very good, there are still people making the effort. I can hear the bloke in the middle of the South Stand; every game, on his own, he will start up a very pronounced chant of 'EE AY EE AY EE AY OH'. Sometimes people join in with an 'Up the Football League we go', on other occasions they don't, which is always funnier. I don't know you Ee-ay-oh man, well actually I probably do, but I salute you nevertheless for your dedication in getting Latics fans to sing up. These are the real people who deserve MBEs.

Just as we bemoan the potential 0–0 half-time scoreline, we get a corner and De Vos spanks home a trademark header to give us the lead. 1–0, get in, now the floodgates will open. Make mental note to get around to setting up spread betting account and lumping on Latics to score between 40 and 45 minutes, every bloody home game without fail! Colchester are a mess, and The Duke nearly doubles the lead when he picks up a poor clearance, runs at their defence and narrowly shoots wide. He's in his third barren spell of the season now, but we're still scoring goals, and he's still on course to get 25 for the season.

The second half sees plenty more Wigan chances and possession but as is often the case, what looks like a drubbing turns a bit nervy. Fifteen minutes to go, and a free kick is sent into the box and the referee blows his whistle. There's a brief pause and then the cry of 'Penalty!' goes up. Don't know what it has been awarded for, in fact I still don't even to this day. Watching the highlights, there was a bit of pushing and shoving with De Vos and a Colchester defender but that sort of thing goes on all the time. However, you don't turn a penalty down, and so it is Andy Liddell who shimmies and slots home his eleventh goal of the season.

In the very final minute of the game, the Colchester substitute Atangana, from Cameroon, breaks free and homes in on goal. Filan charges out and the forward attempts to round him, but has such a poor touch that he will be lucky to retrieve it, so he dives over Filan's legs. The referee waves play on. The linesman, or should I say assistant referee, is obviously pissed off that he is only the number two official in this contest and has other ideas. He is furiously waving his flag, despite being much further away than the referee and on the blind side of the incident. His semaphore actions ensure that we now have a new star of the show. This is a farcical decision, a poorer dive you will not see all day. The players concur with this view and are surrounding the referee, keen to discuss the potential discovery of warheads in Iraq. John Filan, a cool, laid-back Aussie, has a redder face than Brian Clough. The ref starts to brandish cards, which furthers the injustice, but at least doesn't send Filan off as the ageing Dave Beasant has already stripped and is waiting on the touch-line. Rightly so, as whether it was a pen or not, the player had lost control of the ball and was heading away from the goal. Which is why he did his pathetic dive, the key factor which the ref has failed to recognise.

Filan wants to save this badly, you can tell – he's madder than BA Baracus on acid. There's a roar amongst the crowd, much bigger than that for either of the goals as the South Stand faithfully implores the likeable Aussie to claim his eighteenth clean sheet of the season. As he sets himself, he walks over to the goal post, and kicks his boots against it, Barthez-style. If they can do gamesmanship, then so can we!! The penalty is firm and right in the corner, Filan guesses correctly and determinedly leaps full length to get his fingertips to it. He does, but it sneaks in off the post. Bloody hell, Beasant would've saved it. Only kidding, John!

At 2–1 in injury time, Colchester come charging through us on at least two more occasions, sensing blood. When they knock their unsightly niggling and timewasting on the head, they're actually quite a tidy outfit. However, the bulk of the four minutes of added time has been spent debating the penalty decision with the ref, so time is not on their side. The final whistle goes and Jewell is on the pitch holding back Filan from telling the referee yet again what he thinks of him. The whole team are absolutely bloody furious that they have conceded a goal in what they consider to be unjust circumstances. Even 2–1 is seen as a disappointment, especially when the man responsible is another first-year ref with a mere four league games under his belt. The reality is that, even with an incompetent ref, we are still pulling the results out of the bag. Probably just as well, as the dozy bugger wouldn't have got out alive otherwise. I can see it now: he'd be heading for his car, all changed and showered, whistling the 'Skye Boat Song', when some enraged nutter would come steaming out of Rigoletto's with a napkin tucked into their front, brandishing a huge pepper mill . . . 'Jimmy, pack it in, they've just brought your main course out!'

THEY'LL BE STOPPING FOLK FROM GETTING DRUNK IN PUBS NEXT

25 January 2003, Swindon (a). Lost 1–2.

We realise that all teams have to lose sometime, it would just really, really hurt to lose to such a bunch of horrid southern inbreds. It's an 8 a.m. start and a couple of us are recalling our previous trip to Swindon when four of us were harmlessly, if a little unsteadily, making our way onto the ground. A scruffy geezer with long hair and a leather jacket approached us with a camera. 'Fancy having your photo taken with Cathy, boys?' as he pointed to a gorgeous-looking bird with huge breasts. Let's weigh up the pros and cons – CON: We may miss the kick-off; PRO: drool, wibble, wibble, why, it would be rude not to! Unfortunately, as I took up (as ever) a position at the rear, I didn't get to see them in the flesh, until I bought the *Sunday Sport* the day after, that is! A quick search on the Internet would undoubtedly reveal a great deal more of the porn star known as Cathy Barry, but as this has nothing to do with football I'll not direct you there. Fame at last, even if they did show her posing next to a copper for the main pic, with us 'red-blooded Swindon males' (yes they mistook us for home fans) tucked away in the corner. Booo!

As for the pre-match viewing, well, we have a rarity – a video recorder that works, and someone has brought along a copy of that award-winning hoolie film *ID* so we're going to watch it. I'm not sure if there's any law against this, although I know that this sort of thing hit the headlines many years ago and could be construed as somewhat dodgy behaviour. As far as we are concerned it's more a piece of comedy than designed to get us 'in the mood' as many a court case would have it, scary in parts but also very funny in others. What club doesn't have characters such as Gumbo amongst its support if it's honest? We're all avidly playing spot the grounds, although the producer probably should have put a bit more work in on disguising who the main team 'Shadwell FC' are supposed to be, especially for the many of us on board who have recent memories of our clashes with the 'Beasts of Bermondsey'. And is it compulsory for Warren Clarke to turn up in *every* film of this nature? It's gripping viewing. I saw it yonks ago, but never since, so have that sort of half-expectation of what's going to happen. It helps the journey pass quickly, to the extent that I never finish reading my paper and we barely acknowledge (i.e. abuse) a coach of passing Dingles on their way to watch Burnley at Brentford.

Our pub stop is so secluded that it isn't even on the outskirts of nowhere, let alone in the middle, a place called Curney Wick that we've visited before on a previous Swindon trip. We arrive at ten to eleven, and getting a drink isn't a problem. It's not an ideal base – there's nothing at all wrong with a country pub, but most of our mob like the basic small-town creature comforts, a café, a bookies, a cash point, and a lapdancing bar. Just enough to enable us to potter about and stretch the legs due to spending much of the day stuck on a coach.

The ale gets flowing smoothly and, apart from the match itself, this is arguably my favourite part of the day. Propping the bar up with the likes of Les Bagg, Dean Martin and Coopsy talking football while enjoying a few beers. One of the greatest myths surrounding these coach trips is that we're all mates and it's a bit of a clique, a closed shop so to speak. Complete rubbish really – we are mates, of course, but we only become that way through travelling to away games together over the years, with the common love of a few beers and watching our football team. All are welcome, and there's nothing that makes us all more downbeat than when a coach trip has to be cancelled due to lack of interest, something that's only happened a handful of times in the five years or so that Arky has been running them.

This could turn into one of the classic days out if all goes to plan, there's a great atmosphere rising. While I'm sat on the bog, I can hear two Wiganers using the urinals when one of them breaks wind loudly. 'Good aaaarrrrssse,' his mate says in a comedy West Country accent.

'Good aaaarrrrssseee,' says his mate back. They continue this intense dialogue back and forth with increasing volume until I find myself joining in, shouting 'Good aaarrrrsseee!' from the cubicle as well for good measure. The pub itself is slightly surreal. Two rooms are full of excitable football fans playing pool for money and talking shop, whereas there is a quiet restaurant part protected by glass doors which is full of grey-haired grannies quietly enjoying a meal and admiring the view of the yachts on the lake. Dozens of them keep coming in, filing past us, aided by tasteful shouts of, 'Ey up lads, the strippers are here!'

As time and alcohol passes, the inevitable singing starts, with Gerry and The Pacemakers to the fore as the whole pub, as per usual led by Caddy, Rammy and Shannon, let rip with 'How Do You Do What You Do To Me'. Followed up by a few verses of 'Please Release Me' sung with all the compassion of a wounded coyote. Marvellous. And totally irrelevant to boot. The locals are losing patience with our '60s medley, and the landlady starts banging on the bar and gesticulating wildly with a LADLE! This provokes nothing more than hilarity from the masses, who carry on unabashed. 'If you're going to carry on singing and being disruptive, I will have to ask you to leave and get back on your coaches.' Now at first I felt a bit sorry for her here, but shortly after changed my tune: she knew what was coming, there's probably 50 odd of us here spending £20–£30 each, that's a grand in her till between the hours of 11 a.m. and 2 p.m. on a Saturday afternoon. We're noisy and boisterous, but aren't causing any trouble whatsoever. She certainly won't be complaining when she cashes up at the end of the day.

I have resigned myself to the fact that this place is going to get trashed if she carries on being authoritative with us, but she seems to chill out and is all smiles again, ten minutes later. I was talking football with her at the bar the last time I went and I think she knows her stuff and has realised that we probably won't be back next year, as do we. Just weather the storm, luv, until we get back on the coach and business will arrive at a satisfactory closure for all parties.

The coach sets off for Swindon about ten past two, I fail to notice whether the landlady asks us to 'Come again next year' but even I'm getting pretty cocky now that we won't be playing down here again. Twenty minutes later, and after the obligatory wrong turn, we are passing through some dogshit council estate on the outskirts of Swindon. The houses are probably still worth a hundred grand apiece. I am wittering some bollocks about 'southern council estates not having the aura or menace of their northern counterparts. Take Sale or Kirkby for example, they are intimidating to even look at!' Not for the last time today, people are looking at me like I am a bit odd.

We arrive a good 15 minutes before kick-off and I am mooting a visit to the pub on the corner, despite being a good four cans and six pints to the good already. There are surprisingly few takers, as we alight from the coach to chants of 'Shadwell Army, Shadwell Army'. The fascist pigs that masquerade as Swindon's stewards look nervy. As we make our way around to the away end, there are no topless models lying in wait this time, just a bunch of moody stewards, not overly impressed with our singing of 'We are Shadwell, the Kennel is our home'. As I approach the stand, they are harshly manhandling a Wiganer I vaguely know, at which I shout, 'Leave him alone, you twats, he's only come here to watch the game.' This tactful suggestion amazingly cuts very little ice with the stewards who then divert their attentions to manhandling me:

'Have you been drinking, sir?' (Actually, I very much doubt that these oafs called me sir.)

'Well, you know, just a couple, it's not a crime, is it?'

Fear overtakes me and I realise that unless I engage in some fast talking, I ain't going to see this game. I'd be well prepared to go around to the home end to gain umbrage but I guess these stewards would simply notify their brothers and sisters (they all look like they are from the same family, if you catch my drift) and I'm in deep shit.

'Look it's my birthday, if I can't have a drink on my birthday, when can I?'

And so, as it turns out, it is my birthday, as after a quick search and a flash of my £19 ticket I'm in.

As the game gets underway, it becomes apparent that there are absolutely loads of people missing, both off our coach and amongst those who have travelled by train. We estimate that around 20 to 30 have been refused entrance to the stand, what a sad, sorry state of affairs. Reeling off the names, I concede that some of those mentioned might well have been plastered, but some of the others, well they are as placid as anyone you would care to meet. They travel nearly 200 miles across the country, spending hard-earned cash to watch their team just to get turned away by some dickhead in a pink jacket. It's only 3 p.m., how drunk can a person be? Are we expected to go to a dump like Swindon and remain stone cold sober throughout the day? Not blooming likely, in my opinion! It's a long day, personally I left the house at 7.40 a.m. and got in at 4.40 a.m. via the Coops Foyer (don't ask), but Swindon is so far away that we're always likely to make a day of it, where's the harm in having a drink? We're not working, just because they are, there's no need to try and make our day miserable as well. The current theme being sung by the Wiganers of 'We'll never play you again' will hopefully not only be fact, but a genuine emotion from the Wigan hordes present. All in all, we have been made to feel about as welcome as George Dubya Bush at prayer time in a mosque, and unfortunately for us, that sentiment is also being echoed in the only place where it really should apply, out on the pitch.

An unchanged side on offer for Latics against a Swindon team who in all honesty were one of the poorest I've ever seen at the JJB only a few weeks earlier. Today Swindon, to use a northern term, are like whippets. The two lads up front, Parkin and Invincible, are running De Vos and Jackson ragged. Although we're very much in the game, Swindon look a totally different proposition to the team who visited the JJB on 28 December. We can tell from the fact that they should be 2–0 up within the first ten minutes that we are going to have our work cut out today.

The first goal arrives on 23 minutes, following a move on the right-hand side, during which a blatant offside is ignored. While the Wigan players and fans are disputing this, Danny Invincible fires home a beautiful volley to put them 1–0 up. Ten minutes later, and Swindon win a free kick on the same far side. For what I know not. The referee, it seems, has backed Swindon on the coupon. The ball is swung into the danger area, and, with no determined attempt to clear it, Swindon captain, Andy Gurney fires home to put the home side two goals to the good. Gulp! Wigan are shell-shocked, both the fans and the players, and whereas both the goals had a dubious nature to them, there is no denying that Swindon are playing superb football and are absolutely battering us, a credit to the division and no mistake.

Having a leak at half-time, I am looking up at the wall, as most blokes do for fear of the embarrassment of getting caught looking downwards either side. I am deep in thought, because I can't actually remember the last time we were in this position. OK, so we were at Stoke, but I didn't really give a shit to be honest, this is different. I quietly mutter to myself, 'Come on Wigan, we can do these men,' probably not the best words to utter in a public convenience but a surefire sign of the confidence that the players and fans have this season.

We come out fighting in the second half. Keep playing like this and we'll be 3–2 up in no time. I am stood on the seat bawling my head off, and there are a few people looking at me shaking their heads. The Swindon lot offer forward the somewhat predictable taunt of 'Is that all you take away?' to be met by my solo drunken retort of, 'NO IT FUCKIN' ISN'T. THE REST ARE IN THE PUB BECAUSE YOUR WANKY STEWARDS WOULDN'T LET THEM IN THE GROUND!'

Gary Teale goes agonisingly close, hitting the angle of post and crossbar with a fierce shot which keeper Bart Griemink gets nowhere near. Swindon then break clear and Invincible goes one-on-one with an opportunity to seal the game, but Filan makes a great, brave save to deny him and keep us in the hunt. The game's tempo increases, real end-to-end stuff. It has to be said though, Swindon are now relying on chances on the break more, Wigan are pushing forward and look like the home side. With this kind of pressure being exerted, something's got to give, and on 55 minutes. Nicky Eaden sends over a beautiful far-post cross which is met with a superb diving header from Lee McCulloch. 2–1 and Swindon aren't so cocky now. We are as good as back in the game, and patiently await the second (and third). Swindon again have chances to seal it, one shot hits the base of the post and rebounds back goalwards off the grounded John Filan, it looks for all the world like 3–1, but it isn't. This reinforces our view that we're going to get at least a point out of today.

There are several scrambles in the Swindon goalmouth which are so close that I'm in half a mind to run on the pitch and kick the bugger in myself, but I don't. Because I'd miss. As a result of each of these Swindon players take turns to lie prostrate on the ground. The game is halted for a few minutes while one player has his head bandaged up in the penalty area. Get him off the bloody pitch, his legs are OK, aren't they! However, whatever type of bang to the head this player has sustained clearly affects his judgement, as minutes later he decides to take a corner ball off Jason De Vos's head by punching it clear. The distinctive white bandage makes it all the more luminous and a more blatant penalty I will never see. With De Vos already having scored three headers from corners this month alone, we have every right to feel very hard done by, and the players again spend several minutes remonstrating with the incompetent with the whistle.

De Vos stays put up front, but the injustice of this incident knocks the stuffing out of Wigan, and our attempts to claim an equaliser are to no avail. Despite the fact Swindon have been doing as much timewasting as is humanly possible, basically taking it in turns to lie down and roll over, the time added on is shorter than a J-Lo marriage. We applaud the players off, appreciative of their second-half efforts and forgetting their poor first half. Had they been a bit sharper, they would not have ended up chasing the game. Nevertheless, we're dejected, so are they, but they have done us proud as we make our way out of the ground.

Swindon Town have, thankfully, refunded money to those who have not seen the game. I reckon the actions of their stewards have cost their club around £500 today. Considering Swindon were in administration a few months ago, that's particularly galling. Those who have spent the afternoon in the pub (those fortunate enough not to have been nicked as well as turned away) are now returning to the coach. They are now, thanks to the stewards, even drunker than they were before the game and are baiting them. We catch up with Caddy and Doc who were turned away, not for being drunk this year, but because they were drunk on their visit here *last* year, the pair of them are now teetotal of course (er, that last bit might not be true). So being drunk on entry to a football ground is now a life sentence is it? What a shambles. On discovering the final score, Caddy once again turns on the unimpressed 'Pink Army' to say, 'Thanks for that, boys, you've just saved us 20 quid.' Rightly so.

There's a nasty atmosphere in the car park and we've certainly not created it. The stewards are very hostile and are actively seeking confrontation. They don't like us, and the feeling is mutual. We've had just about enough of these bullies for one day and there is a suggestion from both sides that if the police weren't present, we'd both be delighted to get down to business. One lad is having a spat with one of them and before you know it the pair are squaring up to each other. The police intervene – by nicking him, not the steward, of course. We watch the Old Bill haul him off by the throat and take him away, only for him to re-emerge ten minutes later following a spot of Wigan police intervention. The insinuations and allegations that he has 'bought his freedom' don't stop until the coach arrives in Wigan three hours later!

The coach finally leaves Swindon a good half an hour after the game has finished, and the general opinion of this place is that if we never have to play here again it'll be too soon, and we're not coming. Why the hell should we? For all the talk of letters of protest against the heavy handedness dished out, we will simply vote with our feet next time and not visit this shitty little part of Wiltshire. One final call-off point, Sainsbury's in Cirencester for our munchies. I opt for Dairylea Dippers, brunch sandwiches, posh crisps, a Mars and a few large bottles of Smirnoff Ice. Yeah, I know it's wrong drinking alcopops before 1 a.m. but there are never any fridges in these places and there's nowt worse than warm lager.

When everyone's calmed down, the video is put on for the journey home. Which video shall we watch this time? Why SCUM of course! I've never really been impressed with this film, it just seems like endless scenes of youths milling about and being shouted at by the screws. Most of the back-seat boys, however, feel quite differently, especially about one scene in particular and are reinforcing this with constant chants of 'Potting shed, potting shed, potting shed!' Sorry, boys but the public needs to be made aware of these character traits! The front vs. back singing competition gets in full swing, although, as per usual, I struggle to remember much of the madness that goes on during these journeys home. All I know is that the mood very rarely bears any relation to the result of the game earlier on in the day.

I get home in the early hours after somehow combining a good day out (only partially marred by stewards) and a great night out. A costly day, as I have a fiver left in my pocket from £100, after finding myself that £20 down which many Wiganers seem to find goes missing on a Saturday night these days. I couldn't give a shit about the cost any more, or our rough treatment, all I wanted was the three points off

Swindon. We're still nine points clear, but a new threat is emerging from the pack – the total football geniuses, those train-driving titans, those maverick Brazilians from Gresty Road. The team who bought the title versus the team that plays beautiful football and brings its own youngsters through. We're screwed if we think we're the good guys in this one!

BOUNCING BACK TO HAPPINESS

28 January 2003, Mansfield Town (a). Won 2–1.

I could have filled two cars with the amount of people ringing up trying to cadge a lift. I must be the hardest man in Wigan if the amount of mates I know who are 'scared of motorway driving' is anything to go by. Not afraid of sitting in the passenger seat and getting legless though! I'm already about a third of the way there from my place of employment, so I'm not going to drive back up to Wigan to pick up mates who will show their gratitude by coming bouncing out of their houses carrying a crate of ale apiece. Harsh but fair, I think, if we took it in turns I'd accept it, but we don't, it's me or no one. Tonight promises to be a useful test of character following Saturday's defeat. Mansfield are no pushover, certainly not at home anyway, and anything less than three points for the away team tonight and we'll hear the word 'slump' being bandied about. I have meticulously planned my route and have even taken a visit to Tesco's in Northwich to fill up with petrol in my dinner hour and do a 'big shop' (pies, crisps, chocolate and Lucozade, no chance of starving to death then).

Setting off at just gone half four, I head M6 southbound, both hands on the steering wheel fending off gales and torrential rain in the third lane. Down to Stoke, fingers at their stadium for good measure, and as I'm losing WISH (for team news and to ensure the game doesn't get postponed) I am forced to turn to the local signal radio, listening to delightful tales on the news of the local smackheads robbing pensioners. These radio stations are all exactly the same, the same cheesy banter, the same shitey music, even the same shitey adverts: conservatories, bloody insurance, mortgages, solicitors who 'want to be my friend'. I once rang up one of these firms and asked them to lend me £50 so I could go out on the piss. Not that much of a friend then? One programme features someone called Andrew Goulding, who, if I recall rightly, is McCann's old mate and former WISH employee: an advert for his show 'Andrew and some bird at breakfast'. Surely using a real-life couple would be much, much better, him demanding breakfast and her throwing the bloody frying pan at him for having the cheek to ask. Or perhaps even get two blokes from Wigan GPO on at 6 a.m. Monday morning who've been on the ale all weekend to give us their views on Will Young's latest chart offering. 'Coming up we've geet some slack-jawed faggot who's ripped off T'Doors.' Yeah, that'd be good!!

Local radio is putting me into an increasingly psychotic state, I'm on Ram FM now on the outskirts of Derby. On hitting Derby at 6 p.m., a mere 26 miles from Mansfield, there appears the most almighty tailback on the A38. Traffic is wedged solid, and this prompts me to remember why I am listening to local radio in the first place – traffic news.

'Which popstar is the best swimmer?'

'Why, Seal of course.'

Did he really say that? Kill me now.

Twenty minutes and 400 yards later, I catch a bit of 'overturned lorry, A38 Northbound junction with A31, standing traffic for seven miles blah blah blah'. It takes a minute to register and then 'oh bollocks, I'm right in the middle of this'. I have no idea at all as to where I am in this seven-mile queue but my opinion of a few minutes earlier that I'd be sitting in the Early Doors pub by half six supping cool ones (shandy, mind) has now changed to a somewhat more panicky realisation that I'll be lucky to make kick-off. There are cars everywhere, total carnage, you inconsiderate lorry-driving bastards, always shedding your loads, you do it on purpose, I could be here all night, just because you didn't spend an extra ten minutes tightening your turnips this morning. I make a few calls to others on their way, and, needless to say, they are all coming the M62–M1 route. Well, half-time will do I suppose, as long as I get there.

The panic is over at a quarter to seven as the traffic begins to move and as is usually the case, all the evidence has been cleared up by the time the scene is passed. Loads of locals swarming around the ground, certainly compared to the last time I came here, should be a good crowd tonight then. Time for me to shoot over to Early Doors for a couple of quick pre-match liveners. It's packed out and I struggle to get to the bar. There's a few moody glances as the opposing fans aren't mixing too well, but there's no real malice in the air, probably due to the presence of several huge bouncers and the local constabulary.

By half past seven, the pub has all but emptied and we make our way back up the hill to Field Mill. Must say that they have done a very decent job of doing the place up, only the scout hut on the far side remains untouched, with the other three sides looking like three completely new stands. The weather is as shitty as it gets, driving rain and it's blowing a gale. Would now be a good time to admit that the blue long johns are making their second appearance of the season? Hell, why not! I'll wear them in May, OVER my trousers if they turn into a lucky charm. We enter the ground and I purchase a Bovril, another lucky charm for me as the more observant may have noticed. Until Stoke in the FA Cup when I really wanted a pie but there was a nice bird nearby and I didn't want to look like a fat git so just ordered a Bovril. The travelling support of 500 or so are all huddled at the back of the stand as the seats lower down are wet through and the wind is forcing the rain right at us. The team come out to a roar and the home support follows this up with a particularly poor rendition of 'yellows, yellows', I think they come out to a Rocky tune or something equally sycophantic, but pretty soon the Tannoy is drowned out by a forceful version of 'EE-AY-OH'. Once again, our away support isn't the biggest, but is certainly one of the best. The Mansfield lot try to bait us with their taunts of 'Who are ya, who are ya?' Well we all know the answer to this one by now don't we: 'WE ARE TOP OF THE LEAGUE, WE ARE TOP OF THE LEAGUE!' They fall for it every time, the mugs!

The players are ready and the referee is ready so, in the words of Alan Partridge, 'Let battle commence!' The conditions aren't exactly ideal for football but both sides are making an attempt to get at one another. We seem to get a hatful of chances early on, most of which fall to The Duke, a combination of bad luck and good goalkeeping holding us at bay. With the action being right down the far end though, it's very difficult to gauge what constitutes a clear-cut chance.

Mansfield are also lively up front, Iyseden Christie is putting himself about, and they also seem to be winning most of the ball in midfield, whereas we are hitting it long.

The majority of the chances fall our way, and on 38 minutes, The Duke rounds the keeper Kevin Pilkington and slots the ball home from a pass by McCulloch. 1–0. Very pleased for the lad, he's never let his head go down despite not scoring for a few games. Good to see intelligent play too, as he had already been thwarted by the keeper a couple of times – mixing it up a bit by shimmying round him in the blustery conditions. Wigan only have to wait four minutes for the next as Ellington and Teale combine to put Andy Liddell through, who pulls off a carbon copy of Ellington's earlier move to put us 2–0 up. The wind is blowing diagonally towards our corner, but simple, effective passing on the deck is ripping Mansfield to shreds.

No boozer inside at Field Mill so there's nothing else to do but go underneath the stand and have a warm, overhearing the many comments of 'We'll get six tonight' which, I will readily admit, looks well within our grasp. However, Mansfield pull one back shortly after the restart, great passing leading up to it and Matt Jackson goes in for the ball with Christie. Could be an own goal for all we can tell, but I think Christie would prefer to claim it. This serves as a wake-up call for the Latics, who go on the offensive, this time McCulloch has the lion's share of the chances. I count at least three occasions where he brings the ball down beautifully to set himself up, but fails to provide the killer finish. Ellington rattles the post and also creates an opening for Liddell by dragging the entire Stags' defence out of position to lay it off for Lidds, who shoots narrowly wide.

Of course, I am panicking by this stage. The more we try and fail to get a third, the more it enters my head that Mansfield are going to sneak an equaliser from somewhere. Despite the majority of possession, we are unable to make it count. The little blond lad (Disley) is battling hard for Mansfield in the middle, so the ball is increasingly being lofted over the top of him. The typical Wigan moves are just straight passing moves, without any real forward thrust, just playing keep-ball, before Kennedy hits a speculative one into the box. Repeat to fade, but as long as Mansfield aren't attacking this will do me. For once we aren't in any real danger and frustrating Mansfield to death, which results in two of their players making disgraceful tackles on Ellington and Teale. The Mansfield fans accuse them of play-acting which gets my usual retort of 'I'll come over there and do one on you in a minute!' A similar incident occurs when a player kicks the ball out while Lee McCulloch gets treated. The Mansfield player who takes the resultant throw decides to chuck it out of play near to the corner flag while his side is a goal down, rather than directly back to John Filan. Thicker than a Geordie's nostril hair some folk, even if his actions are in protest at McCulloch's play-acting, he must have looked a prize tit when the stretcher appeared. Hope it's not too serious though. Probably not, as McCulloch seems to get carried off every other week. In the absence of any ballboys, Filan walks verrryyy sllllowwllly over to the corner flag to retrieve the ball for a goalkick. We can tell from here that he's taking the piss and the Mansfield fans are going bloody mental. We find it highly amusing, but the referee doesn't and calls him over. The disturbing sight of big Dave Beasant stripping off sobers up our giggles. Just a yellow, phew!

The time added on is about right – four minutes, but we hold firm and send the buggers packing. Held in the car park for about 15 minutes, where matters turn a little interesting, to say the least. The Mansfield muppets are coming past trying to say we have poor support (how original) whereas the Wiganers are shouting 'SCABS, SCABS, SCABS!' (ditto). Looks very dodgy the way a line of stewards are separating the fans with verbals freely exchanged, but it doesn't go any further than that. Later, much later in fact, we are released and allowed back to our cars, still intact. My reward for getting here early is to be parked right at the back of the car park, meaning that it is ten o'clock before we even move. (Yep, I've got some drunken 'yoof' members for company now.) Forced to listen to orgasmic Leicester commentators on Century FM, with not a mention of the Stags' beating to raise a smile. A tiresome journey home, up the M1 and across the M62, arriving home at about midnight. Teletext on, long johns off, and bed. It may not be rock 'n' roll but it'll do for me!

FEBRUARY

FIRING BLANKS

1 February 2003, Cheltenham (h). Drew 0–0.

IT WAS AN AWAY GAME AT MACCLESFIELD IN 1999 WHEN I FIRST GOT TALKING seriously to Vaughanie about the *Cockney Latic*, a day which later turned into a memorable evening around Piccadilly in Manchester. I remember, years earlier in 1987, when the first ever edition came out and I went up and scavenged a copy as a 15-year-old at Brentford. The talk at Macc was of starting the magazine up again and I started submitting articles and attending the regular meetings over the summer in The Brocket to discuss how to get started again. How I became editor, I haven't got a clue, but the frustration of it taking up so much of my spare time is more than offset by the buzz when a new issue hits the streets.

The speculation all week has been that we are signing Peterborough's Jimmy Bullard. I am questioning whether we need another midfielder, as we have four decent central midfielders already. All the noises I have heard about Bullard suggest that he is class, but listening to Jewell on WISH on the Wednesday morning I find myself arguing with him while stuck on the M6. Jewell says, 'We don't need another striker.' I say, 'Yes we do, desperately, it's another midfielder we don't need.' The first half against Stoke made my mind up when Liddell and Roberts were up front. Despite the great qualities that both players have, we just had no presence at all in the final third. Only when Ellington came on in the second half did we pose any real kind of threat up front, by which time the game was over. I believe the reason that we find ourselves in such a lofty position is at least partly due to the good fortune of The Duke not picking up a serious injury during the course of the season. Still, he's the gaffer, not me, who is incapable of even managing a Soccerdome side, and I'm about to veer into the central reservation if I don't concentrate on the road, so best to leave it. Bullard signs for £275,000, Hasselbaink stays at Stamford Bridge.

Cheltenham are rock bottom, we are top; if ever there is a game where we should dish out that 6–0 drubbing it is today. The Robins have managed to take points at Oldham and Cardiff though, so can't be taken lightly. Bullard starts on the left-hand side of midfield in place of the suspended Lee McCulloch. I'm a little concerned that signing him has maybe had an unsettling effect on the other players, but one thing's for sure, the lad's a footballer. A very good passer of the ball, although he's struggling to come to terms with our weather-beaten pitch. The first attack sees Teale put clean through within the first ten minutes, but he hits his shot straight at the keeper. He then puts a lovely ball over for The Duke, whose header is tipped over. It's just a matter of time here. Cheltenham aren't without their chances, and the big fella Alsop is putting himself about a bit, along with Spencer and, latterly, Bristol City loanee, Marvin Brown. The score is 0–0 at half-time but we've had the lion's share of the possession, and are safe in the knowledge that we usually come out roaring at the start of the second half. There's little cause for concern about the stalemate.

Cheltenham are tight and resolute. They are throwing their bodies on the line to get in the way and succeeding in frustrating the home team. It's now possible to see how they are getting results at the likes of Ninian Park. They are doing more than their fair share of time-wasting, but even so we've got a whole 90 minutes to score a goal. Considering we were expecting to score at least five, it shouldn't be so difficult. Midway through the second half, there is further evidence that it isn't going to be our day as the Cheltenham keeper pulls off an amazing double save: first from Ellington and then immediately from Liddell. Both attempts a matter of a few yards from goal and both saved right on the line. Fantastic goalkeeping when both look certain goals. Further chances come our way, but we just can't seem to put the thing in the net today, and to blame the home team would be doing Cheltenham an injustice.

In the dying seconds, Ellington has a cheeky back-heel plucked from the goal line in agonising fashion, and we resign ourselves to settling for a point. Oldham and Cardiff drew the previous night, and, as it turns out, Crewe and Bristol City fare no better today. All things are as they were before the start of play, but there's one less game with which to catch us. The point is taken begrudgingly, because we know we could have had three. Good luck to Cheltenham, a proper club that have come from non-league like ourselves and don't have that chip on their shoulders like some of our North-west neighbours have.

A BLACKPOOL FAN WRITES

8 February 2003, Blackpool (h). Drew 1–1.

Now I pride myself on being 100 per cent fair-minded and unbiased throughout this book. It would take a cynical person to suggest otherwise. I have reported on events as I have seen them with my own eyes. I support a fantastic football team, who are deservedly top of the league playing great football. Why would anyone consider taking offence at a former non-league club 'living the dream' so to speak? After numerous Internet slanging matches between Wigan and Blackpool fans in recent times, I feel it is only fair to give one of 'their lot' the opportunity to offer their point of view. The following review has been gratefully received from the perspective of a Blackpool fan, and is printed in its unedited form. Don't contact me!

'They say that honesty is the best policy, and I'm going to be entirely honest with you. I don't like Wigan Athletic, in fact, let's be brutally honest, I hate Wigan Athletic. In fact I'd probably face the wrath of a few Blackpool fans by confessing that they rate above Preston in my list of most-hated teams! You're right up there lads. Numero Uno, top of the shop, you are the team I despise the most. Congratulations. So why do I hold you in such contempt? In all honesty, it goes back to those Springfield Road days and has escalated since. Indeed, it's strange that at the time I started curling up my lip and screwing my nose at the mention of the word "Wigan", one of the main reasons for my dislike of your club now wasn't even around. Lord of the JJB hadn't got his cheque book out at the time, and you were playing in that hovel that purported to be a football ground.

'So why did I have such bad memories of Springfield Park? Well, for a start we never won there, or if we did I must have been sat in my car refusing to go in. The ground was a death trap! I got food poisoning off the burgers (and why were there never any pies in the away end?), I got flu after standing in the rain for two hours and often felt physically sick as we were dumped out of cups and denied points in the league. Then there was Stuart Barlow – the little peroxide dwarf who always used to score against us – I still can't abide the little nonce to this day! So as you can see my dislike was in place before old moneybags came along. When he did my disdain grew even more. I hated Al-Fayed at Fulham, Hammam at Cardiff, Madjeski at Reading and Whelan at Wigan. How dare they come along with their money and buy their way up the league. Even worse, they did so with irrelevant little clubs whose lives should have been spent in the basement divisions (apart from Cardiff, who should be in the Welsh League). Maybe it's because we had a millionaire owner who didn't plough his fortune into the club that I have this bitter and not particularly flattering view!

'Now, fair play, the JJB is a nice ground but, let's be honest, it's an embarrassment every home game. I'll be first to admit that Blackpool's crowds have some way to go and we started off with a much bigger fan base 50 years ago than you could ever dream of. However, we're not in an over-sized stadium built for egg chasing. Our stands are over 80 per cent full at home games – your stands are only good for playing "spot the spectator" in, and why do you spread out so much! Does everyone in Wigan smell? You want to see the sight from the away side – it's laughable! The first season we were behind the goal and one of the main stands wasn't being used (prompting the chant of "what the hell is that stand for"), at least it made the other two stands look busier. To be top of the table and attract such small numbers is testimony to the fact you'll never be a big club and I don't think Wigan ever deserves to be.

'So on to today's game. Robin Park has got the worst car park of any ground in the country and it would be easier to walk home than sit in the traffic on a Saturday. I can only presume the traffic is generated from people going to Frankie and Benny's rather than those who've bothered to go to the football. Thus we always arrive early and wander around Wigan. I should at this point try and pull back from this turning into a persecution of Wigan and its people because I have nothing against either. I've always found Wiganers to be very affable, friendly and polite folk. I think any problems between the fans over the years has stemmed from ignorance on both sides and the fact that every club has its hardcore lunatics. Just because I have a deep hatred for Wigan Athletic doesn't mean that I won't be courteous and polite to Latics supporters, engage in friendly banter and act like a sane and reasonable human being. I think that's where the minority are misguided. The dislike of a football team is a fairly irrational thing anyway, and therefore to attack someone just because they support that club is irrational. There again, I can't abide these do-gooders who say you should concentrate on your own team and be dispassionate about others! Garbage! I enjoy a Wigan and Preston defeat on a Saturday as much as the next Blackpool fan. It can never come near the emotion of a Seasiders win or make up for a tangerine defeat, but I always listen out for the result in the hope of gleaning some pleasure from your misery!

'It's a big game when we play Wigan and for us to go behind within 46 seconds knocks the Seasiders' sick, I actually felt quite nauseous before the game anyway; such is my desire to win the match. It's probably due to my biased view of Wigan that I feel again totally unimpressed with your team, even though you have the better chances in the first half. "Duke" (why do you nick the Van Nistelrooy chant, that is so cringey!) seems a complete waste of £1.2 million and appears nothing more than a lumbering old donkey who's probably Goater-esque (i.e. flatters to deceive thanks to the number of goals he scores). There are some decent players in your ranks – Andy Liddell is a cheating little runt (straight out of the Barlow mould) but I wouldn't mind him in our side, De Vos, Dinning and Bullard all catch my eye and Filan is undoubtedly one of the best keepers in the division. Paul Jewell is pretty uncomplimentary, though, saying you were the better team in both halves – my arse! Once we swap Taylor for Walker we are by far the better team for the last half hour and thoroughly deserve our point. Clearly the Wigan "crowd" think that as well, as we don't hear a peep out of them second half – always a sign that supporters know their team is under pressure.

'The referee, Mr Laws, is crap for both teams but if you've experienced what we have this season then that will have come as little surprise. I have to say I am amazed at how much you hoof the ball, but then again your pitch is hardly conducive to passing football (either that or your players have mistakenly turned up at rugby training). OK, you are a decent, strong, physical team, but nothing special and I'd enjoy this promotion, as I doubt if you'll see the top half of the first division with this team next year.

'Just finally the pies – absolutely magnificent! A credit to the name of the pie-eaters! So a 1–1 draw which benefits us as much as you and unless we sneak in the play-offs probably our last meeting for some time. I can't say that I'll miss you but you never know, absence makes the heart grow fonder and maybe this time apart will finally heal those deep-rooted scars of hatred that I have for Wigan Athletic and one day I may even be able to come to the JJB without a permanent scowl on my face. Good luck.'

Thank you for your contribution!

DEJA CREWE

15 February 2003, Crewe (a). Don't bloody ask!

I've been to Crewe to watch the Latics on a few occasions in the past, but the one that sticks out most in my mind is Boxing Day 1993, when the game wasn't actually played due to a frozen pitch. Most of us had already arrived and five of us went on the piss around Crewe all day, well what else is there to do when the game gets called off? None of that today as we arrive at Wigan North Western at 10.40 a.m. with dazzling sunshine glaring off the glass façade. Today is going to be a great day, I know this for a fact when I am stood on the platform amongst hundreds of expectant Wiganers. There's a hundred gone on the earlier train and another 300 coming on the next one. The Transport Police have pulled their usual stunt of blocking the station entrance so we are all forced to pay up an extortionate £10.15 for a half an hour train ride. There's nowhere to sit (is there ever?) so I am wedged in a doorway supping a tinnie and trying to sell Neil M some Burberry's paint for his new house. Tickets have been at a premium for this game, Manny thankfully sorting me out using one of his sons' season tickets. Crewe have given us a 1,600 allocation, which sold out in days, and are refusing to give us more despite huge demand.

We alight at Crewe and are faced with a Riot Policeman's Ball. We've heard the 'rehearsal for Cardiff' rumour but this is farcical. Arsenal are coming in on their way to Old Trafford, but there's nothing planned. We can see them peering through their train windows looking terrified, but it's not their firm, just lads on the way to the game. We are penned in on the platform, as 300 people try to depart the police block the exit demanding that we are searched individually. Other passengers are missing trains because of this blockade, how very noble of you. Of course, we are being jostled and filmed and generally treated like criminals. Now I'm not insinuating these people are thick, but their attempts to keep the Arsenal and Wigan fans separate are comical. They stop one lad who is 6 ft 4 in. with floppy hair. 'Are you Wigan or Arsenal?' It's a tough question for the lad with the red and white Arsenal shirt, complete with 'PIRES 7' emblazoned on the back. It takes us half an hour to get off the station where we are each filmed, searched and asked to show proof of match ticket. We head straight for the hotel on the corner because we are parched. The bouncers on the door also ask us to show match tickets. Why, it's a pub, isn't it? And there's nothing to stop one person with a ticket going in and bringing 20 back out with him for the others. Dean gets the Guinness in and we find a good spot to take in the aforementioned United vs. Arsenal FA Cup tie.

It is around about 11.30 a.m. when the news comes through. There is a pitch inspection at half past twelve. It's a formality, it must be, the sun's out and I'm sweating cobs with a big Paul & Shark jacket on. Settle down, watch the game, and watch the streams of Wiganers ambling off the train into Crewe. An hour later and we get the news first from Penky, who is down near the ground with some Crewe mates of his: it's off, the game is off. Not again, what is it with this bloody place? The Chinese whisper goes around the pub, which is by now jam-packed with Wiganers. People are asking me 'Is it off?' I hate to be the bearer of bad news, and am beginning to doubt myself. Must be a hoax, but the people I've spoken to don't do that. We feel completely and utterly cheated. As the rumour goes, it is perfectly playable by the time 3 p.m. comes around, but by this time we're all eight pints of Guinness to the good and cursing anything and everything about Crewe.

There is talk of going to Northwich, or Port Vale vs. QPR, or Stockport vs. Oldham (can't think why!) but I can't do this – I can watch football anywhere at any level, but I do like gearing myself up for a game. I set out this morning to watch Wigan Athletic, now that has been taken away from me, I settle on a drunken crawl around Warrington instead, where events quickly turn very, very silly. The two hours usually spent at the game often serve as sobering-up time, take that away and the coppers have got real problems on their hands. They shut the pubs at three in Crewe, so we simply head off to Warrington and get drunk there. I suppose Crewe will keep for another day, but we could have been 12 points clear by now, and that's the galling thing. Of course Crewe might have pulled our lead back to six, but I don't think so somehow. A few bales of hay or some plastic sheets and an out of the blue postponement could have easily been avoided. Next time we'll have 'em!

WY-COMBE FROM WIGAN AND WE LIVE IN MUDHUTS

22 February 2003, Wycombe Wanderers (a). Won 2–0.

Ah, the contrast of a visit to Wycombe. On the negative side, the ground is in the middle of nowhere with very little to occupy the visiting fans. We usually get around this by paying a visit to the splendid hamlet of Thame in Oxfordshire, an excellent jaunt for a mini pub crawl. The standard script: 8 a.m. start on the coach, an 11 a.m. arrival is perfectly possible but we reckon without the likes of Heeley (who is late and the coach picks him up from his door in Beech Hill after everyone else has had to trudge to the Gas Showrooms) and Caddy (who plays his 'dump stop' card at Frankley services). Abuse aimed at the pair of 'em! Despite my intentions to potter about, have some food and a bet, I don't make it any further than the Sports Bar of The Abingdon Arms and pretty soon the beer is flowing.

We carry on to Wycombe, just time to engage in a bit of scran and a chat and then it's game on. Wycombe are one of the few teams in the Second Division with nothing left to play for this season, not that I expect them to be any less dangerous than any of our other opponents. We have to beat Wycombe regardless and keep the points ticking over – we've only taken two points throughout the whole of February for God's sake!

Wigan's reputation away from home is one to be feared, unless your name is Swindon Town, so with that in mind, Wycombe look edgy. It takes all of nine minutes for the away side to register. I am yapping away to someone behind me and just catch the arse end of a Teale cross being bundled in by Lee McCulloch a matter of yards away from us. Excellent, 1–0 up before we've even broken sweat. Although the occupants of my coach are the same giddy bunch who made Roy Carroll concede a goal a couple of years ago due to their manic Billy Joel sing-along, the atmosphere is much more serene today. We're getting a bit blasé in our old age. 'What what, fine goal, old bean!' and a quick tilt of the titfer is acknowledgement enough compared with the monster pitch invasion of previous years. They just make it too easy at some grounds.

The first half is all Wigan, there are a couple of chances to extend the lead but nothing too clear-cut from the usual suspects De Vos, Lidds and The Duke. Wycombe, the home side, are very off-colour today, and although my view of what is happening at the far end isn't too great, I can just make out John Filan building a pyramid out of playing cards in the goalmouth to relieve his boredom. Jimmy Bullard, playing on a decent surface for the first time, is the Lord of the Pass, the man has a touch so sublime that he must have Bostik on his boots to control it and a geometry set to release it with such accuracy. He's too quick for the rest of them if anything, and by that I mean always one step ahead with his head, not his feet. He will become a real asset, once the other players pass their NVQ in Extra Sensory Perception. He resembles Zinedine Zidane at times, when the Frenchman sports that blonde wig of his.

We appear to have knocked Wycombe off their game before the game has even kicked off by opting to attack towards our own fans in the first half, thus forcing them to attack towards several hundred gurning northerners in the second half. There will be no Wycombe 'Kop End' trying to suck the ball in during the second half, they will have to blow instead which I don't believe has the same effect. Funny how this concept, which seems to have originated at Anfield, has now spread to every ground in the country. Even at Wigan, where both ends are designated home fans' areas, we still seem to perform better with a more vocal atmosphere when attacking the South Stand in the second half. Nevertheless, just time to deal with a chronic digestive problem and purchase a pasty (7/10) before the second half gets underway.

Wycombe come out determined to make a go of it. They create numerous chances, but the Wigan back four holds wonderfully firm. Latics, not for the first time this season, are content to soak the pressure up, which they do admirably. Matt Jackson and Nicky Eaden make two brave tackles to prevent certain Wycombe equalisers. And then, right in the last minute, a foray forward by Steve McMillan sees him felled in the box by a tackle. A penalty is awarded which Andy Liddell gleefully slots home to seal the game. 2–0 and job done. The players milk the applause and we file onto our coaches via some greasy burger van.

It takes bloody ages to get out of the road leading from the ground and, typically, when we do get out, we get hopelessly lost. A quick provisions stop at ASDA and, as our coach departs, we see another Wigan coach parked up by the side of the road. It's the team coach, and, to a man, we are jumping about, singing, cheering and waving like gibbons at them. Jimmy Bullard is laughing whereas David Lowe just looks gobsmacked! Back on the right road home, it must be nearly six o'clock and we're still in Wycombe, no surprise to see that the ground is less than half a mile away as well. In the absence of a video, the next move is to get the karaoke going. Shannon obliges with 'Let's Hang On', while Rammy offers some Meatloaf and Billy Joel's 'Tell Her About It'. His set is interrupted by Caddy walking down the coach completely naked while holding a silver platter (don't ask!), followed by an Elvis medley, and before long everyone's engaged in a sing-along.

By the time we've got back to Wigan and had a few pints in The

Swan and Railway, everyone is steaming and the sight is not a pretty one. Just what is it with Wycombe that everyone ends up in a ridiculous state? Another top day out with our nine-point lead maintained for posterity. The companies formerly known as British Rail have a lot to answer for, but I think they actually did us a favour by making their service so poor. One of the best away trips I ever had was to Wycombe on the train a few years ago. In the home end, shenanigans at Euston, a mob of 20 serious loons and hilarious behaviour all day from a certain Wigan Gunner. All this when Kenny Swain was manager and we couldn't beat the blind school Under-9s. (There go the sales of the Braille version of this book.) From what I hear, fans up and down the country opt for the coach over the train nowadays, although it must be an interesting conversation when the Millwall organiser has to ring up to try and book a pre-match pub! The next stop on our coach travels will be Peterborough away, but not before a crucial rearranged game with Crewe is negotiated. First vs. Second at Gresty Road promises to be a cracker.

YOU'LL WIN NOTHING WITH KIDS

25 February 2003, Crewe Alexandra (a). Won 1–0.

None of the Robocop treatment for me on the train this time, as I decide to work until six and then make the two-junction trip down the motorway from work. Park up on the industrial estate on the other side of the station and then walk into town for a couple of swift ones. In the pub I land in, The Bank, all the talk is of tickets, I've had loads of people mithering me for spares. It's been exactly the same on the website, both for the postponed game and tonight and I don't think I've ever seen such demand for tickets for a Latics game. Mine is safely tucked in a zipped-up inside pocket and I keep feeling through my coat to check it's there. It's hard to get into the pre-match buzz because I'm sober and it's probably just as well, judging by the amount of coppers roaming about. We make our way towards the Alexandra Stadium aka Gresty Road via a ticket check-point and John and I buy a Crewe fanzine. John is berating the poor seller. 'How much? £1.50? For only

32 pages! No colour either! And you only sell 400 copies!' I keep quiet, as my ulterior motive is, as ever, to see if there's anything worth ripping off in there. Hmm, bits and bobs, not a bad read and I always feel a bit of solidarity with a fellow fanzine editor.

Through the turnstiles, following a third ticket check, and onto what passes as the away end at Crewe. The scene five minutes before kick-off is absolute carnage, nobody has got a seat. The original advice for people to sit in their allocated seat has been ignored and it's dangerously overcrowded. Not for the first time, whispers of forgeries are being floated about. A full side of the ground holding 1,600 has been allocated for the away support for this all-ticket game, but the other three sides of the ground fail to fill up despite Wiganers present on all sides due to a variety of blags pulled. The family stand to our left has only a few hundred in it, why didn't they give us that as well? There are heated exchanges going on between fans and stewards, the gangways are full of bodies and the area at the front is full of people milling about as well. In the middle of all this, there's a match to be played!! The teams take to the field to a vociferous roar from one side of the ground, and a muted cheer from the other sides as well. A bloke near me comments, 'That mon looks like the Karate Kid,' pointing to Crewe's Nigerian international Efe Sodje. Possibly the most ironic comment I have ever heard, as within 15 seconds of the game kicking off, Sodje lunges feet first at Lee McCulloch, planting them deep into his chest and thigh. One of the worst challenges I have ever seen and possibly the only time in his career that this particular thug could be compared to Cantona. I used to quite like Sodje, he's a very distinctive and colourful player (no pun intended) with his bandana and has quite a story behind his career, going back to his Macclesfield days. But this time he's gone too far. The referee cowardly gives him a yellow, which is beyond belief, and the only mitigating circumstance I can think of that allows him to stay on the pitch is that we haven't even played half a minute of the game yet. McCulloch is less fortunate and has to be stretchered off (again), to be replaced by Neil Roberts. The Crewe fans, incredulously, boo McCulloch and are now booing the referee. Sodje gets a rousing round of applause off the Crewe fans for his assault. Dickheads!

Both sides are nervous but equally committed to playing football. Like ourselves, getting herded around the away end, they have to keep moving to keep pace with the game. We're at the front of the seats bouncing about and giving the Crewe team a load of shit. I reckon this is good fun until I realise how silly I must look with my nice work-pants on and shiny shoes. We eventually find some seats right at the far end of the stand, where the view is terrible, and at the opposite end to where we are attacking. However, by this point us 'hooligans' have had the police cameras trained firmly on us and have been categorised as key troublemakers for committing the heinous crime of not sitting in a seat that doesn't exist. The view is so awful that we eventually end up stood behind the disabled section, utter chaos, but this'll do. We can see the near-side goal though, and Sodje, not content with maiming McCulloch, attempts to do the same to his replacement, Roberts, by sticking his arm across his face. Roberts drops to the floor and, this time, surely Sodje must go. The referee has no hesitation, or even an alternative, but to get the second yellow card out and send him off.

Now I know Crewe did a lot of whinging the last time we met that they hadn't been able to play us 11 vs. 11, but whose fault is that exactly? We are pleased as punch, simply because this game is so unbelievably crucial: a Crewe win will put them (and Cardiff) just two wins behind us, a Wigan win will put us 12 points clear. Crewe make an immediate substitution, presumably bringing on another defender. The ten men of Crewe come out fighting, as is usually the case, and their front men take turns to carry out spectacular dives whenever they are so much as touched, and on a few occasions when they aren't, in an attempt to level the sides up. Cheating bastards. As the dust settles on the sending off, Wigan start to dominate proceedings, Dinning hits the woodwork and the Alex keeper, Clayton Ince, is pulling out all the stops. Why do we keep coming up against these blinding goalies? Not that I'd swap any of them for the Aussies' number 1, of course!

A goal arrives on 37 minutes and it's in our favour. The splendid Nicky Eaden puts a cross over which isn't cleared, in the confusion a little chip in by Roberts finds Ellington completely unmarked at the far post and he gleefully tucks it home from all of two yards. The travelling masses go barmy, a tap-in maybe, but that could be THE biggest goal of the season. If Crewe weren't up against it before they certainly are now! We come close to doubling our lead when Roberts, from another

Eaden cross (someone's counting, Nicky!) hits the post with a header which looks easier to put away. Liddell is guilty, as well, of not tucking away the rebound, but to be fair to him, the keeper makes a fine blocking save. Half-time comes and goes, one look at the monstrous food queue makes me decide that I'm not hungry after all, and there's bugger all chance of a beer because there's no bar.

The second half sees a lot of football played without the creation of any real opportunities. Crewe defy their one-man deficit with some neat passing and great forward running by the impressive Rodney Jack and Steve Jones. It's not happening for them, though, as their final ball is woeful on too many occasions. The latter of the two is clattered by Tony Dinning early in the second half, a challenge which incenses Crewe fans and sees the young striker carried off with a suspected broken leg. Just a yellow for Dinning as well, and I genuinely 'didn't get a clear enough view' to call it otherwise. Even though Crewe are chasing the game, it's us who look like the ten-man outfit as Ellington is pulled out to the left wing while Roberts is the sole front man. We are cursing the manager at the time for this tactic, but it works as Crewe fail to equalise. The Duke goes down a storm on the left wing, running and dribbling at the Crewe defence, stopping and starting and running the ball down into the corner in front of us.

When Crewe get a corner with 12 minutes to go, their keeper goes flying up the field to join them, but he's not going to be a hero on this occasion. As the ball clears, we break and come close to getting that elusive second but for the covering defender's intervention. We seem to have settled for just the one, but are playing it and passing it around well, much of the play controlled by the wonderful James Bullard. The final whistle brings both relief and elation: we've done our nearest rivals and put 12 points between us and them. If evidence were required as to Wigan's dominance of the match, then it is found when Crewe's man of the match is their goalkeeper, well merited too. As the hordes make their way back to the train station, I face a solitary walk back to my car. I wish I were going back on the train with the masses and then around Wigan for a few joyous beers, but opt out. I am, nevertheless, quietly content with the evening's events which have seen us take a Neil Armstrong-sized step towards Division One, our closest rivals soundly dispatched.

MARCH

NAILED ON FOR DIVISION ONE

1 March 2003, Chesterfield (h). Won 3–1.

MATT'S ON HOLIDAY, SO AS I AM DRIVING ABOUT I AM LISTENING TO GRAHAM LOVETT on WISH FM uttering the above statement about my club. I'm the most pessimistic man alive and refuse to believe that we are promoted until the little yellow 'P' appears next to our name on *Grandstand*. I've got a banging head because I attended a cracking Sportsman's Dinner at Aspull on the Friday night, at which plenty of money was raised. Just as well, really, as a bunch of gypsies have camped on and ruined their pitches. They still look better than the JJB turf at the moment, though. A quick pop into The Brickmaker's to pay some coach money and collect some magazine articles and then on to the JJB. As I nip into the bogs underneath the South Stand, there is a group of mulleted teenagers all wearing hoods and blue-and-black-striped football shirts and they've got the broadest Wiggin accents I've ever heard. On closer inspection, they're actually Belgians, followers of FC Bruges in fact, God knows what they're doing at the JJB, but bloody good luck to them. I can only consider that it's the 'Champ Manager' effect. I've had it two years and still not got further than pre-season, I think I'm scared that it might bring out the addictive streak in me.

The key factor in today's game is whether Tuesday night's massive result has taken a bit of steam out of us. Can we lift ourselves for the visit of an uninspiring bunch such as Chesterfield? The answer, in a season that is now reaching epic heights, is an emphatic YES. Neil Roberts is recalled to the starting line-up in the place of the sawn-in-half McCulloch, who has miraculously made it onto the bench. I notice from Teletext that the 'broken leg' Crewe player also makes a quick recovery, nothing to do with both our respective teams being up at the top of the table and the players being shit scared of losing their places, I suppose. Chesterfield pose very little threat and after 25 minutes a rare foray forward by them is easily cleared and falls to Gary Teale near the halfway line. Teale runs with the ball, cuts inside, beats one man, and then another (and here's where it normally goes tits up) but no, he jinks into the box and hits a great strike into the top corner! Goal of the season, perhaps? Well, I can't think of a better one at the moment. Call it in my top three, along with The Duke vs. Luton and Liddell's chip at Notts County. 1–0 up and cruising.

Fifteen minutes later and we're 2–0 up. All the credit for this goal must go to Ellington – great chasing and hassling sees him dispossess Chesterfield's Steve Payne by the left-hand corner. He runs it in on the byline and pulls it back for Bullard, whose shot is good, but the keeper pulls off a strong reaction save. Unlucky for him, it comes out to Tony Dinning, who smacks it right back past him and into the net. 2–0 up and not even half-time, today's the day we'll get six, I tell you! Well done to the Guv'nor Dinning for tucking that one away, Bullard's getting closer by the minute and The Duke's going through another lean spell, but both are contributing to the game and playing out of their skins.

Listen to the half-times, Cardiff are losing, Crewe are drawing, who cares about the rest? My coupon has ducked like a good 'un – £10 on 3 aways, an easy £150 return, just how easy can it be? Forest, who won 6–1 midweek, at Watford – no. Luton, play-off chasing and playing mid-table Notts County – no. Southend, just released two players including ex-Wigan favourite Graeme Jones – should give the rest the kick up the arse to beat woeful Macclesfield, again – no. Time to give up – yes!

Second half cannot come soon enough, and Latics start it in typical attacking fashion. Ellington is testing the Chesterfield keeper but the young fella between the sticks is equal to everything he tries. The Duke wants his elusive twentieth of the season. The frustration briefly creeps in as Chesterfield have a go back, eventually winning a very dubious penalty. Diving bastard! Still I've seen them given for less. John Filan is fuming again, and is jumping about doing mock dives, insinuating to the referee that the player went down in instalments. It's not going to change the poor old, harassed man in black's mind, though. David Reeves, sadly ignored by the bulk of our younger crowd who are unable to identify his status as a former Bolton bastard, steps up to slot it home and, at 2–1, a murky cloud of doubt starts to emerge over the JJB. What was the other one called? Philliskirk, that was it, Tony Philliskirk – him and Reeves were the two forwards for the forces of darkness from Burnden Park around about 1990. A pair of pretentious blonde bombshells who looked like the brothers from Bros, and played like them most of the time. A third of the game to go and the next goal is crucial.

Chesterfield appear to be slipping towards the relegation zone, so won't be saying no to a point if they can grab one. Their faint hopes are short-lived though, as on 74 minutes, Roberts is fouled in the box, again not the most blatant foul I've ever seen but at least it evens it up. Liddell, taking his fifth penalty of the season, tucks it away in exactly the same manner as the previous four, a quick shimmy then in the corner. Someone's going to suss him one of these days and I'd be amazed if, at professional level, the opposing club isn't perfectly aware prior to kick-off of Liddell's quirky penalty-taking technique. Still, who cares, 3–1 it is and the home crowd immediately perks up again with the current fave, 'We'll never play you again'. Arrogant in the extreme, but those of us who have followed the club through the dark days and even suffered through our recent play-off failures have the right to get a bit overexcited. The game is as good as over, the last 15 minutes are the equivalent of Michael Schumacher doing a celebratory lap at half pace.

I think the players love the JJB on the 'big' days but often find it as tepid as we do for the run-of-the-mill games like today. We may be top of the league but it's only Division Two and we're playing Chesterfield, not Chelsea. Today, ultimate professionals that they are, they grind out a splendid 3–1 result, while Crewe lose at home to Peterborough, and Cardiff can only draw at Stockport. It seems that no one else wants promotion and we're now a mesmerising 15 points clear at the top. Not for the first time this season a planned night in is shelved and turns into a drunken night out.

THE RETURN OF BAMBI

4 March 2003, Tranmere Rovers (h). Drew 0–0.

Once again a lily-livered Welshman is all the talk of the town prior to this game. To boo or not to boo, that is the question. Well for a start, I have doubts whether our home crowd could even muster up half the abuse that poor old Simon copped in the first game over at Prenton Park. And, secondly, there is the nagging doubt that maybe this time it will work against us, and the gangly Taff will fire in a hat-trick to destroy our promotion-chasing confidence. Clearly, the most mature attitude to take here is to ignore the ex-Wigan Athletic player altogether and concentrate on getting behind our own current players, but then football fans aren't exactly known for mature behaviour, so there's fat chance of that. Forget about Richard Hillman murdering Maxine Peacock, there's only one pantomime baddie on the tip of most Wiganers' lips right now, and that's the Ayatollah-ing Simon 'Bambi' Haworth.

With all due respect to Chesterfield, this is an altogether bigger game tonight. The Haworth/Barlow/Mathias factor, a controversial and exciting earlier game at Tranmere, the local derby aspect and Tranmere chasing that last play-off spot. Bring all these factors into play, and it's no surprise that, at last, we are to receive top billing on *Granada Soccernight.* Goals aplenty required then!

There's big, big queues to get in, but as we've established now for night games, it can either mean that there is going to be a decent gate or that there is absolutely no one actually in the ground and all 5,342 are in the queue to get in at 7.39 p.m. It turns out to be the former, as a crowd of over 9,000 is present, with an estimated 1,500 Wirralites making the journey under the Mersey. This is an above-average home crowd, but as regards the ferocity of each team's support – well, it's a complete role reversal from the game at Prenton. The Tranmere fans sing their 'Super White Army' (useful for those watching *Soccernight* in monochrome later on as Tranmere are wearing yellow) and bang their bloody drums with great enthusiasm from start to finish. The home support is a little quiet, only raising a decibel or two to direct the time-honoured chant of 'Simon Haworth is a wanker!'. But it's the game on the pitch that matters, and we settle down to watch our boys take these plastic Scousers apart for the second time this season.

Tranmere settle in no time at all, sitting deep and attempting to counter. They seem to have more men in midfield than us and are passing it about whereas we are knocking it long and hitting the channels. Slight nerves are evident, and the loud Tranmere support appears to be sustaining their team's early confidence. They don't possess any great ideas as to how to break down this superlative Wigan defence, though. The first real chance comes from Liddell whipping a ball in from his unfamiliar left-wing berth, it's partially cleared but when Neil Roberts comes to claim it, he is knocked flying. The usual South Stand crew are debating who is going to take the free kick. Only two players offer themselves forward, Bullard and Liddell. Have you ever seen a team with so many players in possession of so many double letters in their names? Ellington, Dinning, McMillan, Kennedy, Flynn, Jarrett, Mitchell, McCulloch, Brannan (for not much longer) even the manager himself – Jewell, spooky eh? While I am considering this, Liddell steps up from 25 yards out and curls a beauty which hits the angle of post and crossbar, almost too perfect. As it bounces back out, Eaden pumps it back into the danger area, Roberts turns well but sends the rebound over. Change your name to Rrobberts, son!

Tranmere jolt back into action and create a couple of chances of their own, Haworth hits a superb crossfield ball to the youngster Hume, with all the nonchalance you would expect from a naturally gifted player who can't be arsed running with it. There's then a minor bout of fisticuffs with that mopheaded fatty, Jason Price in the thick of the action. I remember saying we should sign him all of two years ago, when he was a slim, pacy, free-scoring centre-forward for Brentford. He's now a sad midfield plodder at 25, although he looks like Kate Moss compared to his accomplice, Gary Jones, who is carrying more weight than Phar Lap. Twenty minutes gone and more Wigan pressure sees Dinning get a clear sight on goal, but his weak shot is easily saved by Achtung-burg or whatever he's called. The ball is hoisted upfield and Haworth once again finds Hume with a superb ball, the lazy Welshman's got himself a great foil here in a youngster who will do his running! Fortunately, Hume knocks it inside and a Tranmere midfielder skies his shot. On the half-hour, Price brings down McMillan near the left touch-line, and the resultant free kick from Bullard nearly goes straight in the net. Ian Hume is proving to be a real livewire up front. Both he and Haworth are getting murdered in the air, but the youngster is making inroads when he runs at pace at the Wigan back four. Another great run sees him lay it off for Rovers' Alex Hay, who hits a feeble shot wide. Plenty of chances, but absolutely no goals to deliberate over. 0–0 at half-time.

Haworth, I have to concede, is having an impressive game. He hasn't had any clear chances, and when he looks like getting one early in the second half and the ball runs away from him, I am very pleased with that outcome. There's no doubting that he has the ability to score tonight, we know that only too well. We also know about his petulant side and really don't want that to rear its ugly head on this occasion either. We'd never hear the last of it. Tranmere's best chance of the game is created by Haworth, who engineers a perfect opportunity for Price, 12 yards out. Please no, another horrible git, don't let him score either! What looks like a routine save by Filan from a weak shot is actually confirmed later on the telly as a great reflex save as the antipodean gets down quickly to smother the goalbound ball. Phew!! As we enter the last half an hour, Tranmere are content to hang on to their point, whereas Wigan go on the offensive to try and take all three. We get about 300 corners but fail to convert any, due to epic rearguard activity from the Tranmere formation scrambling team. At one stage during a goalmouth tussle, De Vos, Lidds and Mitchell all try to force the issue, the ball looks over, but isn't. The only thing in the back of the net is that nark Haworth, pulling faces at the South Stand faithful.

A moment of pie-choking horror nearly occurs as Haworth charges forward and hits a beautiful 30-yard screamer . . . oooh blimey missus (once again can't be arsed running any further), Filan calmly watches it sail over the bar while we plan intolerable revenge crimes against sheep. The Rovers fans continue their unbelievably muppet-ish 'Pigbag' Simon Haworth chant, while we revert back to Plan A by questioning his parentage. More Wigan pressure sees more corners, must be 500 by now, more goalmouth clearances, more clearances pumped back into the box. It's a major bombardment but the Tranmere back line is impenetrable. The travelling fans are jubilant with their point and Haworth yet again treats us to his 'Ayatollah' salute, he'll grow up one day, I presume.

Final score 0–0. A great game for the TV cameras, not. As a Latics fan, though, it's nevertheless a thrill to get good coverage so the video is set and programmed. Jewell and De Vos trot out the clichés: 'We've won nothing yet' and damn bloody right as well. The panellists fail to give us much credit, instead offering it to Tranmere's resilient defence, but we're used to that by now. Exactly what sort of game would it have been had the home side performed in that manner? Answer: none. With the possible exceptions of Wycombe and Cardiff, every team has come to the JJB to defend. Perhaps the reason that our form has been so good is because no one does it as well as we do.

POSH–PISH

8 March 2003, Peterborough United (a). Drew 1–1.

I last went to Peterborough on a Tuesday night a couple of years ago. The journey down was arduous and the performance was one of the worst I've ever seen. We departed to the pub with half an hour to go to nip for a pint and watched Stuart Barlow score three for Tranmere against Southampton in the cup instead. Even though the pub had been full of their firm, it was still ten times more welcoming than watching the likes of an ageing Neil Redfearn going through the motions as the Latics put up a terrible display for those travelling fans. A very, very dark day for Wigan Athletic, all in all.

After enduring a horrible week when everything has gone wrong and I have also turned the dreaded three-zero, I'm not overly ecstatic about today's trip to Cambridgeshire. Caddy has booked a 35-seater coach and Beany has filled it with ease. The coach firm have been on the phone to us a few times giving us the 'no beer' lecture and we have informed everyone that it's a strictly alcohol-free journey. I, of course, comply with this and make do with a large bottle of Diet Coke. Would now represent an opportune moment to thank my work colleagues for buying me a bottle of Jack Daniels for my birthday? Not that any of it could ever get slipped into the coke of course, officer.

There's no police at The Old Gas Showrooms at 8 a.m., only Duffy walking up and down the coach shouting and waving a tinnie about. 'Get that out of the bloody road!' Well, it's Saturday I suppose. To say I'm sick of the sight of the M6 would be a major understatement, but my spirits are high, despite my advancing years, as I anticipate a good birthday piss-up. My thoughts are swaying wildly about today's game: I will be amazed if we don't get beaten as Peterborough's just one of those places where we don't ever win. However, these Wigan boys are shit hot, and who wouldn't bet against our latest acquisition, Jimmy Bullard, banging in a screamer against his former club. We head across the A50 over to Nottingham, through the lovely area of Sneinton, where I used to live, and past Colwick Park and Holme Pierrepoint, where I used to willingly go on five-mile runs. Hawkins is mercilessly taking the piss out of me for turning 30 and having no bird. It would only be fair to point out that I haven't seen old man Joe Hawkins walking around Martland Mill with any supermodels recently.

On through Grantham and disaster strikes as the eleven o'clock deadline is breached. We're going to miss opening time!! We arrive at our destination, the Lincolnshire village of Stamford, at around about half eleven after driving three times around the place trying to find the pub that Arky has pre-booked, much to the bemusement of the gobsmacked locals. I don't know about Peterborough, but this place is posher than Posh Spice herself. A coach full of football lads pulls up outside a shop to ask for directions. A gun shop! We nip in to purchase six Winchester rifles, a couple of Ruger 77/17s and a broom-handled Mauser just in case the Peterborough Terror Squad are planning on getting a bit lairy with us later in the day. Er, that's a joke by the way. We eventually park up in the centre and 35 of us walk through the quiet town of Stamford; it's like aliens have landed. We come in peace and mean you no harm, can you tell us the way to The Black Bull please, and may we abduct your daughters while we're at it? We arrive at our destination and what a pleasant hostelry it is. Good food, decent beer and Celtic vs. Rangers on the box. Simple taste for simple minds. Les Bagg, probably the only Celtic fan on board, stands his corner with all the Bluenoses and cleans up on the result.

Caddy livens things up as there's some sort of medieval mask on the wall of the pub which he manages to get his head into. Unfortunately for the rest of us, he manages to pull his head back out of it, and Peterborough is saved the spectacle of Caddy walking around the away end with a gimp mask on! There are a group of fans who have got funny shirts on and it's bugging the life out of me trying to see which club it is. Turns out that Salisbury City are playing the local Stamford side, but God knows what they think of 35 Wiganers bouncing about in the town. I manage to have a walk around and do a bit of scouting for Northampton away. The usual suspects show interest, the Chorley lot, Les Bagg's mob, Stey, Caddy, Duffy, whereas others are saving their money to go to Twickenham to watch Orrell RUFC the day after instead. Poor show, Mr Hawkins, we could get promoted that night! Two o'clock and half a dozen scoops later soon comes around and we walk back through Stamford suitably refreshed. For a change, we don't get lost en route and make London Road (or Posh Stadium as it will undoubtedly become known in a few years) in good time. A mere £10 for covered terracing, result! Terracing, ah yes I remember that now! The cover is no use at all, though, as the howling wind blows straight into our faces throughout the game.

Time for a quick sausage roll and the travelling support of around about 500 gets ready to strike another one of our few remaining games in this God-awful division off the list. On a cold, windy day the football from either side is hardly inspiring, but Wigan do seem to create the better of the chances. McCulloch goes close and Bullard has a couple of efforts saved by the Posh keeper. Both players then go close again, striking the woodwork, McCulloch from close in, Bullard from 25 yards, all this is against the wind, so second half will be a piece of piss I reckon. Half an hour gone and I finally spot that Ellington isn't playing. Has he been dropped? His form has been a bit wayward of late, but he's still the most likely outlet for a goal. Turns out he's been suffering from some sort of mystery bug, but he's played every league game this season thus far so we're certainly getting our money's worth out of him. I've been fiddling with my new digital camera for most of the first half, but my efforts to try and get an interesting photo are poor. David Bailey need have no worries, although I do manage to take one of a young lady's rear later in the day.

Half-time comes and goes, and the wind-assisted Latics will surely finish Peterborough off in the second half. However, it's actually Peterborough who come out looking hungry for it and they manage to put Wigan on the back foot. They aren't too far away from the relegation zone so certainly have as much to play for as we do. Filan, having had nothing to do in the first half, makes a great double save from 'Boro's Andy Clarke, who must be pushing 40 these days. Ellington is introduced on the hour and immediately we look 100 per cent more dangerous. The Posh respond by throwing on their own talisman, Leon McKenzie, and he creates even more of an impact. The striker was heavily linked with Wigan last year before a cruciate injury sidelined him all season. Four minutes after coming on, he turns and hits a powerful strike past Filan into the bottom corner. This is not good. We can afford to lose one but we don't really deserve to lose today. As for McKenzie, well I've been keeping close tabs on him and he's now scored three in three games since his return from injury, all off the bench. I'm convinced that we're going to sign him, I reason that if he has the same agent as Bullard then it's a done deal. Just a Quasimodo-sized hunch. Soon after his arrival, he disappears up the tunnel, limping. A great talent who I'd love to see in a Wigan shirt, but his penchant for picking up injuries is his Achilles heel, or hamstring in the case of his current ailment. The only player on Peterborough's side who looks like getting them a goal, has done exactly that, and then immediately hobbled off.

Latics aren't looking up to much and it looks like we're in for another unpleasant day in Peterborough. Suddenly, and completely out of the blue, a Nicky Eaden cross is deflected by an outstretched boot, it loops up and over the keeper and is right in my eyeline. It's going in, it has to go in, it is going in, and after what seems like an eternity, it does go in. One apiece and the Peterborough muppets to our left, who were goading us minutes ago, are now strangely silent. There are threats and verbals being passed between the home and away seating sections, but who cares, we're back in it. Watching the goal later on the telly, it was a touch lucky but we'll take them any way we can. In this instance, it was an own-goal from Peterborough's Mark Arber. Thank you for your contribution to Wigan's Championship-winning season, young man!

A draw's a fair result and both sides seem happy with it. Two points dropped maybe, but both Crewe and Cardiff have been beaten by Tranmere and Notts County respectively so we actually manage to extend our lead by a point to 14. If this carries on we could be promoted at QPR in two weeks' time, what a party that would be! The coach is escorted a good 40 miles as far as Grantham. In the end, we just pull up at an ASDA anyway to do our shopping for the way back under the watchful eye of the local constabulary. Not really a problem, as there's bugger all around here and it's the first supermarket we find anyway. The usual shenanigans are evident on the journey home. The singing is a little more restrained than usual, but the old Erasure classic 'Respect' is worth a mention. A little bit camp maybe but it contains the line about being forever blue, which is certainly a sentiment echoed by many of the occupants of Caddy's Tours. I manage to prevent two Latics men from hitting one another later on in Fever and end up blotto as usual. Young James works exceedingly hard to secure an opening with the fairer sex, and as per usual rounds the keeper only to blaze it wide, a characteristic only too familiar in that particular career. Looking 30 and feeling 30, having been drinking since 8 a.m. that morning, it's a dirty job but someone has to do it. A good few more parties to be had between now and May, so having a quiet one simply isn't an option.

RETURN OF THE MOCKNEYS

15 March 2003, Luton Town (h). Drew 1–1.

11 a.m. and the phone is lighting up like a Christmas tree. A thousand copies of the *Cockney Latic* in my house that require distribution. After a daft Friday night where I was pissed after three pints of all manner of daft ciders at the Wigan Beer Festival, I really cannot be arsed. I've been up for three hours but can't face doing anything. We're top of the league, for God's sake man get your act together. Nothing else for it but to slap on one of my many New Order CDs. 'Bizarre Love Triangle' is a classic and if 'World in Motion' doesn't put you in a good mood then you're Scottish. For me, it reminds me of the time when four of us bought a car for £200, and

drove it to Italy. I was barely 17 in 1990, but have a great memory of driving down the Autopista to Rome with this tune playing over and over again on our way to watch Bobby's boys. We never got bored with it, and despite roughing it for the best part of a month and all manner of shit happening it still remains by far and away the best holiday I've ever had. Three hundred quid I spent, it'd cost four grand to attend a World Cup these days, just to sit next to that bastard Angus Deayton. Actually I take that back, I reckon loveable rogue Angus would fit in pretty well on an Arky's Tour. Not a back-seat boy by any stretch of the imagination but certainly sat on the right just behind the bogs mooning at Blackpool fans in the next lane, I should imagine. Just get the magazines delivered you lazy git!

Luton at home will hopefully be the last run-of-the-mill home game that we will ever endure. They're another team in the chasing play-off pack, but we took them to pieces when they came up here for the FA Cup tie, so today should be no different. By the time the next home game comes around (Plymouth) we should be on the verge of promotion, the next one after that (Brentford) will see us lift the Championship, and by the time we play Oldham we'll just take the piss and beat them with our reserves! Not that I'm being presumptuous, mind, but it would take a Devon Loch-style fuck-up of major proportions to blow it now, and everyone knows it. People are talking about us getting promoted in the next week or so, although we still need another 16 or so points to be mathematically secure.

Sales are brisk on the frozen tundra of the Duggy Bridge, the mood of the fans is a good one – the hard work has been ground out through the previous months and we're getting so close now you can almost touch it. The crowd has picked up somewhat, but as the game gets underway, it becomes apparent that some people would be lost if they didn't have something to moan about. People are so much more relaxed at away games, weird really when you consider that they are (in theory) the more passionate bunch, whereas people at home just seem to moan and kick off at the slightest thing. Why can't people just come down to the JJB and enjoy themselves?

The inspirational Tony Dinning is suspended for this game so young Paul Mitchell is drafted in to take his place. Luton (or Lu'on, as they prefer to be called) have found their feet in this division after an iffy spell and promise to be a stern test. Ellington is busy in the early stages, going close on a number of occasions. Goals haven't exactly been flowing freely in recent weeks for the young forward, but he is tenacious and determined and has the presence to wear the opponents down. He works well to put a great ball through for Lidds, who sees his shot saved by the keeper, and shortly after hits a fierce shot narrowly wide. Luton are also a threat up front as Tony Thorpe and the impressive Howard are creating problems for the Wigan defence. The first half is among one of the poorer spells of football I have seen this season, but we are still disappointed not to go in 1–0 up after a Liddell chip lands on top of the net. Not our day, perhaps?

Early on in the second half, the Latics defence have a rare off-moment and are caught napping. A ball into the box isn't dealt with and big Steve Howard powers a header past Filan. I know it's only one goal, but I am still convinced that this is it, we've been found out and will now go on to lose every single remaining game this season. There's optimism for you! Thankfully, the Luton goal serves as a wake-up call. The Latics players finally spring into action and Jewell responds by throwing Neil Roberts into the equation. He takes off Gary Teale, which, not for the first time this season, has me disagreeing, as Teale has been the only player putting balls into the danger area. The strange psyche of football fans is also evident, as people around me who had started to get on Ellington's back five minutes ago are now really roaring the home side back into the game. A Bullard free kick is met by McCulloch, but he nods it over. The pressure on Luton is snowballing.

Fifteen to go, and Ellington is fouled on the near-side touch-line. Nicky Eaden (him again!) floats the free kick over and Big Jason De Vos meets it with a towering header back across goal over the keeper. Roberts, as ever the unsung hero, heads the ball into the open net before joyfully scampering over to the South Stand, pointing to his shirt name. Does he always do that when he scores? I'm not sure because he doesn't get that many! What he does do though, is score absolutely crucial goals, as Man City fans, amongst others, will testify. One apiece and still a quarter of an hour to go and we push for a winner. It doesn't happen, and chances are at a premium, both teams look happy with their point. The post-match ritual of listening to the scores is adhered to, Crewe and Cardiff both draw, which means it's as you were. Fourteen points clear of second, this will do for us. Next stop Stockport.

LUKE VS. THE DUKE

18 March 2003, Stockport County (a). Drew 1–1.

Despite my good intentions to go on the beer beforehand, work has thwarted me and I'm still in the office at six o'clock. My own fault, really, as I'd spent an extended dinner hour trying frantically to find a bookies to put £20 on Bristol City to finish second. I figure that if I can get a decent price, Bristol look certs bearing in mind the amount of points Crewe and Cardiff are dropping. No bugger will take my money, as the book is closed. Yes, even for second spot which any of four teams can still nab, and knowing Wigan Athletic, I'm convinced that we've still got a lot to do yet. Later that day, Mark Robins is called back to Rotherham and Crewe and Cardiff both record wins, so thanks for saving me £20, bookmakers of north Cheshire. Nevertheless, due to my working in the vicinity, I'm driving around Stockport at 6.20 p.m., looking for a parking spot. Twenty minutes later I find one, bloody miles away from the ground.

I potter about that shopping precinct near to the ground where there are loads of pubs but every one is as grotty as the next. A few calls are made, but everyone I know is either on the train, on the motorway or still in bed (at half past six, I ask you). Loads of chippies and takeaways are jam-packed full of Stockport folk. What's wrong with you people, don't you have ovens? Don't you maintain a healthy, nutrition-filled, balanced diet? There's coppers everywhere: on horses, in vans, on foot. A mob of about 20 youths walk towards me, don't recognise any faces so I keep my head down somewhat, enter a pub on my own, Wigan and Stockport in there, atmosphere is uneasy, put some music on for God's sake. Plenty of funny looks from both parties, but nothing more. A couple of bottles of Beck's and I head off to the ground to be greeted by an amazing sight: there's absolutely loads here! There are queues the full length of Stockport's main stand, and the fans are cheerfully airing our latest ditty of 'I'd rather bomb

Bolton than Iraq'. Spot Cockney Latic FC's Spanish centre-forward Manny Flores near the front, a quick 'Alright Manny' and I jump in to make kick-off. We've got half of Stockport's ground and from the looks of it we're going to need it!

When everyone does eventually cram in, the atmosphere is so-so. With a good following the singing always starts up in two or three areas and generally lacks cohesion, but a strong opening from Latics gets us in the mood. Roberts, Ellington, Liddell and McCulloch all register chances early doors and there's only one team in it. Here comes that 5–0 win again! The rare Stockport forays come mostly down the right flank as they play on the inexperienced Leighton Baines. The youngster flies into their right winger with several crunching challenges to put that little ploy to rest. Stockport hotshot Luke Beckett, signing for Wigan in the next few days if you believe every Internet muppet with too much time on his hands, is being kept quiet. He doesn't get any chances, but still looks the part; his running off the ball and lay-offs look confident and astute. The chant, ad nauseam by now, is 'Wigan's going up and Stockport's going down' and the stewards are Man City's stewards, therefore earning them rightful and consistent abuse throughout. I can't help noticing that the building titled 'The Smile.co.uk Learning Centre' is full of coppers with binoculars.

On the pitch the breakthrough hasn't been made. A free kick on the right-hand edge of the box is won, the usual right-footed suspects, Liddell and Bullard, line up but it's crying out for a left footer. Let the kid Bainesy hit it. They do – but his shot is weak and straight at the keeper. On target at least. The second half commences and sees little action of note for Wigan as Stockport seem to be forcing their way back into it.

Midway through the second period, and I'm sat wondering what the hell I'm doing here. We're playing terribly, relegation-haunted Stockport are passing us off the park, even Bullard is finding touch, we're playing park football. I'm sat on a cold plastic seat pondering what the hell I'm doing. We're on the road to the Championship, and this season should be building up to a crescendo, yet we are truly awful at times. This football is no good at all and I just cannot get excited about it. I know a lot of the hard work has been done, but surely the objective of that was to really enjoy games like this. The fans aren't enjoying it, and from the looks of it, neither are the players. It's turning into a desperately dull game. If it was a book it would be akin to *Pygmalion*, some crap or other which I attempted to read while briefly attending sixth form college. I thought *Lord of the Rings* was shite as well, but could possibly be turned into a half-decent film with proper casting and adaptation. We are stumbling our way to the title but we'll all take that, drag us kicking and screaming over the finishing line all you want, as long as we make it, we don't care.

Just at that moment, when my mind has completely rambled (it never wanders, for obvious reasons!), Latics spring into action as Dinning hits a fierce shot which, deflection-assisted, beats the keeper all ends up. The spawny git does somehow manage to get a toe to it to boot it over the bar while grounded. Corner – COME ON WIGAN! The goal arrives amid scenes of pure unadulterated mayhem! Bullard's corner is turned in by Big Jason and the travelling support goes ballistic! The surge down to the front is unhindered by the forces of darkness from Maine Road and there are dozens of Wiganers simply wandering around the penalty area in jubilation. Not sensible shoes here of course.

That's it. That's why I do this, week in, week out. A potent reminder, that buzz of scoring a goal, nothing comes close. Right on cue, exactly two minutes after scoring, the Wiganers are showing great humility by singing 'We'll never play you again' while the home fans, if they weren't quiet before, well they are now. We've barely time to regroup for a second verse before Roberts knocks a ball through to Ellington who shrugs off the chasing defenders. Clean through on goal, and he has an eternity to round the goalie and bury it. Unfortunately, he decides to take an eternity, and rather than slotting it past the keeper, tries a hesitant shimmy while a Stockport defender boots the ball away from under him. Some of the crowd are slating Ellington for this. Why? He's an unbelievable talent and of course he should have scored and it should have been 2–0 there and game over. I know it, you know it, Paul Jewell knows it, Nathan Ellington knows it and so does Uncle Tom bloody Cobbley, so please let it go. Do some of you pricks want Wayne Entwistle back or something? We're on the brink of war with Iraq and the only blood the bloke behind is after is Ellington's. If this had happened five minutes before we scored rather than five minutes after, it wouldn't have even warranted a mention. Later that week, the news leaks out that The Duke has been suffering from a shoulder injury and as soon as the season is complete will go under the surgeon's knife. Ooh, I hate that phrase, makes me wince big time.

From what should have been 2–0 to 1–1 in minutes. Too much space is afforded to them down the right-hand side, the ball is crossed in by the fourth Bee Gee, Ali Gibb, and Stockport win not one but two headers, the second of which (from the head of Andy Welsh) goes past the despairing grasp of John Filan. Well, who didn't see that coming? If only The Duke had taken his chance. Forget ifs, there's ample time to get a winner. Eaden flicks a deft chip over the keeper which just nudges the bar, lovely effort – I heard the 'phhutt' as he clipped the turf with the outside of his boot, pitching-wedge style. Bullard has a long-range effort superbly saved by the keeper. It just isn't going in tonight. The night is summed up when a late attack finds Liddell on the right, he takes a touch and the ball simply rolls off his foot and out of play. We have somehow managed to come up against yet another blinder of a keeper and can't find a winner.

The players trudge off to moderate applause. Nathan looks totally inconsolable, he only wants to please and the sooner a small minority realise that the better. The boy is going to be a football legend but like a certain centre-forward before him, he needs the crowd on his side to really perform. I am amazed to find the car still intact and get on my toes sharpish in order to catch *The Sopranos*. I digest the results: Crewe win, Cardiff win, lead cut to 12 points. Cause for concern? Naaah not really. I'm more concerned about Rochdale manager Paul Simpson's comments on Century about Peter Beagrie, 'If you give a player of his quality time, he'll punish you.' Not at Latics he didn't! Eight games to go and the trip which everyone has been looking forward to all season coming up: QPR away.

'GOOIN' T'THAT LONDON' – A PROFESSIONAL WIGANER WRITES

22 March 2003, Queens Park Rangers (a). Won 1–0.

The professional Wiganer is not me, I'm way too posh for that. I spent a long weekend in the capital, transport courtesy of £80-worth of rail vouchers eventually procured from Virgin Trains due to the Plymouth debacle. A splendid weekend. Myself, Ian, Malc and Griff take in the many pubs of Islington and Camden. High jinks in the hotel rooms, basking in my team's glory, and still refusing to believe that little old Wigan could go to such a great and famous club as QPR and take the piss. My only regret was that while I was still sleeping off hangover No. 1 in my Finsbury Park hotel room, the Saturday morning train journey down from Wigan was getting seriously lively. With this in mind and the belief that I was way too drunk all weekend to recollect anything, I hand over the baton to my esteemed *Cockney Latic* colleague, Mr Les Bagg, to report on the day's events:

'The sighs of disappointment could be heard in Leigh when the fixtures for 2001–02 came out and it was found that QPR away had been tucked away on a Tuesday neet durin' that miserable season, a nine-month dirge lightened only by beating Stoke 6–1 and the end to th'interference of John Benson. Once more as the fixture list was due for 2002–03, the game that most travellin' Laticsmen looked for was Queens Park Rangers away. When it became apparant that it had dropped on a Saturday, folk cancelled all other arrangements in anticipation, people geet on their blowers.

'"Aye, Dave, listen mon, tha's gerrin wed in 2003 aren't yer?"

'"Yeah."

'"Aye, well don't book t'church for t'22nd o' March or yer'll be a best mon missin'!"

'Over t'years we've had lots and lots o' bullshit thrown at us from alleged "sleepin' giants" and clubs fans wi' a very inflated opinion o' themselves, Stoke, Millwall, Reading, and Oldham spring instantly to mind, only Man City have really been able to back up their claims o' grandeur. These men, QPR, are European regulars, FA Cup finalists, League Cup winners and title challengers in t'past, producers of England captains and players of flair, aye, I think we can count 'em as proper sleepin' giants.

'Travelling football fans have allus had a keen eye for a bargain and it seems that some rail tickets were tailor-made for football fans, from th'early days o' Persil vouchers through Boots 'two for one' offers. How many folks sent their mams, girlfriends and wives into Boots for their pit spray, pile lotion and toothbrushes in them days? In this new century, we get Virgin Groupies, this rather kinky soundin' offer allows gangs o' lads to travel down to t'Capital of a Saturday mornin' for a fraction o' the full price (or save 'em bunkin' it!), Luvverly Jubberly! The Tufty Club is our booking agent for this one, and after a few throwin' and screamin' down the line at an answerin' machine phone sessions we find ourselves booked on th'eight-thirty from Wigan North Western, tremendous stuff. A Tuesday neet 1–1er at Stockport gets us all in't mood and text messages start bouncin' around from Wednesday morn' (three more sleeps!) and the like. Wiganers have booked up places on every train from 5.30 (Jesus terneet!) onwards and another legendary London swaree is anticipated. What is it about a trip to "That London" that has grown men behavin' like schoolboys on Christmas Eve? Catch it, bottle it and sell it to folk who need a tonic!

'Well known for turning up wi' just 20 No. 1 and a paper for company on away trips, I'd vowed to be prepared for this one, boiled ham butties and Boddingtons are packed carefully into a Sportspages carrier and loaded into t'fridge on Friday neet. The boiled ham butties go swiftly into a litter bin when I see Galloways open at eight o'clock when I geet into Wigan, replaced by a big bacon barm and a meat an' tater, nice cup o' railway coffee (I don't come alive until I've had me caffeine quota) to wash it down and t'job's a good 'un. Back into little boys at Christmas mode for t'journey down. Papers flicked through (a different tabloid for each group member), horses picked, four draws selected and lots o' meaningless chitter chatter over a can o' Boddies or two makes a journey fly by. We're one down actually, as Foz went down poorly sick the day after Stockport. Foz assures me he was at death's door, and he must've been to miss a trip to "That London", so it's left to me good self, Pilps and The Tufty Club to fly the flag for our four seats. Tufty can be amusin' durin' this chitter chatter period as I don't think he realises at times how loud he can actually speak! I went famously red-faced on one such trip as he informed all the occupants in coach F that a girl he, ahem, used to know, had a "Bloody massive pair once yer geet her bra off!"

'In days (not long) gone by it was always the vista of Wembley Stadium through the smog/mist or the Heinz factory sign at Harlesden that made yer mutter to yerself "Not long now". Nowadays both landmarks have been bulldozed by greedy bastards so it's the sight of "London houses" comin' into view that gives you that nearly-there feelin'. The first group o' said dwellings is spotted and before long we're rumblin' into "That London".

'There's been a few crusty hippy types on t'train coming down, future bank managers, company directors or politicians, designer scruffs, possessing the latest in mobile phone and mini-disc player technology, being different and "not conforming, yeah?" The reason being a big anti-war protest in the City. That, and the total chaos that t'London Underground is turning into, makes lots of Latics folk a bit wary about leaving it too late before settin' off for Shepherds Bush so it's decided that we'll get straight over there (get settled!) and hit as many pubs as we can, leaving the naked attractions o' The Flying Scotsman for another day. One Latics mon is accosted by one too many Swampy lookalikes, complete with dog on a string, offering No War stickers and the chance to autograph a "a massive people's petition to make the fascists aware, yeah?" makes his feelings firmly felt.

'"Kin' 'ell, I thowt you men didn't get up till two in th'afternoon, go and moider somebody else, yer scruffy git!"

'The first task on any away trip once you hit the place is a Ladbrokes spot, just lookin' for t'magic sign has become an art form for meself and Pilps, and sure enough within a couple o' minutes of gerrin' off the station it's located wi' radar-like precision:

'"Theer, just past that little pub," Pilps hollered.

'"Get in theer, mayswell have one in there on t'way eh?"

Too bloody reet! Nice little QPR pub that officially only lets their season ticket holders in of a Saturday, as it's early doors we're given th'honour o' being able to share a pint wi' the R's fans in there. Wow, human beings being allowed into t'same bar eh? Whatever next? Ladbrokes is calling and another familiar bookie dweller has beaten us to it, as I fill out me coupon I coulda sworn I'd walked into a James Bond fillum!

'"Good morning Mr Bagg, we've been expecting you," comes from behind me. Naaah, not some evil madcap nutter after world domination, it's Pompey Lil, who after getting an early train in from Portsmouth (obviously!) had been layin' in wait, it didn't exactly take a genius to suss out did it?

'A big pub on a corner near the Green is our first post-bookie waterin' hole, I'm murder for rememberin' names of pubs 'cos I generally just walk in without lookin' up, and it's packed, mixture o' QPR and Latics fans havin' the crack and watching ANOTHER Man United dinnertime match on the telly. R's fans, like most, find it a bit bewilderin' to come across a large gathering of folk celebratin' the virtues of mudhut dwellin'! "You RRRRRRRS" is fired back and it's only when some R's fans give it a full blown "Rangers" chant that me Celticly inclined (eh?) instincts take over and we head for pastures new.

'It is a grand old day to be alive, sun shinin' down and still time to kill before t'match. We sample the produce in various local hostelries, all, it seems with more Latics punters inside than locals, there's more talk of Peter Houghton and Eamonn O'Keefe than Stan Bowles and Rodney Marsh (tosser, by the way). Eventually it's time to make tracks and stroll on down past the BBC and onto t'Stadium. ("Whereabouts is t'Blue Peter garden then?" being one o' the things mused out loud as we passed, another about what John Leslie may have done in there is better not printed!)

'What can yer say about the ground at QPR? Loftus Road, South Africa Road, Rangers Stadium, whichever o' the monickers yer use it's definitely a fans' stadium, tucked away in a built-up area o' Shepherds Bush (not a theme shopping centre or JD Sports in sight!). The ground is a delight, new stadia (our own included) are all fine and dandy but yer can't beat grounds like QPR for the true football experience, the fans so close to t'pitch they can smell the grass, sweat and wintergreen, four stands with no windy corners and that 'seeing the whites of their eyes' closeness that th'away fans get with a section of homers that just ooozes atmosphere, oh yes, we're gonna enjoy this one!

'Bein' creatures of habit, we throw down t'last flyer of a pint in a pub called The Springbok just as the teams are ready for trottin' out. When directed to this gaff we were expectin' a poncey countrywide chain pub full of phoney Durban accents behind the bar, what we got was a proper boozer (a bit smelly mind) that just happened to be on South Africa Road, hence the name and a healthy gatherin' o' Wiganers lappin' it up outside. Just the sort o' setting yer need for that last drink before enterin' th'arena to see the whole point of comin' in the first place.

'Only the bottom tier bein' open means that the away end is already swarmin' and buzzin' when we make our entrance just as the teams kick off. Stewards are a bit keen but mainly sound as if they don't mind what the hell yer doing as long as it isn't on a stairway! Meself, Pilps and the Tufty Club geet a nice vantage point at the front, close enough to reach out and touch the keeper's arse (if that's what you're into!). O' course the chat goes onto, "Goin' on t'pitch if we score then?" The fascination with jumping over a low wall, runnin' onto a patch of grass and huggin' another bloke and risking, A – ruining yer clobber, B – being ejected and worst case scenario C – bein' arrested, is summat that only football fans can fully comprehend. I once tried explaining it to a non-sporting mon at work after suffering scenario B at Wycombe and it woulda been easier explaining nuclear fusion! "If we score down this end I'm fuckin' on!"

'Again, the creatures of habit resurface as me and the Tuft are just sticking a chicken balti pie into our boatraces when The Duke hits the back o' the net at our end! No pitch invasion from us then, eh? It would enhance my enjoyment o' the football enormously if the first two or three minutes of every match (first and second half) were spent just strokin' the ball around between players, to give 'em a feel o' the thing, goals should only be allowed from three minutes into either half!! We join about 70 or 80 others in jumping about under t'stand, screaming "YESSSS!" with a pie in one hand, coffee in t'other (not spilling either it must be said) celebratin' summat none of us even saw!

'The game itself has more twists and turns than a feature-length episode of *Quincy*, and has a climax to match any cliffhanger of a case the randy coroner had stuck his beak into as Latics hold on under increasing (but ineffective) R's pressure. The final whistle signals, in my opinion, our second most important result o' the season (Bristol City away being THE result) against a team who were bang in form. Another clean sheet, another three points and promotion is so close I can touch it with me tongue! It seems our great leader Kaiser Dave Whelan can also taste Division One as he runs down to th'away end to meet his people, embracin', shaking hands and kissin' the babies of any Latics fans who happen to be in his path, the dream is coming true, any doubters back home needin' confirmation only have to see Dave Whelan today to allay any jitters that they may have been having.

'Comin' outta the ground the amount o' bonhomie and clenched fist greetings between Latics fans in the street illustrate how important this result is. Next thing on the agenda, where to celebrate it? As luck would have it after walkin' into bolted doors a few times, we chance our arm at one o' the earlier pubs we'd visited which looks open.

'"We alreet fer a drink then?"

'We'd stumble on a welcome we hadn't expected as Arky's yed pops out between two doormen and put their minds at rest: "Aye, these men are alreet." Just how th'intrepid Mr Arkwright had wangled his way into th'affections o' these men, so much that they saw him as pillar of Wigan society, is anybody's guess, but get a drink we do! A call from Penk and Pilps who are roamin' the streets looking for a pint.

'"Full o' bloody crusties and bobbies, where are yer?"

'"In that second pub from dinnertime, tell them men on t'door you're friends of Arky's."

'A couple o' minutes later we're all one big happy family again!

'By t'time we've legged it to the tube back to Euston Square we are a band of very merry men, some of whom have started to entertain some po-faced locals goin' about their daily business wi' a pull-up competition on the tube train hand rail! Sterling efforts by most, pulling their normal body weight up with an added ten pints o' liquid. A little bit less than sterling is one mon who thinks swinging on the bar will suffice (a mon well known for his ability to eat five burgers during the course of a game so he can, however, be excused).

As the train hits the Square I think Penk comes out of it all looking like Brian Jacks to everyone else's Jack Duckworth! He is only a young pup, though, so not an altogether unexpected outcome!

'A little bit too late to spend time in t'Flying Scotsmon so it has to be The George on the corner of Eversholt Street for t'last pints before headin' back to the hills, the usual mixture o' football fans and local misfits in attendance. Sheffield Wednesday are about but don't fancy a drink in there among others, an excellent place to sit outside and watch t'world go by when yer've got the time but we're on a mission to poison ourselves (minus Pilps, who on losin' his bearings a little ended up on th'earlier train) so it's two pints thrown down the throat at speed while catchin' up with other 'Tic tales from the day then a carry-out for the journey home.

'Always a pleasure (I'm certain not shared by "normal" passengers) to travel back to Wigan wi' a full complement o' Latics fans from "That London", card schools on the go (thanks for all them pound coins by the way!), folk trying to chat up (very badly it has to be said!) any unfortunate lady travellers, when will they learn that t'railway system is taken over by football fans on a Saturday, eh? Little drinking groups up and down t'train holdin' passionate conferences wi' as diverse subjects as, "Aye well, I reckon yer shoulda decked yon mon on the spot" to "Blair? fuckin' Blair, biggest bloody Tory since Thatcher, and I'll tell yer summat else . . . " All different folk, different views, different backgrounds, different jobs, some very differing home lifestyles but all united in one common cause. As the train snakes its way back up north the drunk, the very drunk and the almost comatose are singin' it loud and singin' it proud:

WE COME FROM WIGAN AND WE LIVE IN MUDHUTS
OOH AAAAH, OOH, OOH AAAH,
OOOH TO BE A WIGGGINAARR!'

Thanks to Les for reporting on 'that London'!

MARINO KEITH IS FATTER THAN ME

29 March 2003, Plymouth Argyle (h). Lost 0–1.

I will freely admit to having a tear in my eye the previous week when departing from Loftus Road, but today finds me tearing my hair out. Far be it from me to gloss over our defeats and concentrate on our victories, but today was one of those days where our championship train gets seriously derailed. Beyond belief. As me old mucker Dunc might opine, it can flip 180 in a matter of days. A bad day at the office of arse-photocopying and fire drills in weather of February proportions. Easily our worst performance of the season, even thinking back to our defeats back in August. This game was a Newcastle midfielder, first name Kieron.

We should know what to expect from the opening minutes when Plymouth break free and Filan manages to tip a screaming volley over the bar. A sign of things to come, and Plymouth spend the first half peppering the Wigan goal, closing down the home side's unimaginative play and winning all the 50/50s. The Latics simply don't look like they want it at all, but full credit to Plymouth, despite wearing a sickly luminous orange away kit sponsored by every hungry away fan's favourite savoury manufacturer, Ginster's. With the obvious exception of Blackburn, the Greens are by far the liveliest and most industrious outfit to visit the JJB all season and look a good outside bet for promotion next season.

The Plymouth goal, while in every sense a deserved one, is highly spawny and occurs after the exotically named Jocko, Marino Keith, is given way too much time on the edge of the Wigan penalty area. Filan, who is performing miracles just to keep the score in single figures, manages to tip his piledriver onto the post. A valiant effort from the Aussie but, agonisingly, just that little bit not good enough as the ball trickles towards the other post and rolls over the line. 1–0 Plymouth, but plenty of time to go.

The away team scoring has usually been the rallying call to give the home side the kick up the backside it has needed in the past, but today Plymouth look remarkably like us and continue to control and dominate. The influential Tony Dinning is out injured and missing from the centre of the park, his replacement, Jason Jarrett, although long overdue a recall, fails to recapture his early season form. Half-time and changes need to be made, but with only three recognised forwards at the club, and all of them on the pitch, we can hardly bolster our attack. Andy Liddell finds himself with a couple of chances but fails to make anything of them, and then, in the ultimate tribute to our firepower, the patient Ian Breckin is brought on at centre-half and Jason De Vos is moved up front. Alas, the balls launched up to the big fella all go over his head for him to chase after, rather onto his head and he is as ineffective as the rest of our forwards on this by now freezing afternoon. Needless to say, memories of Chesterfield away come flooding back as I have turned out with a T-shirt on and am now shivering, willing the final whistle to be blown.

A couple of late corners and we're beckoning Filan up. Not out of desperation, but because if anyone deserves a goal this season it's him. Now there's an idea, if we get a couple of games at the end of the season when we're already promoted, let him take the penalties. Can't see Lidds buying it, nor could I see it going down too well at Ninian Park, whose home speccies may interpret it as blatant showboating and proceed to come and join us in the away end! I can't hear any booing at the end, and rightly so, they've earned the right to have at least one truly shit game over the course of the season, let's just hope it isn't repeated.

The respectable Plymouth following is waving us 'Cheerio' but I console myself with the knowledge that I live ten minutes away whereas they have a six-hour drive. The scores filter through, and Crewe have won, meaning our lead is cut to nine points with six games to play. Cardiff are thirteen behind, but with two games in hand, which could cut the lead to seven. All of a sudden, that doubt starts to creep in again and our lofty spot is starting to look a little precarious: we need three wins from six games. Two are against teams battling relegation and two are fighting for promotion. The other two are safe in mid-table, just like Plymouth! Transfer deadline has gone so we're stuck with this lot, who, it has to be said, looked completely knackered and devoid of ideas today. They have, however, always managed to bounce back from all their previous disappointments, a totally necessary scenario if a bad dose of the jitters is to be avoided.

APRIL

NOT AN APRIL FOOL

1 April 2003, Disaster Strikes.

DRIVING TO WORK DOWN A COUNTRY ROAD NEAR NORTHWICH I PULL UP BEHIND A BUS which is letting schoolkids in as I can see there is traffic coming the other way. The car behind me doesn't stop. I will never forget that banging sound, and I suppose it's the same for anyone else who's ever been in a car crash. He's swerved into me, smashed all my rear end and the fuel tank, the car's a write-off and I am pacing up and down a country lane in Cheshire muttering obscenities under my breath for a good hour. Ring around a few people, including my boss, the office, my family and a few mates. They think it's a clever ruse to get the morning off on April Fool's Day. I wish. The next five hours are spent in hospital, as my neck, shoulders and back have all suffered painful bruising. My head's not in the best of shape either, as I have turned a ghostly shade of white and am sat in the waiting room staring blankly at the wall shaking my head, a depressing place. My season nearly finished prematurely, but I'll live to fight another day.

ARE YOU TURKING THE PISS? (AS THEY SAY IN WIGAN)

2 April 2003, England 2 Turkey 0. European Championship Qualifier.

The mother of all hangovers, like I've been on the beer for a week, even though I haven't had a drink since the weekend. Holidays already booked, tickets and coach paid for, and it's rare that I actually get the opportunity to watch England these days, so there's no way I'm giving this one a miss. I don't recall Jack Daniels being on the recommended list of painkillers on the prescription note upon my release from hospital either. A coach of 20 or so Wiganers have sorted a coach up to the Stadium of Light and the journey up is going great guns until we are pulled over at Washington for half an hour by the plain clothes mob. Alcohol and other is all hastily disposed of, as we are taken off the coach and individually searched for 'bladed articles', all while several carfuls of flag-waving, murderous Turks cruise past, taunting us. There's a reasonable humour about the exercise though and I get off quite well with my 'Medium Build W1' description, compared to Stey who is described as 'stocky' and a delighted Neil M, who is allegedly 6 ft 2 in and blond; definitely not ginger.

Arrive in Sunderland and met by a heavy police presence on every corner, with loads of English-based Turks milling about around the stadium. We head into town to find most boozers either shut or chocker, eventually settling in The City Tavern after a good half an hour's strolling about, not a Turk in sight and nor do I see any trouble at all before the game. A good drink and chat is had, both amongst our lot and with other England fans, good to see so many old faces as a former England regular. Great lads from up and down the country, although, worrying in these times, outnumbered by face-painted, flag waving 'footie' fans. I don't recall seeing too many of these nuggets in Sardinia 1990 nor Dublin later on that year when 10,000 of those lovably friendly Irish fans decided to have a pro-IRA march through the centre of Dublin and several hundred of us were left to fend for ourselves.

Many of the England lot follow smaller clubs and I've recently seen a lot of Premier League clubs slating the England support, in particular United fans and their apparent love of all things Argentinian, which has strangely died a death since the last World Cup. It's been fashioned by greed, in my opinion, as I am firmly of the belief that this hasn't always been the case. Are you seriously telling me that fans of top-flight clubs back in 1966 weren't arsed when the likes of Bobby Charlton and Geoff Hurst were winning the World Cup? The anti-England bias which prevails in this day and age at certain clubs is solely caused by those same clubs paying ridiculously inflated salaries to their players, thereby thinking it gives them some kind of rights to prevent every young lad fulfilling his dream of playing for his country. If players can't play for their country then are they saying that there shouldn't be qualifiers and there shouldn't be Euro Championships or a World Cup, the greatest sporting event in the world? I don't buy it.

I follow my local side and my national side and am proud to do so. I've read comments in various fanzines scoffing at lower division fans backing England because they'll never see their own club play in Europe, but what is the alternative option? Football's not just about the Premier League and money-printing Champions League, we, as a nation, not Newton Heath FC, gave the world the beautiful game and I enjoy being part of the passion generated by the national side. If it was a choice between Latics or England then that would be no contest, but I don't see the harm in taking an interest in the national team. And it's not just the Man Uniteds and Liverpools of this world who suffer through lost players. I mean, Peter Kennedy's been out injured for a month, you know!

The Stadium of Light is awesome, and we will almost certainly be visiting it again next season in the league. We eventually find our seats 15 minutes in, after circling the ground several times. High up in the north-west corner, the view is spectacular and the ground is buzzing. The players look like gerbils knocking a marble about I'm so high up, so when people tell me afterwards what an exceptional game Rooney had then I'll have to take their word for it. I can see everything that's going on, I just can't see who's doing it. The first half is pure Wigan Athletic, little is created, neither side dominant with tense performances prevalent. The national team's record of underachievement bears uncanny resemblance to Latics' recent seasons although I'm struggling to find comparisons between the mild-mannered Swede and the brash Scouser. Hmm, Jewell for England anyone?

The second half gets underway and the result can go either way. The atmosphere is fantastic and we speculate on what it will be like next season when there are 40,000 Mackems being outsung by 500 Wiganers rattling around in one of the vast corners of the ground. Young Wayne dazzles the Turks as England start to take the game to them. On 75 minutes the deadlock is broken as substitute 'Cerraig Daavidd', or should that be Darius Vassell, pokes home a shot and the stadium roof lifts off. Bo Selecta! The Turks are not singing any more. James earns his corn by making a splendid save a few minutes later and then Dyer wins a penalty, which is converted by Beckham. 2–0 and what was that about lack of passion for the national side?

Now we've been warned by Clandon that it took his lot till midnight to get off the car park last time Everton played there on a Monday night, so we stroll off in search of an open pub. All we find are large mobs of angry young men awaiting the Turks, who are being protected by the entire Northumbrian police. Just like Istanbul, I don't think. We end up in a hospitable local Phoenix Nights-style club near the ground and have a couple of pints, not before the old codger on the door fastidiously demands a 20 pence entrance fee off each of us. We then sort some carry-outs and visit the remnants of a disgusting local burger stall. At 11.15 p.m. we're still on the car park, eventually getting out around 11.40 the last ones off, due to our complete disorganisation and disorientation. Stuck in traffic all the way out of Sunderland, we're at the top of the hill and can see a huge mob of lads, Leeds fans, looking for Turks to fight and offering them out of their cars and vans. I'd rather not comment further, but bearing in mind the history I can kind of understand their actions, even though two wrongs don't make a right. When the police turn up to disperse this angry lot, it holds us up further and the journey home is a tortuous one. We are kept awake by Appley Bridge Blue's constant shouts of 'Who's your feeder?' and 'that Thora Hird's a right lazy cow'. Arrive home at gone 3 a.m. by which time all intentions of getting a few scoops around Wigan have been long abandoned.

NO BOG, NO STYLE

4 April 2003, Northampton Town (a). Won 2–0.

Oh Jesus, I'm going to get lynched! My foray into the murky world of away-match travel has certainly had its ups and downs. Ably assisted by Brasso, we've been registering interest for this Friday night trip. I've got 40 paid-up names, with another dozen or so names ranging from the 'definitely be there' to 'well, I've not booked the afternoon off work yet, so will I be OK to turn up on the day'. Cancel the 49-seater, we'll have the 52-seater just in case. What do you mean no bog, no telly? The natives aren't going to be happy with me at all. I'm convinced it's a wacky wind-up at my expense as no one suffers from the weak bladder syndrome as much as my good self.

On the morning of the game, I'm in danger of wearing my shoes through due to all the pacing about. I come to the conclusion that whether tonight will be a success or failure will solely depend on the performance of those blue-shirted heroes of ours. A defeat will leave us nervously scanning Teletext over the weekend and in midweek while Cardiff and Crewe play catch-up. A win and we can forget about the 'two Cs' and concentrate on winning the 'Big C'.

Arrive at The Moon at 11.45 a.m. for a couple of bottles of Weston's cider and break the news to those assembled. 'No bloody bog'. I'm not popular. Baker, bless him, nips to the market to buy a bucket. He doesn't even drink! The beer flows, or Thunderbird Blue in the case of travelling companion Moore, and we make our way down to the OGS for pick-up. Fifteen minutes later, and there's still no coach, let alone a luxury toilet. A quick phone call is met with the standard taxi firm 'it's on its way' response. 'Liars!' I scoff as the coach pokes its front end around the corner of the Deanery School. Cock-up No. 2, as there appears to be a shortage of seats, not helped by Johnny Mentalhead turning up on spec after he just happened to be boozing in The Moon at the time. There's at least one other sneaked on, but throughout the day I can't for the life of me work out who's pulled a freebie. The coach driver seems a sound enough geezer, as most of them always are, on his first job as it seems. Quite what he makes of the back-seat chorus of 'The wheels of the bus go round and round' as we pull off past The Galleries I don't know!

Eventually everyone squeezes on and I'm pleased to report that all present have adhered to our 'strictly no alcohol' directive. I think they must have dropped the 'no' part as we set about negotiating the Friday afternoon M6 sprawl. We get as far as Knutsford before Thai Blue is screaming for a piss stop. It's going to be a long haul. We pull off at Stoke, but the driver takes a wrong turn and we end up stuck in traffic at Burslem and at least one more occupant departs for a piss stop in Port Vale country. Two hours and we've still not gone through Stoke! Tempers are frayed and certain folk are hurling abuse at me, 'Capitalist Bastard' being one of the more choice accusations, despite the fact I was well prepared to put money up for this coach had it fallen short on numbers. Eventually, we get back on track and I optimistically ring up the landlord of The Fitzgerald at Naseby and tell him we'll be there for four. Another toilet break and we reach the M1. Total journey time four hours and the bucket has been called into operation by various parties, including yours truly, at least twice.

And the pub is only bloody shut! One of the coach party, clearly familiar with housebreaking, creeps around to the back and leans into a door which opens. Result at last, and what a cracking little boozer. Beer and burgers are the order of the day and all is well with the world as we manage a good two and a quarter hours of unspoilt drinking, only marred by one daft idiot abusing the staff for getting his order wrong. He hasn't even come on our coach, but I manage to take the pretty barmaid to one side (if only) and apologise on his behalf for his behaviour. There's a gaggle of Cobblers fans in and it's good to hear that their confidence for tonight's contest is as high as in a turkey farm on Christmas Eve. Seven bells and everyone is well oiled and letting rip with their vocal chords as we board the coach bound for the Sixfields, if anyone can vaguely remember where it is from here. Moore is blurting out 'Championi' to himself at five-minute intervals suggesting that the Thunderbird has taken its toll, good job he jibbed on the Red! I'm on the phone to a player because I've got a result sorting the comps out for some of the lads and myself. We arrive in good time to pick our tickets up and take a pew in the away end to watch the game.

There's probably three times the crowd that there was last time I came here, but the atmosphere is non-existent. The home crowd seem to have read out the Last Rites as far as their team is concerned and are as vocal as Trappist monks. The away end is packed, not difficult as it isn't the biggest in the division, and it's good to be able to report an excellent following from Wigan making themselves heard. In stark contrast with the previous Saturday's game against Plymouth, we bloody murder them right from the off. Nine minutes in and Liddell feeds Roberts who slips the ball into the danger area. Hesitancy from the Northampton defence and The Duke could drive a high performance sports car through there. He instead settles for barging through and tucking the spherical home to make it 1–0. Excellent! Twenty-one for the season for the young man with the dicky shoulder, I love seeing him score more than anyone else, simply because it shuts all the fuckwits up amongst our support (not here tonight) who seem to enjoy watching him fail. I remember writing a *CL* editorial a couple of years ago saying how we were crying out for a number 9 who the whole town, and especially the kids, could look up to. I had Zamora in mind but we tried and failed on that score. Nevertheless, I personally think we are unbelievably fortunate to have such a talented footballer wearing our colours. I knew he was special the first time I saw him jinking his way through our defence a few years ago at Bristol Rovers. I'd go as far as to say he was nearly as good as the pasties.

Ellington is unlucky not to force a second with a blistering shot which just clears the bar and Wigan are totally and utterly dominant to such an extent that we could almost be mistaken for thinking that we were the home side, if this ground weren't such a ten-bob affair. Johnny Mentalhead appears to have had a mishap and is hobbling about at the front of the terrace, accompanied by the St John Ambulancemen. Highly amusing as the *Steptoe* tune is whistled in his direction. And a tall lad off our coach is orchestrating the singing with a few verses of 'Wake me up before you go-go'. Why, I don't know, but it's bloody funny and much more original than 'We'll never play you again' which is by now getting just a little bit tiresome and winning us no friends. The Cobblers fans, like their team, are meek and completely clueless but I don't like rubbing it in too much as I've had the misfortune to watch a Wigan Athletic team sink haplessly into the basement in recent times. Full credit to them for turning up in such good numbers really.

Close to half-time and Roberts ambles his way into the box and is hit with a heavy challenge which sends him tumbling. Penalty it looks and penalty it is. Lidds slots home his sixth penalty and sixteenth goal of the season with ease and from here on in it really is plain sailing. Seconds later and, while we're still celebrating, Ellington gets his legs taken in the box following the restart. A clear penalty, but no referee in the world is going to give it, no matter how certain, with the home fans still baying for his blood over the last decision, so 2–0 it is at the interval.

Whereas it might possibly be feasible that Northampton could come out fighting for the second half, they looked a beaten side before the first half kicked off, and sure enough, very little changes as Latics set about extending their lead. The Cockney rebel, Jimmy Bullard, is the man pulling the strings as time after time he releases Teale and Lidds down the wings, the pressure is unrelenting but somehow we fail to add to our lead. Teale runs through the entire defence, bobbing and weaving, but his final shot is disappointing. A sub comes on for Northampton and the crowd is in uproar about the player being taken off. Blimey, what's all the fuss about, they all looked crap to me. Latics give Mike Flynn a deserved run-out for the last quarter of an hour or so as the chant of '2–0 to the Champions' reverberates around the ground and the Cobblers fans make for the exits. Their time will come again, tonight's our night and we're doing it in style.

The final whistle is blown and we've got what we came for and moved ourselves that little bit closer to the promised land. There's a brief discussion as to whether to return to The Fitzgerald for a couple but it's such a great ground for access that pretty soon the driver has the hammer down up the M6. We'll be back in Wigan for 12, I reckon. Wrong! The journey back is a complete and utter nightmare as we shelve the A50 route and get caught in 30 miles of standing traffic on the M6. Little red lights as far as the eyes can see both in front and behind, there is no escape, we could be here all night. How the hell do you get stuck in a traffic jam at midnight? When they decide to shut two lanes of the motorway, perhaps?

The bounty of another win and our 89-point tally is the only thing that keeps us sane, and I shudder to think what would have happened had we lost. When we do eventually reach and pass through the 'roadworks', the tea-drinking, £20-an-hour morons are suitably abused for costing us our Friday-night drink back in Wigan. At 2 a.m. all thoughts of more alcohol have been forgotten for the weary heads on board. It's a weird concept walking around Wigan in the early hours having sobered up when all the natives are completely blotto so I settle for a toast with a can of Tango purchased from Jamal's kebab house, full of drunken Disco Daves arguing over who's drunk the most Bacardi Breezers. Was it seven or was it eight each, they really can't decide, with stupid pizza-smothered grins on their faces. One day, people in this town will see the light, until then the educated minority will continue to appreciate what we have. Five more games in this poxy division.

SCOREFLASH

5 April 2003. A Free Saturday.

Eighty quid spent in the bookies in less than an hour. Bolton beat Man City – oh how we want to play those terrors from the Shitbok next season, what a shame they keep pulling the results out of the bag, and it looks more likely that the Happy Hammers will be paying us a visit instead. A trip to The Pagefield to watch the Grand National, no luck there either, and my football coupon is a complete waste of money and effort as well. Nothing else to do but watch the results roll in. A youngster is asking me whether I'm Liverpool or United, 'Neither, me little fella, just Latics!' is my response.

One scoreline in particular is being monitored hawk-like. Sixty-four mins – Cardiff 0 QPR 1. Seventy-eight mins – Cardiff 1 QPR 1. Eighty-nine mins – Cardiff 1 QPR 2. Undoubtedly the second best result of the weekend where Latics are concerned. Although many Latics fans will have their own preferences over whether they want Crewe or Cardiff (or even Oldham) to go up, I simply don't care. All I do care about is that we put the required gap between us and third spot to ensure that we make it, another three points dropped by Cardiff makes our goal that little bit more achievable. Later on that evening, the great minds on the *CL* website are trying to work out the various permutations until we eventually come to a definitive conclusion: if Cardiff lose again to Wycombe midweek and we beat Brentford next Saturday, we are promoted! It's scary how close we are now.

A QUESTION OF MATHEMATICS

12 April 2003, Brentford (h). Won 2–0.

The day begins with champagne, cigars, chips and cheese butties in The Bowling Green at Newtown, Arky's way of saying thanks to all the members who have travelled on his coaches this season. I've been in a bad way all week with neck and shoulder injuries. As someone who always considered whiplash to be a myth, I can confirm that it is not pleasant and akin to a 12-pints-of-Kronenbourg hangover. Manchester United get us in the mood early doors by putting in a devastating performance to trounce Newcastle 6–2 and we envisage more of the same later in the day at the JJB.

All week the permutations have been floating about, until inevitably, it all becomes clear and only two eventualities need to be considered. We need to win and Crewe need to lose or draw away at Blackpool. Cardiff play tomorrow, and if they lose we're also up. If we beat poor, hapless Brentford we'll have 92 points and, although Cardiff and Crewe can both match that total, they still have to play each other, meaning that any more dropped points by either of them will make it impossible for both of them to catch us up. We are closer than a Vincent Jones bodycheck.

A bigger crowd than usual, heavy queuing for the South Stand, and I am riled by some cheeky twat wearing £2.99 shades who pushes in front of me. I've never seen the bugger before in my life, and certainly not at the likes of Plymouth and Colchester and mutter, 'Who the fuck are you?' just loud enough for him not to hear me. The woman behind me is asking her hubby, 'Which stand is it we're going in?' You're in the bloody queue for it, love, it's written in six foot letters in front of you and you don't bloody know!! Still, some people can't win in my eyes. We moan at them when they don't turn up and we moan about what a bunch of dickheads they are when they do. Just get in to see the kick-off, the crowd isn't much larger than normal but then there's still a horde of people outside waiting to get in.

Three home games to go, and each one should increase in tempo and excitement. It's hard to build up a rapport with the few Brentford fans rattling away in a corner of the East Stand, and we are once again debating the idea of booting them out of there, or at least giving the home fans half the stand so that banter can be more easily exchanged. Being able to see the whites of their eyes is great fun, and although there's always the chance that vendettas may go too far and you end up lamping 'that tosser in the orange jumper' outside after the game, it would certainly enhance our own Wigan Athletic watching experience. The scare of the week concerns our everpresent and omnipresent keeper, John Filan, and his wonky shoulder, but there's no hesitancy as he leaps effortlessly to pluck an early Brentford cross out of the air. The Londoners are quick and inventive and are receiving plenty of early possession but their finishing is wayward. Looks like we're going to have to fight tooth and nail for this one after all.

The first clear home chance is 20 minutes in when Gary Teale is put through on the far side and uses that pigeon-catching pace to run purposefully at the red-haired maniac in the Brentford defence. He does everything right – he takes a good touch and draws the keeper, but his final shot is slotted agonisingly wide. Should have buried it! More Wigan possession and chances follow along with text updates from Bloomfield Road. Oh, for the heady days when the chap with the weather-beaten wireless was the most popular and informative chap in our little corner at Springfield (formerly known as Haitchie corner). It's 0–0 between Crewe and Blackpool.

The dodgy Aspullite in front of me with the Arabic-sounding moniker is trying to get the singing going but is so pissed everyone else is just laughing at him. This is the same bloke who, a couple of years ago, decided to run at a huge mob at Burnley single-handedly, waving a Galatasaray scarf and yelling 'GALATASARAY!' A complete loon, our support takes all kinds I suppose. The Duke is having a stormer and this is underlined when he runs at the Brentford defence and hits a great strike, which their keeper manages to fingertip over the bar. Half-time sees 0–0 at the JJB and 0–0 at

Blackpool between the donkey-shaggers and Crewe.

The second period sees the home side trying to force the issue, but it's not looking good. There's a major scare when Ellington leaps for a ball and spends several minutes walking around dazed clutching his troublesome shoulder. He's going to have to go off, he looks in pain. He slowly builds himself back up to full pace, taking his arms away from his side, and as a Liddell cross is sent over, he turns and hits a great low strike into the far corner from 25 yards, which slips in off the post. It's a 24-pointer maximum score on that electronic football game facing the beach in San Antonio, Ibiza. Major celebrations all around me. This is it, this is the one, and a great finish from a great player. And it would be amiss not to mention Liddell's contribution, capitalising on a defensive lapse to sweep the ball over.

The next ten minutes are barmy. The Crewe game is still 0–0 and we're convinced that today really is THE DAY. 'Wigan's going up', 'Champions' and 'Stand up for the Champions' rings around the stadium with absolutely the whole ground on their feet, bar the overweight rugby fan still stuck in his seat from their game the previous Friday. Cheesy maybe, but a sight to behold, and another great moment when we sense our destiny is getting that little bit closer. The Duke has now hit 22 for the season, not a Beckett- or Earnshaw-type tally, but very respectable considering he's not been fully fit throughout.

Our joy is short-lived, as a few minutes later the news filters through that Crewe have scored against Blackpool. We will savour the win but not promotion; that must wait until another day. The opportunities continue to fall Wigan's way, but getting that second goal at home is always the most difficult, like the bit under Homer's nose that he can never quite reach with the blade when he's shaving. Another good chance for Teale is saved by the keeper and there is the obligatory scare as Brentford come close to sneaking a cheeky equaliser. The 3 points will put us on 92 points, meaning that promotion has been more or less guaranteed, if not today then soon. Latics' dominance is emphasised in the final minute, when McCulloch slams home a second just to add a big, fat underline to the score. The assist on this occasion goes to The Duke who caps a fine game by dispossessing a Bees defender and rounding in on goal before tucking it back for Lee to control and smack into the net.

More delight and mutual appreciation between players and fans occurs and there is clear evidence of loitering by both parties as we await news of whether Blackpool have slipped in a late equaliser, but it's not to be. We're three points from the promised land and champagne on ice is all well and good, but you can't get properly pissed until someone cracks it open. It's difficult not to feel a little disappointed, as it now looks likely that we will win promotion on a day when we won't even be playing. Cardiff play twice and Crewe play once before we next kick a ball; any dropped points will see a large escape tunnel being formed from the JJB into the First Division.

Opinions differ: some don't care who wins just as long as we keep winning, others want our promotion rivals to lose so we can seal it asap after all the previous near misses. Others would prefer it to still be in the balance when we visit Huddersfield next Saturday, whereas others, the ones with balls of steel, are happy for us to lose a couple and then clinch promotion on Easter Monday against those repulsive nearly Yorkshire types. I can certainly sympathise with people's views that they actually want to physically be at the game when we clinch promotion, so that is what I intend to do . . .

PLAYING AWAY

15 April 2003, Crewe 1 Bristol City 1.

Cardiff do the honours by walloping Chesterfield to keep their own promotion ambitions on track. I've got a funny feeling about tonight, so after much deliberation and a spot of working late, my mind is made up. It looks very likely that we will be promoted tonight, as Crewe's home form isn't the best – just like Cardiff's, and, dare I say it, ours. Contact Mark, another every-game merchant, he'll be there, a half an hour drive and I'm outside the ticket office with a dozen or so other Wiganers buying tickets for the Bristol end. Well, you have to haven't you?

Big queues to gain entrance, although nothing like the hysteria or police presence that greeted Wigan's visit six weeks ago. The Bristol following is large and vociferous, complete with 'Cider Army' chants.

The away end isn't full, but it's not far off, there must be 1,500 here tonight from the West Country, great support, only slightly boosted by the North-west contingent. That bloody drum's still annoying though. The atmosphere at Gresty Road isn't very good at all, despite the efforts of the cidered-up Bristolians to crank it up. With this kind of backing, it is no surprise that it is the away side that begins the game on the offensive.

The Bristol side aren't a million miles away from us. They can play it short or long, are neat and tidy and hit the flanks with regularity. They lack someone to control the line up front, but Scott Murray (not slating him tonight then?) is lightning fast and little Doherty in the middle has a great bag of tricks in his armoury. We all know the view from the away section isn't the best at Crewe and due to our outsider status we have taken seats right at the far end near the family side. Bearing this in mind, is there really any need for some old dear from Bristol to come lunging towards me when Bristol get a corner, bawling, 'Would you please sit down, some of us are trying to watch the game!' The Bristol fans, who by now are perfectly aware of our allegiance, are laughing out loud at my rollocking received off the bitch-cow grandma of Pam Ayres. I sit down as sheepishly as a Tranmere centre-forward's premature walk to the dressing-room.

The Bristol fans are a good mix, like our own, and to a man, thank us for coming and say 'Good on you boys!' We respond by giving them our ticket stubs in the hope that they can utilise them for the play-off final. Their good nature takes a turn for the worse, however, when the lively Rodney Jack twists and turns in the box before planting himself on his arse following the most innocuous of challenges. A penalty is awarded and Kenny Lunt pours himself a large whisky and sticks it home. Bristol 1–0 down yet Crewe have never been in it.

The rest of the half sees the home side buoyed by their undeserved goal and pushing for a second. They are well on top and look every bit like getting it. Bristol are struggling to make the ball stick up front, Christian Roberts is making little impact and the linesman is making some perilous offside decisions a matter of yards away from the City fans. One old bloke of pensionable age gets thrown out by the steward for over-disputing these, Pam Ayres bitch-cow grandma's hubby perhaps? Crewe continue to play their patient passing game and thwart any Bristol raids coming their way, but at half-time the score remains 1–0 to Crewe. Where there's hope and all that.

Bristol are by no means overawed by Crewe, who, of course, are playing football akin to the Magyars of '53, the Brazilians of '70 or the French of '98. Any team with the awful Efetebore Sodje playing for them can't be that good. Bristol come out second half fighting hard. The forwards, Roberts and Peacock, who looked like a right pair of donkeys in the first half, are now chasing every ball, and Scott Murray is making some dangerous, probing runs. Peacock hits a scorching drive which just clears the crossbar and then narrowly heads wide. It's all Bristol at the moment, and the goal can't be far off, although the other linesman is now incurring the wrath of the City fans.

And then, a moment in time: arguably one of the most significant moments of our season. A poor Crewe clearance is controlled by Christian Roberts who, 25 yards out, fires a low, hard drive beyond the full stretch of the Crewe keeper. 1–1. Stay seated or jump up is the quandary? No contest, it comes naturally and, before you know it, I'm up and bouncing about like the biggest scrumpy-monster in the ground. The other Wiganers are no different, bollocks to the ratty old bird. It would be unjust to the efforts of the staff of Wigan Athletic to say that Christian Roberts has just scored the goal that has got us promoted, but it certainly feels that way and, indeed, proves to be the case.

Crewe respond by throwing on top scorer Rob Hulse and former Leigh RMI forward Steve Jones, but create little of note; it is Bristol who come closest to taking all three points in an exciting finish. As the minutes tick down, we get closer to our dream, for some reason it isn't really registering as it should, but we still go daft at the final whistle while the Bristol lot are just clapping a bit. I drive home alone and sober, in contrast to many Wiganers who have been sat in pubs all night getting blotto and staring blankly at Teletext. Every tune on every radio station makes sense from Jah Rule to Lisa Stansfield to Coldplay to Sash to The Real Thing. 'You To Me Are Everything' is particularly apt, if a little on the cheesy side, I'm amazed that no one's ever taken it up on the terraces. No, I'm not. On arrival back in Wigan I pull up at the lights alongside a car with a Latics kit in the back. I turn and nod with a smile in that way that we all used to do to fellow believers back in the days when we struggled to get 2,000 at home and Latics fans nearly all knew each other by name and were genuinely excited to meet a fellow fan.

Unfortunately, I've forgotten that my previous car is no more and I'm driving a hired Ka with no distinguishing Wigan Athletic marks on it, not even an infamous and now highly sought after 'Mudhuts' sticker. In fact it's absolutely spotless, bar the remnants of a cheese pasty I had for my dinner. The driver picks up her mobile and is mouthing the words 'sex pest' into the phone. That was never proven! It's tempting to find an accommodating pub and get quickly pissed, but I refrain because I know that there's a bigger party on the way. The Second Division Championship: destination as yet unknown.

STAND UP FOR THE CHAMPIONS

19 April 2003, Huddersfield Town (a). Drew 0–0.

This is it, the big one. Cardiff lost on Wednesday to Peterborough, so can no longer catch us. The scenario is as follows: one more win and the title is ours. A win will secure it, but even if we don't get one, who would wager against us doing it anyway, considering how the results of our rivals have been going. Certainly not the convoy of 4,000-plus Wiganers making their way across the Pennines fuelled with euphoria, beer and probably a few other items besides. We've got three coaches heading down to the Y–M–C–A (perform actions) in Huddersfield, hundreds on the train, every third car is a blue one, not to mention the 16 other coaches in our convoy. We might not have been able to watch our team get promoted, but today is going to be THE day we're going to sit on the throne and the Wigan public wants a piece of it.

I turn up for the coach bang on time, looking resplendent in my finest dress: Paul and Shark corduroy shirt and Adolfo Dominguez chinos, the quintessial Englishman abroad (i.e. wearing Italian clothes). It's boating at Henley Regatta on a glorious summer's day. It's a Paris café under the twilight sun. It's Rik's Bar by moonlight. It's the debonair James Bond, equally at home at a polo match or in a house of ill-repute. 'You look like a twat!' announces the back seat and we get as far as Aspull before I seriously want to get off and go home to my mummy due to the abuse. Bullies. Wearing light-coloured jeans is a strict no-no when there's a possibility of a pitch invasion, coupled with the probability of ending up in the gutter in the early hours.

At half eleven we pile into Huddersfield YMCA ARLFC, immediately double up on the Buds and Naylor immediately suggests a few liveners for accompaniment. Not a problem. After a couple of hours, I reckon the score is 12 each on the Bud front and constant bog trips as more faces enter the club. I'm keeping quite a low profile in fear of more sartorial abuse, but I have to laugh when seven Huddersfield scrotes put their boats through the boozer doors. A quick look around at 200-plus Wiganers drinking like it's going out of fashion and they shrug their shoulders and walk out meekly. It may be rich for me at this stage to make a cutting-edge comment on fashion, but I swear blind that one of them has on a pair of jeans with the 'Fred Flintstone' patches woven into them. The sort that were sold on Wigan Market *circa* 1990, price £5. Nice! Their demeanour suggests that they won't be telling their 40 or so chums in the next pub to pop in for a drink after all.

Half one and sold completely out of Bud with barely a clean glass in the house, I thought these rugby teams were big drinkers. Not to fear, though, as we spot an old friend lurking in the corner of the fridge – Skol Special, a choice tipple I used to drink regularly in my youth while frequenting The Crofters and the infamous Bricklayer's Arms (RIP). Another four of them, please, mine host, who is a ringer for Brian Glover (also, sadly, RIP). Soon after, the coach is on the move, and we're on to the main event. Wiganers swarming all over the ground, huge queues for the pay turnstiles, yours truly feeling smug as he's in possession of a ticket.

Fifteen minutes until kick-off and no chance of a pie or a pint, so we head out to the fine arena that is the McAlpine to savour the atmosphere. It would be remiss not to mention at this point that the famous Yorkshire weather has surfaced once again and mid-April feels like mid-January and I and many others are physically shivering. Utterly brass monkeys. Surprised to see the home lower tier at the opposite end is closed, and the home crowd in general is quite sparse. The Wigan end, well what can I say, absolutely breathtaking – 4,000-plus all singing their hearts out. We take a spot next to the particularly animated bunch of Huddersfield fans towards the left-hand side. There's barely a spare seat to be had in the away end, emphasised by the fact that the black-mesh netting covering the front few rows has to be pulled away a good ten minutes before kick off. Several hundred never move from the aisles throughout, and several hundred never move from the bar, only up and down on tiptoes with cranked necks when the volume rises from the stand.

The team come out wearing that awful red kit that Nathan Ellington himself allegedly called 'minging'. And it's going to be worn on our greatest ever day. Oh well, small penance for great glories, I suppose. Huddersfield are deep in the relegation mire and are in desperate need of points. There's no need to elaborate on our own situation too much. Great applause for the Wigan team – the home crowd is somewhat subdued, but the group immediately to our left flare up as we start to cheer our team on. This must be the youngest football firm I have ever seen. Never really rated Huddersfield as a rough lot but they've turned out in force today and look very silly.

Sixty or seventy fifteen-year-olds all wearing their identikit Burberry caps and Aquascutum scarves, coupled with gloves and Henry Lloyd and Stone Island jackets. Very 1998. At least the little dears won't get cold like many of our lot. It takes a second to register but I hear a distinct 'chinking' sound on the floor a couple of feet away where a young Latics fan is sat. Coins. They're chucking coins at us! Only pennies mind, but they are from Yorkshire. These little muppets, plus a few old enough to know better, proceed to spend the whole game gesturing and insinuating what they would like to do us and doing that mock 'trying to get forward' past the stewards and netting thing, as if they can't wait to rip us limb from limb. Right in front of the CCTV cameras, silly boys. I wouldn't fancy their chances even if they did manage to get near us, although if you're asking me to put money on the outcome I'd be backing the smug yet fierce-looking Alsatian patrolling the dividing line. It's reassuring to know that football violence between hundreds of fans can often easily be prevented by employing one Pedigree Chum-munching German Shepherd.

Anyway, game on, and Wigan immediately pour forward with intent. Roberts gets a half-chance but snatches at it and the ball goes skywards. This attack serves as a quick headcount check: no Nathan

Ellington. He's had his shoulder operation this morning and won't play any further part in the 2002–03 season. Get well soon, Duke, and thanks for all your efforts in this historic season. Huddersfield weather the early storm and regroup to come at us. This sparks the home crowd into life and their team comes close to opening the scoring for the day. McCulloch gets crudely knocked flying midway through the first half, a challenge for which a Huddersfield player receives the first yellow card of the day. I pass the time taking pics of the Terriers teeny terrors with my digital camera, which I still haven't worked out how to use properly. At least the coins have subsided, that's their pocket money wasted for another week. There's a few menacing older faces at the back of the stand, but who cares, no one's going to spoil our party as the old 'Going Up/Going Down' chant gets a strong airing along with 'Sunshine'.

With The Duke already having seen his season finished, Andy Liddell is the next one to go, worryingly limping off before the half-time break, to be replaced by Peter Kennedy. A dull, inoffensive game only livened up by the half-times – Crewe are 0–0 versus Swindon, it's still on! The second half sees the Latics now attacking their huge and excitable travelling support. A revised strike force of Neil Roberts and Lee McCulloch push on, with McCulloch going close with a header, a goal would do just the trick to shut the Huddersfield whoppers up. I think it's a bit sad to see them in their current predicament, but I'm not in a situation where I can hand over the points to them, and even if I could, I don't think I would. Chances for Huddersfield too, as Martin Smith is proving a handful for the away side's defence.

The best chance occurs 20 minutes into the second half when a Huddersfield clearance sits up beautifully for Peter Kennedy, who smashes a screaming 30-yard volley which nearly breaks the crossbar in two. A great dipping shot, which would have lifted the roof off the South Stand, Huddersfield version, had it registered. Teale follows up the rebound but can only hit the outside of the post with another fierce shot. Hitting the woodwork when it doesn't go in is both painful and exciting, but with the keeper beaten on both occasions, the home side can consider themselves fortunate still to be in this game.

If this was exciting, though, the moment which seals the day is the electric scoreboard reporting the news: Crewe 0 Swindon 1. Very few spot it first time as it's behind us at the back of the stand and everyone is watching the game. The noise is vaguely familiar, it starts with a handful of people, shouting and cheering and the buzz starts to travel Mexican wave-style. 'Crewe's getting beat!' And sure enough they are. Within seconds the whole crowd is bouncing up and down and cheering, John Filan turns around, mouths a few words and before long all the team knows. If it stays this way it's over, Crewe need to win to have any chance at all of stealing our prize. 'Champione, champione ole, ole, ole' is ringing around the away end as we seek confirmation of what we have known for a long time now. Should be 'CAMPIONI' but never mind!

The news lifts the players, as twice Jarrett charges through the middle to find himself clean through on goal, but cannot finish. At least he looks like David Trezeguet! The remainder of the action on the pitch is completely uneventful, it's the party on the terraces which is taking priority. The scoreboard is flashed up again, still 1–0 to Swindon, amazing! Even if Crewe equalise it won't be good enough. It's going to happen, we're going to be champions: 19 April 2003. 'Let's Hang On' is aired with gusto, we don't need to for much longer. The referee's assistant signals three minutes of added time. Who bloody cares, we've waited a lifetime for this, three minutes isn't going to make a difference. Never again will a goalless draw be greeted with such jubiliation as grown men start crying. 'You Are My Sunshine' again and again, louder and louder. The whistle is blown and the cheer is a prolonged, purposeful one. We've only gone and done it!

Everyone wants a piece of the away support. The Huddersfield coin-chuckers are trying to get at us, or at least pretending that they want to, knowing full well that the banks of netting, stewards and police prevent it. They won't be spoiling our day and make for the exit. The players come charging over to the away end and produce a 'We're going up' flag, bouncing and singing, the photos are taken and their reaction is a wonderful sight. Outsiders just can't appreciate what this means for a small club like ours to go from the Northern Premier League to the First Division in 25 years.

There's been a special bond built up between the fans and the players over the course of the season and an outflow of emotion is evident from all concerned. What a buzz, what a high. The people who mock our crowds from near and far don't realise that there's more to it than the numbers who follow us. Save a few moaning twats at home games, we've backed them from day one and supported them to the hilt. We got through our bad patch in August and the players have been truly fucking marvellous ever since. They didn't even concede a goal throughout the months of November and December, and have only conceded nine goals all season away from home! They've carried off a fantastic achievement, we've watched them do it and the players have every right to milk it as much and for as long as they want to. Of course, their efforts deserve a wider audience, but that's not to the detriment of those of us who have been watching them. Every one of the players and every one of the fans deserves this success, and if you don't believe that then you simply aren't a football fan.

I might be on my own here, but I'll wager there's probably a few thousand others who feel the same when I say that this is the greatest moment of my life. I was too young to fully appreciate our promotion from Division Four in 1982. Beating Millwall at Wembley in 1999 was as good as losing to Gillingham in the play-offs was bad. Winning the Third Division Championship in 1997 was fantastic, but apart from the daft Torquay weekender which half of Wigan attended, I don't really look back on that season that fondly. I suppose the only thing that can come close for a Latics fan was the day we got into the Football League in 1978. It was well before my time, but this feels pretty similar – we're going somewhere that we've never been before and we're doing it in style. Wigan Athletic have given me every bit as much pain and suffering as they have given me pleasure over the years. Following a football club hurts, it costs money and is immensely painful and distressing at times. If I went wild in the away-team dressing-room with a baseball bat, I couldn't even get close to causing half as much pain as they've given me over the last few years. But at this particular moment, what else can I say other than what the crowd are singing, 'We love you Wigan, we do': I love 'em, I really do. Bollocks to women, fast cars, drugs and music, you're the one for me Latics. (Although obviously a bit of the others now and then wouldn't go amiss.)

Laughing and smiling faces everywhere, none more so than Paul Jewell's. Modest and unassuming, he has refused to celebrate until now, with the standard 'One game at a time, we've won nothing yet' managerial mentality. He's a winner and has produced a team of winners. Enjoy that champagne, Paul. One other man who deserves the credit is Dave Whelan, no doubt toasting the boys from his Barbados holiday home. Just a fan like the rest of us, yet his wealth has allowed him and us to live the dream that we all thought wasn't possible. The man who saved the club from going bust and turned us into CHAMPIONS!

After much delirious stumbling about outside, we board our coaches and clear off back to Wigan. A spot of ridicule and abuse for a coach full of 'Cumbrian Reds' on the M62, completely dumb with that 'Why do you hate us?' look. Does it really need an explanation? News of minor shenanigans at the station are of little interest, there's a party to be had and party we do. Manage a consolatory drink with some West Ham lads in The Raven, who have just seen their side face relegation from the Premier League after a defeat at Bolton. We wish them well and then proceed to Little Fifteen's for some Moet-swigging with little fingers in the air. The rest of the night inevitably gets blurry – wild scenes in The Moon and a jam-packed Rik's Bar, standing up, sitting down and rolling over for the Champions, and how I get home is a complete mystery. Spend the evening knocking back the beer with all the faces that matter, the diehards who have waited years for today, many are just stood around with a glazed look on their faces, as the reality of what it all means slowly sinks in with the Stella. No more trips to Colchester or Chesterfield, we've got Sunderland and Forest to look forward to. Forget the heartache, tonight is the night to enjoy the moment.

BITTER BUNNIES

21 April 2003, Oldham Athletic (h). Won 3–1.

More like it, not quite a stuffing, but certainly a ritual humiliation of our closest rivals with none of that foot-off-the-gas business to wreck their promotion dreams!!

Spend Sunday out on the beer again, culminating in a night at the inaugural 'Like This, Like That' club night at the JJB Marquee, where great music is only marred by Wild West scenes at the end, chairs and tables flying and everything. I've come out of some house in Ince at daft o'clock and I've been off my head for three days solid. I've had barely any sleep and I'm looking like a million lira. Turkish lira to boot. If ever I needed a break today was the day, but there is absolutely no chance of that at all. Because if ever a team in our division deserved a walloping, then that team is Oldham Athletic.

They are the worst set of fans in the division bar none. I have never seen such a collectively ill-mannered, unknowledgeable and unsporting bunch in all my time as a football fan. The world begins and ends in Oldham in their opinion, and all outsiders have got it in for them. They drone on and on about their Cup semi-finals and Premier League seasons, totally oblivious to the fact that it will do them very few favours in the future. They have delusions of grandeur and detest the fact that our nickname is the same as theirs. We are a club with a sugar daddy who don't deserve any success, not like the 'Real Latics' who will one day regain their rightful place in the Premier League.

Oh how ironic that today sees a bumper Bank Holiday crowd watch Wigan Athletic, newly crowned Second Division Champions – that bit I can't stress enough – stand in the way of Oldham's own promotion challenge. We, on the other hand, having won the title with three games to spare, have nothing to play for but pride and local rivalry. Entering the ground I decide to get a pie and a drink to try and settle my nerves and stomach, when a roar goes up. Not a home crowd-type roar, but an (admittedly) large away following roar. Bugger – Oldham have scored with 11 seconds on the clock. I could not stand losing to this lot and am considering turning right back around and getting some much needed shut-eye. Great to see a healthy crowd in, but disappointed to find my team behind in the first minute, 4,000 gloating Nearly-Yorkshiremen. Liddell and De Vos have gone the same way as Ellington in that they have completed their footballing contribution for the season due to injuries. We've got a scratch side on display and it's not looking good. Getting turned over by Oldham at home isn't exactly my favourite Bank Holiday pastime.

Unfortunately for Oldham, the home team haven't read the script, and an understrength Latics go steaming right back into them. Eight minutes later, Teale hits a peach of a ball into the box and Roberts out-leaps the Oldham defence to plant home a great header. 1–1 and jubilation, or is it relief that we are back to level pegging? A rousing yet completely typical chorus of 'You're not singing any more' is offered by the lively and packed South Stand. Tealey and Das Bomber both look well up for this game, as do the rest of them. I sometimes wonder whether they are in tune with all that bollocks flying about via the Internet, maybe they are, and maybe they have decided that the gobby Oldham tossers are going to get their come-uppance for the second time this season.

A further setback for Latics, as the model of consistency, Matt Jackson picks up a worrying knock, forcing him to retire. Those loveable Oldham fans spend the whole time he is prone on the floor booing and calling him a cheat all the way up the tunnel. Scumbags. Not really impressed with their players either, a dirty set of individuals, many of whom who are so fat they possess stretch marks. Paul Mitchell comes on to fill in at centre-half alongside Ian Breckin. Neither is a first-choice centre-half and that dirty little shit Wayne Andrews has been following through and leaving his boot in after every tackle. Breckin in particular is filling the boots of De Vos admirably, winning every ball and taking no crap off anyone. More problems still midway through the second half as Jarrett is the next one to get carried off following a particularly nasty kick to the head from another cultured Oldham challenge. Jewell later quips, 'Hopefully it'll knock some sense into him,' but he's got a bump on his head the size of Parbold Hill and yet, once again, the Oldham lot are screaming blue murder at Jarrett, rather than remonstrating at their own players' poor attempts to play football.

Fortunately, we have a returning-from-injury Tony Dinning to bring on for Jarrett, giving him at least an hour of the game to make his mark and resume his friendship with that little nark Darren Sheridan. Now I've seen Sheridan play plenty of games for the proper Latics in the past and he's a tough nut, but he ain't the world's best footballer and his tackling is dubious to say the least. The Oldham fans can't see this and spend the entire game hollering away at the referee, blaming everyone but themselves for every minor event. I mean what sort of bad sports boo not one, but two players getting stretchered off with serious injuries? I'm considering getting a load of mates together and hanging around Oldham Infirmary next week to wait until one of their fans gets injured in a household accident and requires treatment. We'll follow them in on the stretcher, watch them squeal like the squealers that they are, calling them 'cheating wankers' to see how they like it. A more bitter set of fans you will never meet, trying to mask their own team's shortcomings by blaming everyone else. We've got to beat this lot, they really do deserve it!

So back to the game and the second half is just getting underway. A near full-strength Oldham may be expected to turn over a half-strength Wigan but we are just about to show the scruffs from east Lancashire exactly why we are the Champions of Division Two. We give them a pasting! McCulloch hits a firm shot which is tipped wide, Dinning hits a blistering drive which is palmed over. Teale is having a field day and the McCulloch–Roberts partnership up front is starting to bear fruit.

Cometh the hour and cometh the man. As Roberts is fouled by another pathetic Oldham challenge just outside the box, the names are lining up to take it – Bullard, Dinning or Kennedy perhaps. Bullard is looking favourite, but during that lull I am ranting away that 'it's about time this lad delivered something, hogging all the free kicks like that'. Jimmy aka The Perminator blows my legs off in no uncertain terms, curling a sublime free kick into the top corner while the keeper barely moves. A great moment as the world seems to stand still, only for three sides of the ground to erupt seconds later as we see the ball nestle high in the inside netting. Oh dear Oldham, there goes your hopes of automatic promotion! A nothing game for us perhaps? Looking at the reaction of the players, they are celebrating wildly, they really want to win, and Bullard gets seriously mobbed. A deserved 2–1 lead. Needless to say the South Stand are giving it to the away support with both barrels, including those tools from the FYC or whatever they call themselves who seem particularly agitated, no doubt keen to impress their mates from Hibs and Stockport.

Oldham's away record is second only to ours in the division but they are simply getting ripped to pieces by a team that is completely on top of its game. It comes as no surprise a few minutes later when Neil Roberts convincingly wraps it up with another stunning finish after beating the last man. Two more for The Bomber; who says this man can't score goals? The 'other' Latics fans are now leaving in their droves, 'Bye-bye, bye-bye' and 'Champions' is ringing around the ground, as the away support heads for the door. All except one that is, who attempts an impromptu streak but he can't even get that right, as he is stopped a few yards short of the pitch, without even getting the chance to whip his smalls off. Not a sight we were really looking forward to in any case, but possibly the only time throughout the day that the humourless Oldham fans actually go up in my estimation. Nearly 13,000 at the JJB cheer the boys on until the end and the last few minutes turn into a carnival atmosphere as the Wigan team takes the piss out of their opponents in their search for a fourth, resulting in a spot of showboating. They want those three points to go with the 93 already accumulated.

Despite all I've said about them, I really do hope Oldham make it up through the play-offs as they're great entertainment value and always good for six points. Ever since the game in December when we outplayed them at home, we've had to listen to their constant moans about how they would have stuffed us had it not been for all their injuries. The tables are turned as a decimated Wigan outfit puts on a class performance to smash a near full-strength Oldham. They just never learn do they? They argue that we are just a rich man's plaything – wrong: Dave Whelan is a Wigan Athletic fan. If Dave Whelan were an Oldham fan worth 200 million quid would the Oldham muppets be telling him to go and invest in Man United because it would be wasted on Oldham? Would they bollocks. Bad losers and jealous to the core.

As the final whistle blows, what is left of Oldham's support looks dejected and downbeat, whereas the home fans are joining in the chorus of 'We Are the Champions' over the Tannoy. Yeah, it's a completely naff record for 99 per cent of the time, the only exception of course being when your team ARE the champions and it's completely impossible not to get carried away with it. The usual kids have been banging on the perimeter, signalling their intentions to run on the pitch. Not my cup of tea this time, I may have a quick saunter over after the Barnsley game, but only after the players have done their bit. A shame really, as the players today have earned the right to take a bow on the basis of this performance alone, a stunning display to put our close rivals to the sword. Dun 'em good and proper.

LET'S HANG ON

Putting our rivalries aside and despite all I've written about our dislike of Oldham, I was nevertheless disappointed to hear about the club's financial difficulties. I'd like to genuinely wish them all the best getting out of it, as no genuine football fan wants to see a rival club go bust, and I am no exception.

NEW TROUSERS PLEASE

26 April 2003, Cardiff City (a). Drew 0–0.

With the Championship now safely wrapped up, I don't think I'll bother making the trip to that fine hospitable venue, Ninian Park, Cardiff. What's the point of wasting time and money risking life and limb in that shitehole? It's not like I'm a coward, everyone knows I'm a lean, mean fighting machine and when I turn up in Cardiff, the Soul Crew will take one look and flee en masse if they know what's good for them!! Ahem, brown underpants it is then!

In all seriousness, it wouldn't be fair if the players or the fans were to travel to Cardiff half-heartedly. After all, we've already gone to Oldham, QPR, Crewe, Bristol and Tranmere and taken the piss. I suppose we now owe it to them to do the same to Cardiff, although quite why they all expect our by now skeleton squad to do them all a favour is beyond me.

More importantly (boo, sob) it's going to be our last away bash for a few months. Cardiff or not, I wouldn't miss it for the world. There are, of course, other ways of occupying your time over the summer. Cricket, gigs, holidays, golf, races, even writing a book, heaven forbid. But there's nothing like having the craic on a great away trip and I know full well that 99 per cent of our party will be feeling that cold turkey by mid-June. The other 1 per cent will have run off with a one-legged can-can dancer, never to be seen again, but then he's always been a bit weird.

At least three coaches full of lads is enough to put the frighteners on the locals at most away games, whether the occupants are going for the beer or to cause bother. At Cardiff it's a source of amusement, or like a red rag to the proverbial bull. It's a rough old trot at Ninian

Park, but to chicken out would be tantamount to treason and we chortle away to ourselves at the OGS at the various 'got a wedding to go to' tales of cowardice others missing have offered. Cardiff's a big ground, hostile atmosphere and should give us all a taste of what Division One is going to be like every other week next year.

I spend the previous evening throwing up all night with barely a drink inside me and look like a ghost on Saturday morning – ideal for scaring irate Welshmen, but not ideal for my comfort. I am also aware that to admit that I have been suffering from pre-match vomiting to anyone would, of course, cause great mirth and bugger-all sympathy. Several coaches pull off from the Gas Showrooms at the unearthly hour of 7.30 and we're cruising. Strange observations are made on the way down as a trickle of funny-looking fat fellows wearing badly designed replica shirts is witnessed, which turns steadily into a fat man's motorised conga. Yeah, it's the rugby Challenge Cup final day, and if the traffic's not bad enough to Cardiff on a normal day, it's going to be far worse with all the chubsters cleaning all the services out of tasty yet pricey savoury snacks. It could be worse, but only if our own rugby league heroes (*sic*) from Wigan had managed to make it through to the final.

We have already established that if we nick one of those silly Bradford Bulls flags or a scarf or two, and stick it to our coach (emblazoned with 'Hursts of Wigan' in foot-high letters) we could possibly pass ourselves off as rugby men and breeze into Cardiff unhindered. However, looking at the state of some of them and the state of some of us, you can spot the difference a mile off, rugby and football fans are a totally different breed. Although they would probably dismiss the majority demeanour of our coach as loutish football hoolies, every one of them is wearing an XXXXXXXL replica shirt and bad trainers. Beam me up, Scotty. Football fans are from Earth, Rugby fans are from . . . well most of the ones who watch Wiggin Bugry appear to be from Preston. The tragic thing is that not one of them looks even the slightest bit excited about their trip to Cardiff, as if wearing garish clobber alone is some kind of expression of their mood. We're on our way to Cardiff for an end-of-season non-event and everyone, and I mean everyone, is bouncing around on the balls of our feet in anticipation.

A trip to the services just before the M50 turn-off. Pulling over always seems to be a bad move, and today is no exception as it's crawling with the buggers! The coach next to us has one Bradford mon who must weigh 30 stone and can barely get out of his seat, whereas a walk outside proffers another like-minded soul walking around with a shell suit on and a belt around his waist. I attempt to start a vicious rumour that Selina Scott and Jeff Banks are in the food hall filming a new series of *The Clothes Show* but unsurprisingly no one believes me. I know the lads on our coach aren't always the smartest but Wayne Hemingway would be bemoaning in Burnley-ese if he took a look around here. So fat and so young: what a tragedy. Queues a mile long (and half-a-mile wide – and they're in single file!) the coffee smells great, as does the Harry Ramsden and not even the sight of an amusing 'Captain Beak' chicken hut can appease us. It's been completely emptied by hundreds of the stripey buggers. 'Could all the well-dressed people please return to their coaches please?' As football fans we are only too aware that we will get the blame for this wanton destruction and looting.

Unfortunately, we end up stuck in the car park for half an hour, as the drivers have decided to use their vouchers, and what with the queues everywhere, have barely started chomping on their hors d'oeuvres thus far. Nothing left but to engage in large-scale piss-taking, aimed at a family of kitted-up Warriors fans. 'We're just here for the day out,' they say. 'We go every year, regardless of whether Wigan get there or not.' Nope. The arrogant gits bought their tickets in January, fully expecting to get to the final, and now can't get rid of them after their team has been knocked out. It's too much for us and the only action is to give the hundreds of RL fans a quick chorus of that old *Addams Family* fave:

> They're scruffy and they're smelly,
> They come from Scholes and Whelley,
> They haven't got a telly,
> The Wigan Warriors!

They are also eagerly reminded that 'There's only one team in Wigan!' It's no wonder this country is in such a bad way when there's such downright scruffy buggers parading their wares. We eventually get onto the M50, and it's absolutely gridlocked. Nerves have set in as we meander towards Wales. It's just gone eleven o'clock and we're nowhere near Cardiff, or a pub, and to make matters worse, the pubs we had booked in advance in some Welsh village have rung us and told us to piss off on police advice. All dressed up and no place to go. A less than tasteful game is in progress which involves shouting out the names of dead people, while the chief brains on board consider whether to stop off at Monmouth or Ross-on-Wye.

The boozers/anglophiles get their way and Ross-on-Wye is chosen to play host to 200 Wiganers for a couple of hours. A very good choice it is too, taking away the irony that we're not even in the same country to which we are going yet. Once the locals have got over the sight of dozens of lads all piling off coaches mid-morning asking, 'Where's your Wetherspoons?' they make us very welcome in some great pubs. The Wetherspoons is full of all the Goons making their presence felt, whereas we go on a mini-crawl ending in the magnificent Charlie's Bar, possessing the country's finest ever barmaid. Compliments, marriage proposals, requests for Guinness, constant ogling and finally a wonderful serenade of 'Hey, did you happen to see the most beautiful girl in the world' are all flung aimlessly at this dusky beauty. Admittedly, the last occurs some five hours later on the trip home but she did take some serious coming to terms with.

Half past one and half-time in the Bolton–Arsenal game and it's time to get moving, we're still a fair trot away from Cardiff but at least we've avoided all the rugby traffic now and we've got a clear run. We're soon in the land of sheep and all the St George's are coming out. Now, I'm not sure about this – is it because we're English and proud and letting the Taffs know we're coming or is it really a cry for help (or a police escort)? Only the individuals themselves can answer that one, but we don't get any escort and we're greeted by lots of posturing and gesturing as we near the ground from various red-faced Welshmen, along with torrential rain. Pride of place goes to the Taffy 'Disco Dave' on his way to the match and obviously around town straight after as he is wearing a flimsy shiny shirt and is now soaked to the bone. There's nowt worse than a bogus weather call at the football, when you take a coat it's 70 degrees and when you go in shirtsleeves it ends up minus five!

The ground doesn't feel even a quarter as intimidating as last time I was there, both times when there were barely more than 3,000 in.

There are a few more fences up, and there's still the odd prick knocking about jabbering into a mobile but I honestly believe that they've lost their bottle in the same way as their team has. Having said that, we still need an escort across the road where the coppers hold us just long enough for us to get our first soaking of the day. Quite impressed to see a very reasonable following from Wigan, including a good contingent of 'normal' fans, singing their hearts out and taking the piss out of the home fans. So much for my prediction that 'It'll be like Millwall – 400 daft lads will go and absolutely no one else.' The whole away end is suggesting to the home fans that their team is, in fact, staying down.

On to the game, and our subs bench is made up of kids we've barely heard of, such is the player shortage. The game is unmemorable in the extreme, apart from the performance of the unbeatable antipodean between the sticks. I defy anyone to witness a finer display of goalkeeping at any of the other 45 grounds in the country this weekned than that of Mr Johnathan Filan. The home side may as well fling elephant dung at him from catapults he'd keep it all out. Absolutely outstanding from first to last, pulling off several world-class saves to keep Earnshaw, Thorne, Kavanagh et al. at bay. That's not to say he's doing it all by himself as Breckin is outstanding in defence and Bullard is making his Division Two select team-mate Kavanagh look like a clockwork plum. And it's certainly not all one-way traffic as Teale and McCulloch are unfortunate not to score.

The home fans are somewhat subdued, and erratic, switching with ease from 'Lennie Lawrence's Super Blue Army' to 'Lawrence Out' seconds later. The away speccies are belting out a great repertoire from 'I love you baby' on to our latest ditty of 'We'll be running around Wigan with the Cup' coupling it up ingeniously with 'You'll be running around Cardiff with fuck all!' I am pointing out to anyone who will listen that there's a lad in the home end wearing a Hackett coat with a big St George on the front, but no one bats an eyelid. So why the hell did I nearly get a good hiding off 40 of Wrexham's mob last year when we went to the ticket office to pick some rare comps up, simply because Ian had a little Hackett marque on his shoulder? Strange folk, the Welsh.

Half-time and, I am not joking here, the ground is like a swimming pool. If there was a feature when selecting the weather options on *FIFA 2003* for the PS2 entitled 'Pissing down', then the designers should have modelled it on a trip to Ninian Park. The ref is out on the pitch jogging up and down on it. Surely, we're not going to have to come back on Tuesday, I really don't fancy that at all. I've been keeping quiet about the fact that I haven't missed a game all season on the journey down just in case some wag decides that it would be fun to strip me naked and leave me on the M4, but a Tuesday night rerun would be a complete no-go. Turns out it's just the fourth official – the original referee has had to retire, suits me sir. A few words of praise for the half-time tunes: don't know whether it's as a tribute to Wigan's Northern Soul roots or Cardiff's Soul Crew but 'Ghost in My House' and 'Feel the Need in Me' sure get me in the mood for an evening chilling out in Rik's. A splendid change from the usual guff and even the sun comes out for the second half as a mark of respect.

A quick burst of 'Rocky' – back to normal then – and we're underway and there's a mad, mad atmosphere for the first 15 of the second half, so THIS is what a trip to Cardiff is about. The whole ground is turning up the heat and the feeling is both exhilarating and scary in equal measures. If only they had been doing this from the start they'd probably be 3–0 up by now. The replacement ref is definitely a Valleys boy as he proceeds to give the home side everything, and no bloody wonder as the place is on the verge of eruption. All three and a half home sides look ready to steam the pitch at any moment as they bellow out their rousing national anthem. Respect to Cardiff as 14,000 of them briefly attempt to lift the roof off. A real, passionate, hostile football club with absolutely no flag-waving, horn-wearing, drum-beating muppets in sight unlike the Millennium Stadium a mile up the road. And yet Cardiff still cannot score.

Wigan Athletic remain confident and nonchalant throughout all this spell. Jimmy Bullard cleans out the uninterested Kavanagh with a brilliant hard-but-fair challenge. Cardiff throw everything but the bathroom bidet at us, yet our retort is a simple one: thou shalt not pass. They'd be better off joining the Wiganers who are punting a blow-up sheep around the away terrace, prompting Hawkins to utter the inevitable one liner about them playing 'sheepy-uppy'. Cardiff look knackered, Gareth Ainsworth, former Wigan target, looks like the Honey Monster trudging down the wing and after a while simply stays rooted to the spot. Thank God we didn't sign him, he's fatter and slower than me, in severe need of a hair cut, and it takes Cardiff about

20 minutes to realise that they have effectively been playing with 10 men for most of the second half.

Just time for Filan to deny Cardiff's Andy Campbell from point-blank range and it's over. Crewe are promoted, and Cardiff aren't. I'm half expecting a riot, but they quietly file out, heads shaking, wondering where their season went wrong. A good 15-minute wait inside the ground is passed by applauding the players who have come out to warm down and listening to a spot of U2. A scruffy-looking fella in a trackie and a flat cap comes over to the away end clapping us, and bugger me if it isn't Sam Hammam. He comes over, warmly congratulating us on our great season and naturally all he receives back is 'Hammam is a Taliban', 'One Dave Whelan' and 'We're going up and you're staying down'. Bit harsh I think, he seems a good enough egg, if a tad eccentric. Word of advice: buy yourself a suit if you want to command respect, son.

Crewe have now been promoted with us by getting a result at QPR to put them on 85 points. Their tally now is the same as ours was on walking off Loftus Road a month ago, so in an ironic way, we also got promoted at QPR. We're now on 97 and officially indestructible. Ninety-seven bleeding points!!! An amazing feat! Any chance we can carry some of them forward to next season? Huddersfield have been relegated and Tranmere's game has been abandoned due to some loony on the roof. The post-final traffic is appalling and it takes an hour or two to get out of Cardiff, and needless to say it's completely impossible to tell who has won the rugby because both sets of fans look equally as miserable as they did several hours earlier.

For us, it's a brief refuel at Stroud, and then, you know the score by now, you name it, we'll sing it. It's like the Last Night of the Proms. From Showaddywaddy's 'Under the Moon of Love' to The Drifters' 'Saturday Night at the Movies', right through the card including the theme from *Happy Days*, Rick Astley, Meatloaf, Tight Fit, Billy Joel, Deacon Blue's 'Dignity' and a good deal of chino-related abuse in my direction despite dressing down today in cowardly Armani jeans. The encore gets an airing as from the Thelwall onwards the entire coach partakes in an inventive variation on the going up/going down song with the surreal lyrics of 'I can't believe it's not butter, I can't believe it's not butter . . . WE ALL LIVE IN A TUB OF MARGARINE!' And of course the numerous ditties in honour (!?) of various public luminaries and sex cases which cannot possibly be reproduced here. We arrive back in Wigan just in time for a few goodbye beverages with some seriously daft folk, half of whom I now probably won't see until August. The arse-twitching of early morning has long since disappeared as the travellers can be heard to mutter, 'Cardiff, yeah, walk in the park, mate!' Now, if they'd had something to play for, things could have been very, very different.

THE YOOF IS ON FIRE

30 April 2003, Lancashire FA Youth Cup Final vs. Preston North End. Lost 0–4.

Time to pick up a spot of pre-title silverware at this Youth Cup final at Deepdale. A great neutral venue! On arrival at the three-sided enigma, things turn a little surreal as there are heavy queues to get in and the kick-off's been delayed ten minutes. I must be one of the last half-dozen to enter and catch up with the others in the half of the one stand that's open.

A quick scan of the programme sheet and I've already decided that it would be great if a couple of the Preston lads make it as pros as we have Carl Clampitt at centre-half and Warren Beattie on the bench. Meanwhile, the blond-haired lad wearing number 9, if we're to believe the programme, is called Fola Onibuje. Ah well, the game kicks off and it's even stevens, Preston are the favourites but Wigan are matching them. Very impressed with the Wigan midfield pairing of Greg Traynor and Chris Lynch and their fierce tackling. The huge black lad up front wearing 11 and who, it is safe to assume, is called Fola, is strong and quick but can't do much with it. The Latics keeper is called into action several times and performs valiantly. We get lucky as a professional foul only merits a yellow but the moment that changes the game is about to happen.

A Nob End youngster clatters the Wigan keeper with a disgusting challenge. Anthony Meakin eventually gets stretchered off with a broken leg, the PNE offender walks away scot-free. Our own allegiances are clear now, as Hawkins is out of his seat ranting, thank

God well-known referee baiter Golly didn't come. Matt McCann further up the stand lets me know that there's no replacement keeper, just like the first team in that respect, and from the moment the little right-back takes the gloves, we know it's game over. I don't know what they teach their kids at Preston but they aren't half dirty little shits, leaving their foot in after the ball and, in the case of big Fola, elbowing the remaining Wigan full-back out of the game. He's bleeding heavily, and Joe Hawkins is off again. This time, Bob Monkhouse, sat in front wearing his Baxi manager's jacket, turns around to defend his lads, 'He went for the ball.'

I'm tempted to tell this complete tosser to take a look at all the blood streaming out of his nose, and for a minute or two it looks like it's going to go off between two old-timers in the form of B. Monkhouse (Preston, No Shorts) and J. Hawkins (Wigan, Brown Shorts). Typical Nob End, as there's maybe 40 Wiganers scattered across the stand amongst 800 or so PNE fans, so they can be as cocky and as ugly as they like, and carry both off beautifully. To call them Dingles would be unfair on the residents of Burnley; I'd prefer to liken them to Dexy's Midnight Runners, all earrings and in need of a wash. We weather the storm, as do the players for a while, with the little fella between the sticks making a save or two, but just before half-time a ball into the box is punished making it 1–0 Nob End.

The second half is a write-off for the young Latics as PNE dominate, playing some good stuff. The big black fella notches two but the other goal is the best, as a midfielder runs through about three or four men (or should that be boys) before hitting home a screamer. Subs are on, but sadly no Warren Beattie – I wonder whether it's because he's round the back of the stand shagging Madonna? Good value I suppose, pleasing for PNE, and not totally disheartening for us, as the Wigan lads worked hard and there is definitely some talent coming through.

Final word of advice to anyone making the journey to Deepdale next year: if you leave your car across the road on the car park (roll those rrr's), be prepared to get battered across the head. Not in that park, where it used to be open season after the game, but when you walk into the house later that night with your shoes caked in shit. Not the best of evenings, but what do you want for four quid?

MAY

ENCORE UNE FOIS

3 May 2003, Barnsley (h). Won 1–0.

APOLOGIES FOR MENTIONING 'THEM LOT' ON A DAY LIKE TODAY, BUT HAVING HAD THE misfortune to catch a bit of the rugby the night before, I chanced on a young Wigan RL player being interviewed and I was astonished by his words. He wasn't a literary genius, he was simply trotting out all the usual stuff: 'Yeah, it's every Wigan lad's dream to play for the Warriors, ever since I was a boy, you know, the cherry and whites, the town's rugby mad, you know.' Without the crafty insertion of the phrase 'you know' after every third word you might think he had been primed for the camera. Nevertheless, what bollocks! And yes, I do know, because you've just told me. Still wonder why we hate them? What I will tell you is that in my role as fanzine distribution executive I get to drive around Wigan on Saturday morning in the company Lexus, and the town is a sea of blue. Young and old, man and woman, happy smiling faces and all football fans. Not a rugby fan in sight. Great isn't it? Er, you know?

The rumour early Saturday suggests that the South Stand is going to be a sell-out, so I nip to the JJB to buy a ticket, I want my usual spot for this one rather than end in the North or West stand with all the . . . oops better not. My lost gym card has turned up in one of the returned mags. There's a relief – the irony of my gym card falling out of a copy just as the reader is perusing one of my many scathing anonymous attacks on gymgoers doesn't bear thinking about. It's a hassle bringing one out today but everyone mucks in and we sell with ease. Get in The Brick for 1 p.m. for a couple of scoops. A trip to the South Stand bar for two, not my usual manor, but the atmosphere under the stand is really starting to rock. Catch a glimpse of Showaddywaddy on the pitch, gloriously miming their many hits, along with the opera singer Martin Toale and our biggest celebrity Latics fan John Finch aka Marti Pellow. The pre-match entertainment is a good call, but with all due respect, they all know the real reason we're here today.

All the main faces are here, and plenty more besides, some new, and some we've not seen for a while; all are welcome, today is the start of a new beginning, and the day we say goodbye to Division Two, hopefully forever. Next season, well, for Northampton read Norwich, it's Preston not Port Vale, Sunderland not Stockport, and we're here to give the best possible reception to those players who have made it happen. The players emerge to rapturous applause from 12,000-plus Wiganers; packed South, North and West stands, and several hundred bemused Barnsley fans in the eight-and-a-half-thousand-seater East Stand. Once again, we've got a very patched up side, but not one soul in the crowd is in any doubt that the adrenaline will carry them through the magical 100-point barrier.

Barnsley, with nothing to play for, start off attacking, with Filan being forced to make an early save from Dyer. However, it takes a matter of 12 minutes from kick-off for the game to be effectively sealed, as a well-worked move, typical of our season, cuts Barnsley apart and Tony Dinning slams home. 1–0 Wigan, how many times have we heard that this season? And how many times have I heard that roar while downstairs buying a pie? Once more won't make a difference, like I have a choice in the matter when my stomach/bladder calls. I could make out that I'm really bothered about missing the last goal we'll possibly ever score in Division Two, but to be perfectly honest, I couldn't give a shit, I'll just go out and buy the video. Massive respect to Tony, though, for getting yet another from midfield, and turning into the player we all knew he could be.

The game ebbs and flows without ever promising fireworks. The songs ring around the stadium, and at times the whole arena is on its feet 'standing up for the champions'. Wonderful scenes, but as if to illustrate what funny folk us Wiganers are, the centre stage of the pinnacle of our season appears to have been hijacked by a pigeon. The little bugger has landed in the centre circle, and due to an injury sustained during warm-up, cannot get off. The crowd love it, every time the ball or a player goes near it, there is a sense of anticipation that it's about to meet its maker. Good job we're playing Barnsley and not some haughty southern boys, as they might be tempted to jump on the stereotype here. It's a gutsy northern pigeon, though, and resists all attempts to get trodden on, plus John Filan's efforts to pick it up or shoo it away. They should get Gary Teale on the case, as according to Paul Jewell, he can catch them.

Barnsley fight hard to get back into it and, as with the earlier game at Oakwell, it's the dangerous Betsy creating most of the problems and finding himself with at least three clear chances where Filan is called upon to deny him. The third is a stunning one-handed save proving that the God-like Aussie hasn't turned his mind to planning summer barbies just yet. Absolutely no chance of a pint and who cares, bearing in mind the quantities of alcohol likely to be imbibed following the conclusion of this game. The second half sees Wigan up the tempo a notch with some crowd-pleasing stuff. Neil Roberts's stunning 30-yard volley stands out, alas the Barnsley keeper manages to tip it over. McCulloch comes sliding in at the back post following a Teale cross, but the ball gets scooped over.

Everyone is nervously clock-watching, but just for once it's with good reason. A Roberts shot hits the post as it looks increasingly like we're just settling for the one today. The 100-point barrier is a great psychological boost, but we all want to see that trophy. Eight minutes to go: bye bye Layer Road and Saltergate, hello Stadium of Light and Upton Park, how good does that feel. The pigeon's still flapping about, is the little feathery twat going to upstage our Championship presentation as well?

Never has a final whistle been greeted with such emotion, relief, jubilation, celebration, ecstasy. You watch a football club for a lifetime and find that disappointment is never far away, but moments like these are all too rare and should be cherished. I feel a tear coming from somewhere but hold it back, eager to avoid being categorised as a soppy git. The feeling inside is impossible to describe and unlike anything else in the world. First time sex? Yeah, it was good but my spirits were dampened when I found out she'd nicked my wallet as well as charging me twice as much as the other lads in my scout troop. (Er, that's a joke, Mum.) Put simply, there's nothing legal that beats it.

The after-match drill runs like clockwork. The requests to stay off the pitch are adhered to by the usual brigade of young scrotes and old-enough-to-know betters. This perhaps dilutes the occasion, but also makes it a great one as a proper ceremony gets underway with Matt McCann calling the players and staff out two by two, allowing them to receive a great reception. The Duke's got his shoulder strapped up and Jarrett's got a huge shiner that I can see from here (he's a cheat isn't he, Oldham fans?), but it's great to see all the squad out there despite their assorted ailments as they all deserve to be. Just one notable exclusion – Scott Green, who is probably enjoying the promotion celebrations at his new club Wrexham at this precise moment, but he chipped in with some crucial goals for us earlier in the season. Dave Whelan and Brenda Spencer come out next to last with the final pairing being the captain, Jason De Vos, and the manager, Paul Jewell. One hand apiece, a brief pause and up the trophy goes. The JJB Stadium has lift off! How do you eclipse a moment like this?

I know that it's not a great day for everyone, there will be clubs and fans up and down the country who experience almighty lows as well; relegation, missing out on promotion or the play-offs, or in the case of Exeter or Shrewsbury dropping out of the league altogether. They have my utmost sympathy, but they will have had great days in the past and their time will come again and they will undoubtedly have great days in the future to counter their current woes. Even today's opponents, Barnsley, are a cracking club that have fallen on hard times, but they will return and I have massive admiration for the bulk of their support who stay behind to applaud our team on the lap of honour, long after their own had departed. This, however, is a tale of a little non-league club from a Lancashire mining town that rose from the Northern Premier League to Division One in 25 years. Today is a great day for Wigan Athletic – for the fans, for the players, for the backroom staff, for Paul Jewell, for Duncan Sharpe (RIP) and for Dave Whelan. Thanks to one and all!

Uptown and in Springfield there is the mother of all parties. The Pear Tree is standing- or rather, singing-room only. Me and Naylor nip to the John Bull for a quiet moment and cigar apiece, in through the side door, no daft football celebrations in here thank you! The Moon is complete carnage with hundreds upon hundreds of lads and lasses joyfully clearing the place out of beer and singing a medley as diverse and as large as John Peel's record collection, coming from all over the pub. Although 'Paul Jewell's Barmy Army' takes the honours as it rings around the pub for a good solid hour. Bolton are at the forefront of the minds of quite a few as they are rumoured to be coming to gatecrash the party after a load of Wiganers decided to stop off there last week. They don't turn up, and just as bloody well for their own sakes, as every lad in Wigan must be uptown tonight, with a good 500 or so in here. Dare I say that even the most hardened of hoolies is probably glad as well, as today is about the rise of Wigan Athletic, not settling scores with the Horwich scumbags. We don't need or want the bad press, it's a day where only good things should happen as the footballing gods smile over a small part of Lancashire.

The party inevitably moves to Rik's Bar, where the queues to get in snake back to King Street, seriously silly events happen inside, and as queue-jumper extraordinaire, a quick scout about reveals it's exactly the same all over town. I'm the last one out and simply don't want the evening to end, wandering around town with Jay T from the Frees. I'm no big drinker, but tonight I'm invincible and could easily manage another gallon, however it's 4 a.m. so I stagger merrily home. A fantastic day that many have waited a lifetime for. If you really want me to moan about something, then I could always point out that earlier at the game I accidentally swallowed a fly. Now if that had happened at an away game, we'd be singing about it.

Of course, on Sunday morning the head is not in the best of condition and not aided by receiving an 8 a.m. wake-up call off Neil Goon, bawling 'Championi, Championi' several times before putting the phone down. He's gone through his entire address book and delivered the same message. Jimmy White, the snooker player, was none too impressed and called him a 'northern crackhead'. Not got a clue what he's doing in possession of a snooker player's mobile number, but priceless all the same. Stand up for the Champions, Jimmy!

EPILOGUE

'I HATE YOU, BUTLER'

5 May 2003

It would be rude not to follow up Saturday's frivolities with another gargantuan session on the Sunday; inevitably this leads to the scenario of me sitting in The Red Robin at half past eleven on a Bank Holiday Monday knocking back Guinness and muttering the word 'detox'. I'll keep going for another day or two regardless. The realisation that we have finally made it as a proper football club is evident as we are about to witness an open-topped bus ride by the staff of Wigan Athletic.

At noon, there are great scenes at the JJB, where thousands of excitable fans have gathered to wave off the champions of Division Two 2002–03. The players arrive to cheers and more 'Championi's, many of them with their children, and make their way up onto the top deck. Ever the clothes spotter: Filan has a ridiculous Hawaiian shirt on, ensuring he couldn't look more Australian if he tried. McCulloch's got a brown leather jacket with white shirt, James Dean are we? Only joking, I was drinking with his mates down from Glasgow the previous night in Liquid, top geezers, so I'd best stay clear of offending his clan. Gary Teale takes the honours with a cream-coloured Paul Smith trackie top. It's a little bit out there, the sort of garment I'd get sent home for turning out in on a Saturday night, but after a spot of deliberation with my peers, we concur that it is a very smart piece of kit.

Endless camera shots for the papers and television and myself and Statto make the front page of *The Observer*, peering over JDV's shoulder from below with daft grins on our faces. The bus is, very much On The Buses, bright green and considerably older than Neil Redfearn. Despite this, it moves a hell of a lot faster than him, and we potter back over the canal bridge with the intention of having a pint in The Springy and watching it pass there. Unfortunately, we're beaten to it. Now I'm not going to lie and say that 100,000 people have lined the full three-mile stretch. However, it's clear that, along with all those at the JJB, there are pockets of people all the way down the three-mile route, and a few hundred at certain strategic points on the way, i.e. pubs.

I arrive at The Pagefield just in time to stand with my mates and several hundred others outside the local as the bus whizzes past, collecting speeding tickets on its way. It's the same uptown, as the pubs and bars of King Street are packed out, but the bus takes about a minute to travel through. I don't know why this is, and I am loathe to conclude with a moan, suffice to say it's great to see such huge crowds out cheering on the club and to add one more comment: rugby town, my arse. Before we know it, it's done and dusted, and we get down to the serious business of drinking, recalling the season and contemplating our movements in the summer, a pre-season trip to Holland being at the forefront of matters.

Later that day, we make all the local and national TV bulletins, and Dave Whelan is quoted as saying he wants to give Paul Jewell a three-year contract and a pot of money to take the club further and 'doesn't want to be the richest man in the graveyard'. A rich man, a football man, who is living the dream and has the vision we all share. No one can say with any certainty where the future lies, but one thing's for sure, Jewell's management and Whelan's financial backing have given all Wigan Athletic fans a historic season we will never, ever forget. Thanks, Dave. Thanks, Paul.

EXTRA TIME

This is not the end. This is just the beginning. Wigan Athletic Football Club: coming to a Premiership ground near you. Sooner than you think.

LAST WORD

By John Heeley

MARTIN TOLD ME ABOUT HIS INTENTION TO WRITE THIS BOOK DURING THE SUMMER. About time, I thought, but what a year to do it, putting pen to paper (well, fingers to his QWERTY keyboard) has enabled this season to be documented for all to see for many years to come.

Yes, there will be books full of statistics that will periodically find their way onto the shelves but to relive the season from a fan's point of view, a different angle, will bring back the emotions of a year that ultimately saw the Division Two championship trophy lifted aloft at the JJB Stadium, bringing tears of joy to even the most hardened of fans.

To coin a phrase used by a regular contributor to our fanzine, 'Only those who have been disappointed can truly appreciate success', and to say that those profound words sum up the feeling of fans of Wigan Athletic at the end of the 2002–03 season would be a major understatement.

Formed in 1932 following the demise and subsequent folding of Wigan Borough, Athletic made attempt after attempt to bring league football back to the town but all to no avail, even though they were seen by many as one of the top amateur sides in the country.

Election to the Football League was finally achieved at the expense of nearby Southport in July 1978, leaving behind the memories of the Lancashire Combination, Cheshire League and Northern Premier

League and they began a journey that has seen a lot of ups and downs.

Reaching Division One may not seem like much, especially to those who have been brought up as followers of clubs such as Manchester United, Liverpool and Arsenal. However, when you've been used to watching your side, with no disrespect intended, play the likes of Halifax Town, Rochdale, Worksop Town and Gainsborough Trinity, the prospect of taking on the mighty West Ham United, amongst others, is mouth-watering to say the least.

The way they achieved promotion brought with it a number of club records, a few that will take some beating. Firstly, a total of 100 points has only been bettered in any division on 6 previous occasions and, in fact, only once at this particular level. The final table was impressive reading, 100 points and 14 points clear said it all really.

Wigan began the season with a record-breaking start of four straight wins, bettering their previous best of two set in 1985. The start prompted the bookmakers to slash their pre-season odds on Wigan dramatically, recognising that they were serious contenders for the title, a decision that eventually proved to be a correct one as the season progressed.

However, back-to-back defeats at the end of August saw Wigan lose top spot, but that proved to be a minor blip and after regaining pole position at the beginning of November in front of the watching nation, following a win over Lancashire rivals Blackpool, they never once relinquished their hold on the summit.

A 21-match unbeaten run between the beginning of November and the end of January, which included 11 consecutive wins, meant that the chasing pack had more or less thrown in the towel as early as January, resigned to chasing the second automatic promotion spot.

Defeat at Swindon Town's County Ground at the end of January may have brought a little optimism to the chasing pack but it was only their third loss of the campaign and other than Plymouth Argyle nobody else took all three points from Paul Jewell's side for the remainder of the season. They tasted defeat in the league only four times all year, yet another club record set, eclipsing the one set during the 1980–81 season, when they were beaten on seven occasions, and again equalled over the 1999–2000 campaign.

Well, we know the manner in which promotion and the title were brought to the JJB Stadium, but how did they do it? Wigan weren't exactly the most prolific in front of goal but, looking over the final table, it's easy to work out that they were extremely difficult to break down, scoring against them proved to be a major feat in itself.

A total of 25 clean sheets in the league, added to the 4 in cup competition (now there's another story) was testament to a certain Australian goalkeeper, but let's not forget the defence, two of whom were selected for the PFA Division Two Team of the Year alongside the likeable antipodean shotstopper.

Keeper John Filan has been ever present, apart from one LDV Vans Trophy game, since making his debut at Oldham midway through last season, and at £600,000 has proved to be one of the bargains of the century. It is often said that a goalkeeper is only as good as the defence in front of him, and with Canadian international Jason De Vos leading the back four alongside former Everton centre-half Matt Jackson few strikers got the chance to test Filan, but when they did the man from down under was well up to the task.

Filan conceded only 25 goals all season in the league, another club record, and just 9 of those were conceded on the road, again a club record. Awesome is the word I am looking for here.

However, the success was a team effort, both on and off the field, and it would be foolish not to thank our chairman Dave Whelan for bringing success to the town, for building a superb stadium in which to enjoy it and also for employing Paul Jewell, a man that at only 38 has already achieved more as a manager than most can dream of.

So to summarise, champions of Division Two and the quarter final of the Worthington Cup (defeating THREE Premiership sides en route) means that the 2002–03 season has been arguably the most successful in their 71-year history. What does the future now hold for the Latics from Wigan? Well we will have to wait and see but let me leave you with one more thought:

> Success is not a place at which one arrives but rather the spirit with which one undertakes and continues the journey. (Alex Noble, 1979)